What's in the Bible for . . . ™

Women

Georgia Curtis Ling

CARTOONS BY

Reverend Fun
(Dennis "Max" Hengeveld)
Dennis is a graphic designer
for Gospel Films and the
author of *Has Anybody Seen
My Locust?* His cartoons can
be seen worldwide at
www.reverendfun.com

STARBURST PUBLISHERS ®

P. O. Box 4123, Lancaster, Pennsylvania 17604

To schedule Author appearances, write:

Author Appearances
Starburst Publishers
P.O. Box 4123
Lancaster, Pennsylvania 17604
(717) 293-0939

www.starburstpublishers.com

CREDITS:
Cover design by Dave Marty Design
Text design and composition by John Reinhardt Book Design
Illustrations by Melissa A. Burkhart and Bruce Burkhart
Cartoons by Dennis "Max" Hengeveld

Unless otherwise noted, or paraphrased by the author, all Scripture quotations are from the New International Version of The Holy Bible.

"Scripture taken from the HOLY BIBLE: NEW INTERNATIONAL VERSION®, NIV®. Copyright © 1973, 1978, 1984 by International Bible Society."

Reverend Fun cartoons ©Copyright Gospel Films Incorporated.

To the best of its ability, Starburst Publishers® has strived to find the source of all material. If there has been an oversight, please contact us, and we will make any correction deemed necessary in future printings. We also declare that to the best of our knowledge all material (quoted or not) contained herein is accurate, and we shall not be held liable for the same.

First Printing, November 1999

ISBN: 1-892016-10-9
Library of Congress Number 99-63784
Printed in the United States of America

READ THESE PAGES BEFORE YOU READ THIS BOOK . . .

Welcome to the *What's in the Bible for . . .* series. This series is the result of a belief that no matter who you are—teenager or senior citizen, pastor or plumber—the Bible is the most important book for you to read and understand. You could start with the first page of the Bible and start plowing through, but doing so can be a little overwhelming. This series aims to help you navigate your way through the Bible so the time you spend reading it will be as rewarding as possible.

The *What's in the Bible for . . .* series is a sister series to Starburst Publishers' *God's Word for the Biblically-Inept™* series. The following is a list of previously published and soon-to-be published books in each series. You'll notice a "Title Code" for each book in the upper right-hand corner of the description. This code along with page numbers is used throughout the books, allowing easy reference from one book to another.

What's in the Bible for . . .™ Women

Georgia Curtis Ling　　　　　　**TITLE CODE: WBFW**

What does the Bible have to say to women? Women of all ages will find biblical insight on topics that are meaningful to them in four sections: Wisdom for the Journey; Family Ties; Bread, Breadwinners, and Bread Makers; and Fellowship and Community Involvement. This book uses illustrations, bullet points, chapter summaries, and icons to make understanding God's Word easier than ever!

(trade paper) ISBN 1-892016-10-9 $16.95　**AVAILABLE NOW**

What's in the Bible for . . . ™ Mothers

Judy Bodmer　　　　　　**TITLE CODE: WBFM**

Is home schooling a good idea? Is it okay to work? At what age should I start treating my children like responsible adults? What is the most important thing I can teach my children? If you are asking these questions and need help answering them, *What's in the Bible for . . . Mothers* is especially for you! Simple and user-friendly, this motherhood manual offers hope and instruction for today's mothers by jumping into the lives of mothers in the Bible (e.g., Naomi, Elizabeth, and Mary) and by exploring biblical principles that are essential to being a nurturing mother.

(trade paper) ISBN 1-892016-26-5 $16.95　**AVAILABLE SPRING 2000**

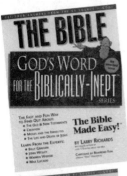

The Bible—God's Word for the Biblically-Inept™

Larry Richards TITLE CODE: GWBI

Get serious about learning the Bible from cover to cover! Here is an overview of the Bible written by Larry (Lawrence O.) Richards, one of today's leading Bible writers. Each chapter contains select verses from books of the Bible along with illustrations, definitions, and references to related Bible passages.

(trade paper) ISBN 0914984551 $16.95 AVAILABLE NOW

Daniel—God's Word for the Biblically-Inept™

Daymond R. Duck TITLE CODE: GWDN

Daniel is a book of prophecy and the key to understanding the mysteries of the Tribulation and End-Time events. This verse-by-verse commentary combines humor and scholarship to get at the essentials of Scripture. Perfect for those who want to know the truth about the Antichrist.

(trade paper) ISBN 0914984489 $16.95 AVAILABLE NOW

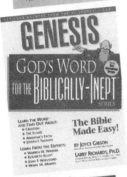

Genesis—God's Word for the Biblically-Inept™

Joyce Gibson TITLE CODE: GWGN

Joyce Gibson breaks the Bible down into bite-sized pieces making it easy to understand and incorporate into your life. Readers will learn about Creation, Adam and Eve, the Flood, Abraham and Isaac, and more. Includes chapter summaries, bullet points, definitions, and study questions.

(trade paper) ISBN 1892016125 $16.95 AVAILABLE NOVEMBER 1999

Health & Nutrition—God's Word for the Biblically-Inept™

Kathleen O'Bannon Baldinger TITLE CODE: GWHN

The Bible is full of God's rules for good health! Kathleen O'Bannon Baldinger reveals scientific evidence that proves that the diet and health principles outlined in the Bible are the best for total health. Experts include Pamela Smith, Julian Whitaker, Kenneth Cooper, and T. D. Jakes.

(trade paper) ISBN 0914984055 $16.95 AVAILABLE NOW

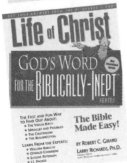

Life of Christ—God's Word for the Biblically-Inept™

Robert C. Girard TITLE CODE: GWLC

Girard takes the reader on an easy-to-understand journey through the gospels of Matthew, Mark, Luke, and John, tracing the story of Jesus' life on earth. Icons, illustrations, chapter overviews, study questions, and more make learning about the Virgin Birth, Jesus' miracles and parables, the Crucifixion, and the Resurrection easier than ever!

(trade paper) ISBN 1892016230 $16.95 AVAILABLE MARCH 2000

Men of the Bible—God's Word for the Biblically-Inept™

D. Larry Miller   TITLE CODE: GWMB

Benefit from the life experiences of the powerful men of the Bible! Learn how the inspirational struggles of men such as Moses, Daniel, Paul, and David parallel the struggles of men today. It will inspire and build Christian character in your walk with the Lord.

(trade paper) ISBN 1892016079 $16.95   AVAILABLE OCTOBER 1999

Prophecies of the Bible—God's Word for the Biblically-Inept™

Daymond R. Duck   TITLE CODE: GWPB

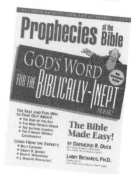

God has a plan for this crazy planet, and now, understanding it is easier than ever! Best-selling author and End-time prophecy expert Daymond R. Duck explains the complicated prophecies of the Bible in plain English. Read with wonder as Duck shows you all there is to know about the End of the Age, the New World Order, the Second Coming, and the Coming World Government. Includes useful commentary, expert quotes, icons, sidebars, chapter summaries, and study questions! Find out what prophecies have already been fulfilled and what's in store for the future!

(trade paper) ISBN 1892016222 $16.95   AVAILABLE FEBRUARY 2000

Revelation—God's Word for the Biblically-Inept™

Daymond R. Duck   TITLE CODE: GWRV

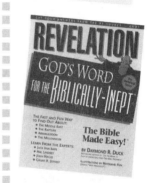

Revelation—God's Word for the Biblically-Inept™ includes every verse of the Book of Revelation along with quotes from leading experts, icons, sidebars, and bullets. Learn and enjoy as end-time prophecy expert Daymond R. Duck leads us through one of the Bible's most confusing books.

(trade paper) ISBN 0914984985 $16.95   AVAILABLE NOW

Women of the Bible—God's Word for the Biblically-Inept™

Kathy Collard Miller   TITLE CODE: GWWB

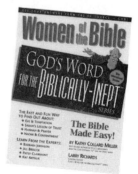

Finally, a Bible perspective just for women! Gain valuable insight from the successes and struggles of such women as Eve, Esther, Mary, Sarah, and Rebekah. Interesting icons like "Get Close to God," "Build Your Spirit," and "Grow Your Marriage" will make it easy to incorporate God's Word into your daily life.

(trade paper) ISBN 0914984063 $16.95   AVAILABLE NOW

New Titles Are Coming!

Starburst Publishers will continue expanding the *What's in the Bible for . . .* and *God's Word for the Biblically-Inept* series. Look for these future titles:

☞ **What's in the Bible for . . . Couples**

☞ **What's in the Bible for . . . Teens**

☞ **Acts—God's Word for the Biblically-Inept**

☞ **Mark—God's Word for the Biblically-Inept**

☞ **Romans—God's Word for the Biblically-Inept**

Purchasing Information

www.starburstpublishers.com

Books are available from your favorite bookstore, either from current stock or special order. To assist bookstores in locating your selection, be sure to give title, author, and ISBN. If unable to purchase from a bookstore, you may order direct from STARBURST PUBLISHERS. When ordering please enclose full payment plus shipping and handling as follows:

Post Office (4th class)
$3.00 with a purchase of up to $20.00
$4.00 ($20.01–$50.00)
8% of purchase price for purchases of
    $50.01 and up

Canada
$5.00 (up to $35.00)
%15 ($35.01 and up)

United Parcel Service (UPS)
$4.50 (up to $20.00)
$6.00 ($20.01–$50.00)
12% ($50.01 and up)

Overseas
$5.00 (up to $25.00)
20% ($25.01 and up)

Payment in U.S. funds only. Please allow two to three weeks minimum (longer overseas) for delivery. Make checks payable to and mail to:

Starburst Publishers®
P.O. Box 4123
Lancaster, PA 17604

Credit card orders may be placed by calling 1-800-441-1456, Mon–Fri, 8:30 A.M. to 5:30 P.M. Eastern Standard Time. Prices are subject to change without notice. Catalogs are available for a 9 x 12 self-addressed envelope with four first-class stamps.

CHAPTERS AT A GLANCE

PART THREE: BREAD, BREADWINNERS, AND BREAD BAKERS

PART FOUR: FELLOWSHIP AND COMMUNITY INVOLVEMENT

ILLUSTRATIONS

For a preview of the icons in this book, check out the sidebar in this Introduction!

INTRODUCTION

Welcome to *What's in the Bible for . . .™ Women*. I'm glad you picked up this book. Like one of those fun, adventurous tour guides in amusement parks, I'll be your personal escort as we open the pages of the Bible and see what secrets are revealed.

Now, this is not your father's "Oldsmobile" kind of commentary. It's a "let's sit down and chat over a cup of Starbucks® grande skinny mocha, no whip espresso" kind of commentary. You are about to discover a REVOLUTIONARY COMMENTARY™ that will change your outlook on the Bible. Reading this book will improve your life!

Why Look to the Bible?

Several years ago, *Writer's Digest* magazine carried a feature in their seventy-fifth anniversary Special Edition entitled, "75 Books Every Writer Must Read." These books were chosen by published authors, an exclusive list of "must-reads" to update your own bookshelf. According to these literary professionals, the number one book every writer must read was . . . the Bible! Yes, the Bible. One writer commented, "Lay your chosen faith aside and experience this beautifully written book."

The Bible has been the number one best-seller of all time, and it's no wonder—it has the answers to all of life's questions. Contrary to popular belief, **Freud** did not write the book on human relationships, nor did Dr. Spock write the book on raising kids. Someone else did: God, our Creator. Of course it's the world's greatest book! Our Father knows best!

Scripture opens the door to understanding. It is <u>living and active.</u> Once you discover the <u>truth</u>, you will understand its

---

WHAT'S IN THIS CHAPTER

Here We Go

SNAPSHOTS

EXAMPLES

GEORGIA'S TIPS

☞ **GO TO:**

Hebrews 4:12 (living and active)

Psalm 119:159–168 (truth)

Freud: Sigmund (1856–1939), well-known neurologist

☞ **Check It Out:**

Exodus 1

☞ **GO TO:**

Matthew 24:35
(timeless advice)

**What Others
are Saying:**

KEY Outline:

Key to Intimate Faith

*Listen as God speaks
through Scripture*

ACT OF GOD

creation of Adam (man)
and Eve (woman)

Think About It

relevance for your life and be able to apply it each day. The Word of God offers hope when a crisis hits, comfort in time of grief, encouragement when you are weary, and guidance in relationships. The Bible's <u>timeless advice</u> for women has guided countless lives across the millennia.

Luci Swindoll: The best advice I ever received was in 1955. I was twenty-three. Somebody had the good sense to say to me, "Luci, if you want to give yourself a gift, learn all you can about the Bible. Start going to a Bible class and don't stop until you have some knowledge under your belt. You won't be sorry." More than forty years later, this wonderful storehouse of truth is my standard for living, giving, loving, and learning. It is my Rock and Fortress, the pattern for enjoying abundant life on earth, and for eternity. I know what I believe, and why.[1]

> **2 Timothy 3:16–17** All scripture is God-breathed and is useful for teaching, rebuking, correcting, and training in righteousness, so that the man of God may be thoroughly equipped for every good work.

Women of the Bible

God gave us snapshots of women's lives in the Bible to provide us a wealth of inspiration, wisdom, and encouragement. Though separated by thousands of years, drastic cultural differences, and divergent customs, the ancient Bible woman and the modern woman still share the same joys, sorrows, anxieties, disappointments, pains, and dreams of a safe, stable life. Just like we do, Bible women longed for an intimate faith in their Creator and struggled to develop rewarding relationships. Because these women looked to a loving God during confusion, disappointment, and suffering, they lived rewarding inner lives no matter what the external circumstances were.

Enjoy their stories. May these newfound friends step out of the pages of the Bible and walk alongside you as you reflect on how relevant their examples are for today's modern woman.

**What Others
are Saying:**

Kathy Collard Miller: The women of the Bible can show us how to live, what choices to make, and why. These women faced sticky problems and difficult situations just like we experience.[2]

How to Use
What's in the Bible for . . . Women

- Sit down with this book and your Bible.
- Start the book at Chapter 1.
- As you read through each chapter, read the "Check It Out" passages in your Bible.
- Use the sidebar loaded with icons and helpful information to get a knowledge boost.
- Answer the Study Questions and review with the Chapter Wrap-Up.
- Then go on to the next chapter.

It's simple! Now, if you like to hop, skip, and jump, go ahead. The book is laid out in a carefully planned order, but if you are yearning for answers to a specific need, go ahead and play leap-frog, but I hope you return to those chapters you skipped. You may think a given chapter doesn't apply to you, but try reading it anyway. Odds are, you'll be pleasantly surprised as you find gems of truth specifically for you. Even if you don't use the information now, it will be a great resource for later.

Why Use the New International Version (NIV)?

I want this book to be easy to read and understand; that's why I chose to use the New International Version (NIV) of the Bible. It is a scholarly translation that accurately expresses the original Bible in clear and contemporary English.

The Features

This book contains a variety of special features that can help you learn. They're illustrated in the outside column of this introduction and in the following sample page. Here they are again, with a brief explanation of each.

Sections and Icons	What's It For?
What's in This Chapter	the most prominent points of the chapter
Here We Go	a chapter warm-up
Bible Quote	what you came for—the Bible
Commentary	my thoughts on what the verse means
What Others Are Saying	if you don't believe me, listen to the experts
Go To	other Bible verses to help you better understand (underlined in text)

REMEMBER THIS

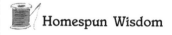
Everyday Life

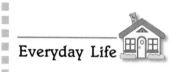
Homespun Wisdom

Laugh Out Loud

Flashback

COFFEE BREAK WITH GEORGIA

Sections and Icons	What's It For?
What?	the meaning of a word (bold in text)
Check It Out	related Bible passages you should look up
Snapshots of Women in the Bible	focuses on specific women from the Bible
Examples from the Bible	scriptural examples to follow or avoid
Georgia's Tips	a list of practical tips
Key Point	a major point in the chapter
Key Outline	a mini-outline of information
Act of God	indicates God's personal intervention in history or people's lives
Think about It	interesting points to get you thinking
Remember This . . .	don't forget this
Everyday Life	brings a concept down to reality
Homespun Wisdom	wisdom for everyday people
Laugh Out Loud	something to tickle your funny bone
Flashback	learning from looking back
Coffee Break with Georgia	stories from my heart to yours
Study Questions	questions to get you discussing, studying, and digging deeper
Chapter Wrap-Up	the most prominent points revisited
Georgia's Bookshelf	favorite books I recommend

CHAPTER WRAP-UP

GEORGIA'S

BOOKSHELF

A Word about Words

As you read **What's in the Bible for. . .™ Women,** you'll notice some interchangeable words: Scripture, Scriptures, Word, Word of God, God's Word, etc. All of these terms mean the same thing and come under the broad heading of "the Bible."

In most cases the phrase *"the Scriptures"* in the New Testament refers to the Old Testament. Peter indicated that the writings of the Apostle Paul were quickly accepted in the early church as equal to *"the other scriptures"* (2 Peter 3:16). Both Testaments consistently demonstrate the belief that is expressed in 2 Timothy 3:16, *"all Scripture is God-breathed."*

One Final Tip

There's a wonderful promise given when we turn to the Bible to answer life's questions. As we read the inspired Word of God, he himself promises that his Word will make a distinct difference in our lives, and he is present whenever we read it.

As you read, pray, and open your heart to God, ask him to speak to you. You will find your life enriched and changed forever as you find out what's in the Bible for women.

Here's a Sample Page!

Bible Quote: This is where you'll read a quote from the Bible.

James 1:5 If any of you lacks wisdom, he should ask God, who gives generously to all without finding fault, and it will be given to him.

Decisions, Decisions: In or Out?

Commentary: This is where you'll read commentary about the biblical quote.

James, the brother of Jesus, is writing to the new believers who were scattered about the Roman world (see GWBI, pages 213–214) when they fled from persecution. James knows that godly wisdom is a great gift. He gives a simple plan to get it: need wisdom, ask for it. God will give it to us.

Up 'til now we've concentrated on finding the wind sails of your drifting marriage and overcoming marital lems. But you may be the reader who is shaking her head, thinking that I just don't understand what you're going through. You can't take the abuse any longer; you've forgiven the **infidelity** time after time; and in order for you and your children to survive, you see no alternative but divorce.

So let me make this clear: in no way am I saying to allow your husband to abuse you or your children. If the abuse continues, get out and seek profess... keep the a... only dam... physical a...

"What?": When you see a word in bold, go to the sidebar for a definition.

infidelity: sexual unfaithfulness of a spouse

"Go To": When you see a word or phrase that's underlined, go to the sidebar for a biblical cross-reference.

When you feel you've depleted all of your options, continue to ask God for wisdom in order to have the knowledge to make the right decisions. Wise women seek God. God is the source of wisdom and wisdom is found in Christ and the Word.

☞ **GO TO:**

Psalm 111:10 (source)

REMEMBER 👍 THIS

Gary Chapman, Ph.D.: Is there hope for women who suffer physical abuse from their husbands? Does reality living offer any genuine hope? I believe the answer to those questions is yes.[6]

What Others are Saying:

Give It Away

You don't have to be a farmer to understand what the Apostle Paul wrote to the Corinthian church (see illustration, page 143). A picture is worth a thousand words, and Paul is painting masterpiece. He reminds us of what any smart farmer knows in order to produce a bountiful harvest, he has to plan for it

What Others Are Saying: This is where you'll read what an expert has to say about the subject at hand.

MONEY, MONEY, MONEY • 5

127

Feature with icon in the sidebar: Thoughout the book you will see sections of text with corresponding icons in the sidebar. See the chart on pages xv–xvi for a description of all the features in this book.

Part One

WISDOM FOR THE JOURNEY

Reverend Fun

"I am taking my thoughts captive."

1 SPIRITUALLY FIT

Renewing and Strengthening Your Intimate Walk with God

WHAT'S IN THIS CHAPTER

- Visiting the Great Physician
- Spiritual Exercise Routine
- A "Soul Food" Diet Plan
- Rest for the Weary
- How to Last

Here We Go

> **Psalm 19:7–11** The law of the Lord is perfect, reviving the soul. The **statutes** of the Lord are trustworthy, making wise the simple. The **precepts** of the Lord are right, giving joy to the heart. The commands of the Lord are radiant, giving light to the eyes. The fear of the Lord is pure, enduring forever. The **ordinances** of the Lord are sure and altogether righteous. They are more precious than gold, than much pure gold; they are sweeter than honey, than honey from the comb. By them is your servant warned: in keeping them there is great reward.

statutes: *established customs*

precepts: *directions for daily living*

ordinances: *authoritative commands*

We all have questions about life. Among those questions may be this one: Can I have an intimate relationship with God? The key to finding the answer and strengthening your connection with God is in listening for him as you read the Bible, often referred to as "God's Word."

David, who wrote most of the Old Testament book of Psalms, was the most famous king of Israel and ruled his kingdom under God (see GWBI, pages 62–67). He points out in Psalm 19:7–11 what is special about God's Word:

1. It is perfect and true.
2. It makes us wise.
3. It brings joy in life if we follow its guidelines.

 **GO TO:**

1 Chronicles 11–29 (David)

KEY Outline:

Key to Intimate Faith
listen as God speaks through Scripture

Look to the Bible,
God's Word, for
guidelines on becom-
ing spiritually fit.

4. It leads us only to do what is right.

5. It is a treasure better than gold and sweeter than honey as it satisfies the appetite of our souls.

Our search for an intimate faith is fulfilled first and foremost in discovering what's in the Bible for women. Just as God created ways for our bodies to stay physically fit, he also gave us ways to become spiritually fit using his Word.

What Others
are Saying:

Everyday Life

Dean Ornish: Working with heart patients has convinced me that the nation is suffering from an epidemic of spiritual heart disease and that people are turning to food, alcohol, and other bad habits out of loneliness and despair.[1]

As a New Year's resolution, I declared 1994 "The Year of the Body." Four years had whizzed by since the birth of our son, and in that lovely pregnancy I had gained several pounds. Those extra pounds were with me for quite some time, so I gave them a pet name: Baby Fat. That year I decided to say farewell to ol' Baby Fat. I declared war. I laid out a strategic plan, set goals, and obtained advice from diet and fitness experts. Realizing "friendly fire" could help me, I shared my plan with my family and enlisted them in the Battle of the Bulge.

Let me tell you, it was a long hard battle. It took commitment, discipline, and hours of physically demanding work. But as the months passed I reached my weight goal, going from a size six-teen dress *back* to a size six. I felt like a new person!

To get physically fit, I went back to the basics and followed five steps. I'm sure you know them by heart; we're bombarded with them every day (see GWHN, pages 6, 145–146, 220–221):

1. Have a regular check-up by a physician.

2. Exercise regularly—at least three times a week.

3. Eat a proper diet.

4. Drink plenty of water.

5. Get adequate rest.

Hang on! Don't put this book down! This is not a "mini-fat farm" book. In this chapter, I use basic health and fitness prin-ciples as guidelines to show us how to shape up and become fit spiritually.

> **Matthew 9:20–22** Just then a woman who had been subject to bleeding for twelve years came up behind him and touched the edge of his cloak. She said to herself, "If I only touch his cloak, I will be healed." Jesus turned and saw her. "Take heart, daughter," he said, "your faith has healed you." And the woman was healed from that moment.

☞ **Check It Out:**

Mark 5:24–34

Is the Doctor In?

In the culture of first-century Jews, women who bled as this woman did were ceremonially unclean. That meant she could not participate in worship at the Temple in Jerusalem, and against her will was counted out of other activities that faithful Jews enjoyed. The gospel of Mark tells us *"She had suffered a great deal under the care of many doctors and had spent all she had, yet instead of getting better she grew worse"* (Mark 5:26). Her illness was not just a health problem. It grew into a social problem and a financial problem. No wonder she fought through a large crowd for a chance at healing. I've done as much just to snag a great bargain at a sale!

When Jesus healed her, the healing touched every aspect of her life the illness had touched. In the same way, when we open our hearts to Jesus, he can transform every aspect of our lives. That's why he's called the "Great Physician." But first this determined woman had to put forth effort. So must we.

 *EXAMPLES FROM THE BIBLE*

The pages of the Bible are filled with women of faith who put their trust in God to heal their hearts or build their lives.

- **Eve**, the first woman God created, disobeyed his commands, but turned back to God as he renewed their relationship. (Genesis 3:1–8, 20)
- **Sarah** put her faith in God as she followed her husband, Abraham, and waited upon God's promise of the miracle birth of her son **Isaac**. (Genesis 21:1)
- The extraordinary faith in God by Mary, the mother of **Jesus**, enabled her to surrender herself to God as he chose her to give birth to his son Jesus. (Luke 1:35; Matthew 1:18–25; see GWWB, pages 104–108)

Eve: Hebrew for "Mother of all living"

Sarah: "Mother of Nations"

Isaac: "son of promise"

Jesus: "the Lord saves"

submitted: *yielded to the authority of another*

☞ **GO TO:**

Luke 4:23 (Great Physician)

Think About It

surrender: *to give up possession or control*

psalmist: *the author of the book of Psalm*

children of Israel: *God's chosen people; the Hebrews*

Jerusalem: *home to the Jewish people*

exile: *a period of seventy years that the Israelites were held captives*

I served as a missionary intern and even married a minister. I showed all the signs of faith and I felt like I had a relationship with Jesus, but not until I fully **submitted** myself to God did I encounter him on a personal level. Fifteen years ago, it looked like I had it all: a successful career, a wonderful husband, and a baby on the way. I thought I was in control. Then we relocated, I left a successful business behind, and we lost our baby. I was spiritually, physically, and emotionally sick until I turned it all over to Jesus Christ, the <u>Great Physician</u>. That was a defining point in my life. Many writers refer to it as "brokenness." It took total surrender of every aspect of my life, my marriage, my career, weight, children—I had to yield everything to God every day. I allowed God to have control, and he took this broken woman and made her whole. *"Draw near to God and he will draw near to you"* (James 4:8). Once I put God in the driver's seat, my life's journey became amazing.

No matter where you are in your spiritual walk with God, you're not as close as you can be. As we use basic physical health steps to symbolize spiritual fitness, our first step is to have a regular check-up with the Great Physician. The first step may be the hardest because it is built around the verb **surrender**.

It's against our nature to surrender. But spiritual healing begins only when we give in to the lordship and loving guidance of Jesus Christ.

When you surrender:

1. You give up control.
2. Spiritual healing begins.

• • •

David, the **psalmist**, knew a thing or two about brokenness. He declared in Psalm 147:1–3, *"How good it is to sing praises to our God, how pleasant and fitting to praise Him! The Lord builds up **Jerusalem**; he gathers the exiles of Israel. He heals the brokenhearted and binds up their wounds."*

David gives praise to God for his ability to heal. He is gracious not only to see to the physical needs of his **children of Israel** as he rebuilds their city, he also sees to their spiritual needs and heals their hearts that were broken from their suffering in exile.

SNAPSHOTS OF WOMEN IN THE BIBLE

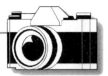

Mary of Bethany

The first snapshot we have of Mary of Bethany finds her at the home of Martha, her sister (see GWWB, pages 257–273). Martha had opened her home to Jesus and his disciples as they traveled. Mary, Martha, and their brother Lazarus were friends of the Lord. We find Mary sitting at the <u>feet</u> of Jesus, listening to his every word. She not only knew the Savior as a friend, she knew and understood how important it was to know his heart. Her sister, who evidently was doing all the work, complained to Jesus and told him to order Mary to help her. Jesus replied with that double name sing-song, "<u>*Martha*</u>, *Martha*." (You know the tone. It's that "I'm disappointed in you" tone. I can easily picture him shaking his head.) He said Mary had chosen what was important, and he wouldn't ask her to leave.

Mary surrendered her time and attention. Nothing was more important than being with Jesus.

In the next snapshot, we find Mary with Jesus. Lazarus was gravely ill. The family had sent for their friend and healer Jesus, but he came too late. By the time Jesus arrived, Lazarus had been dead for four days. When Mary saw Jesus, she questioned his methods, but she still <u>fell</u> at his feet and called him Lord. In her time of sorrow, Mary surrendered her suffering soul to her Great Physician for healing. He not only comforted and wept with her, but also raised her brother from the dead. There is no such thing as "too late" for Jesus.

The third snapshot of Mary occurs as Lazarus hosted a dinner in Jesus' honor. I'm sure it was a celebration to honor the man who gave him life. Mary, who listened to Jesus' teachings, understood because she listened with her heart. The men did not understand; they only listened with their ears. She knew Jesus talked of the day that his death would come. During the dinner as Jesus reclined around the table, she surrendered all she had by breaking a costly bottle of imported perfume (see illustration, page 8). For the third time she was at Jesus' feet, this time anointing him for burial. If the perfume was like the perfume of a separate story in Mark 14:3–9, she <u>poured</u> away a year's worth of wages. She surrendered her most precious possession as a **sacrifice** to the One who would soon be sacrificed for the world. As the perfume lingered in the air, the **disciples** complained of the waste of money, saying it could have been given to the poor. But Jesus commended

☞ **GO TO:**

Luke 10:39 (feet)

Luke 10:41 (Martha)

John 11:28–32 (fell)

John 12:1–11 (poured)

ACT OF GOD

the **resurrection** of Lazarus

resurrection: *physical renewal of life after death*

sacrifice: *an offering*

disciples: *followers; in this case followers of Jesus*

her, saying she'd done a beautiful thing. Imagine the stirring of her soul as Mary heard her Master speak those words.

What Others are Saying:

Jill Briscoe: Jesus loved Mary. He loved her because she was discerning, disciplined, and delighted with Him. He loved her through her periods of doubt and despair, and he loved her for her grand display of adoration as she poured upon him her costliest sacrifice, putting her future in his hands.[2]

Think About It

Jesus is the Great Physician—get check-ups regularly. When Mary's heart broke in the face of death, Jesus removed her sorrow. Similarly, he will heal your broken heart and give you a fresh outlook, a revived hope, and an inner image of a new faithfully fit life.

> **Psalm 86:11–12** Teach me your way, O Lord, and I will walk in your truth; give me an undivided heart that I may fear your name. I will praise you, O Lord my God with all my heart; I will glorify your name forever.

Exercise Your Way to Fitness

In Psalm 86, David prays to God during a time of crisis. David is running for his life as King Saul, jealous of David, attempts to kill him.

David asks God to teach him how to live, and pledges to trust and walk in the path of God's truth. He wants his heart united with God's, and David **pledges** to **worship**, **obey**, and **praise** God forever.

pledges: promises

worship: to revere, honor, or be devoted to

obey: to follow God's commands and instruction

praise: to express admiration or appreciation

As we exercise our way to spiritual fitness, like David we need to pledge to worship, obey, and praise God daily.

Carole Mayhall: In order to know God in a deep and personal way, it's critical that you be convinced that spending time with him—primarily through his Word—is essential . . .

My heart aches when I see a woman start strong in the Christian life and then wither, much like the seed sown on shallow ground or among the rocks. There are a number of reasons for this, of course, but one is that she isn't convinced of how important time in God's Word is for her walk with God.[3]

My friend was having a hard time battling the bulge. I asked if she had a regular aerobic exercise program. "Yes," she said with a sly grin. "I walk a few feet to the mailbox every day."

The biggest complaint about exercise is that it takes too much time. There are even programs with just ten minutes of exercise a day designed for the hurried woman. But experts tell us if we want to make a difference in our health it takes a minimum of thirty minutes of aerobic exercise at least three times a week. Our spiritual fitness also needs an aerobic workout as we walk with God.

What Others
are Saying:

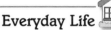

Everyday Life

KEY Outline:

**Mary of Bethany
Surrendered**

time to Jesus

sorrow to Jesus

*precious possessions to
Jesus*

Three Ingredients for Spiritual Fitness

	Scripture	Description
WORSHIP GOD:	Exodus 20:5	Worship God only.
	Psalm 29:2	Worship the Lord in the splendor of his holiness.
	Hebrews 12:28	Worship God acceptably.
OBEY GOD:	1 Chronicles 21:19	David obeyed.
	Hebrews 5:7–9	Jesus obeyed.
	Romans 5:19	Obedience of Jesus brings righteousness to all.
PRAISE GOD:	Hebrews 13:15	Offer praise to God.
	1 Peter 1:7	Trials come so that praise, glory, and honor will go to God when Jesus is revealed.
	Psalm 111:10	To God belongs eternal praise.

Flashback

On our son's fourth birthday he received his first real bike. He thought he was big stuff. No more Big Wheel toys! He had moved on up to a manly two wheeler (with manly training wheels), where he could ride faster, weave in and out of obstacle courses, and ring his bell as he passed by. He said his bike was "really cool."

We spent many hours out on the driveway. To make those minutes productive, I decided to join the bicycling ranks and pull out the old exercise bike. (You may be familiar with this bike; it's usually the one in your den that serves as a coat rack.)

Tucked away in the dark shadows of the garage, the bike weighed a ton as I struggled to pull it out. Finally I climbed on. I tried peddling but it wouldn't budge. I turned the bike upside down and began tinkering. When I looked at the tension pads, they were rusted to the metal wheels. Does that give you a clue as to how long it had been since that bike had a good workout?

Laugh Out Loud

Have you found yourself wanting to get spiritually fit only to find that when you turn to your first exercise of reading the Bible the pages are rusted shut? Maybe you start to pray but since you're out of the habit, you're spiritually short of breath and you quit early. Have you dropped out of regular worship and can't remember the church service times? Don't worry, help is on the way. You are not alone if you turn to God and <u>rely</u> on his promises and great power.

REMEMBER THIS

EXAMPLES FROM THE BIBLE

In our "spiritual aerobics," what is special about walking with God? One who walks with God . . .

Psalm 15:2 .... is blameless
Psalm 26:3 .... walks continually in truth
Psalm 89:15 .... is happy and blessed
Psalm 119:45 .... walks in freedom
Proverbs 6:22 .... has guidance in life both day and night
Proverbs 10:8 .... walks securely in **wisdom**
Isaiah 2:3 .... learns God's ways and walks in God's paths

☞ **GO TO:**

Ephesians 1:19–20
(rely)

KEY Outline:

Walk in His Truth
worship
obey
praise

wisdom: *having knowledge and the ability to apply it to life*

Romans 6:4 .... walks in the newness of life in Jesus
2 Corinthians 4:2 .. walks by faith, not by sight
Galatians 5:16 .... lives and walks by the Spirit
Ephesians 5:2 .... walks in love, just as Christ loved us

As with physical fitness, spiritual fitness requires regular exercise. I encourage you to loosen and turn those pages— give your Bible a workout. Strengthen your stamina by communicating longer with God in prayer. Don't let anything keep you from worshipping God with others as you gain encouragement from believers. Discipline yourself. Make the effort, and you'll reap the rewards. *"I will instruct you and teach you in the way you should go; I will counsel you and watch over you"* (Psalm 32:8).

REMEMBER THIS

KEY POINT

If you seek God daily, walking with him becomes easier.

SNAPSHOTS OF WOMEN IN THE BIBLE

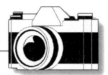

Elizabeth

This snapshot of Elizabeth records one of the most flattering descriptions I think any woman of the Bible ever received. She, along with her **priest** husband Zechariah, were described as *"upright in the sight of God, observing all the Lord's commandments and regulations blamelessly"* (Luke 1:6). Wow! What a compliment! I think the greatest **epitaph** on a tombstone would read, "She walked with God." If there had been tombstones in that era, that's what Elizabeth's would have read.

Elizabeth and Zechariah suffered greatly as a couple because they were <u>childless</u>, a condition that was humiliating in their culture. Elizabeth may have questioned God: Why had he not blessed them with a child? What had she done wrong?

As Zechariah performed a once-in-a-lifetime priestly duty of burning incense to God (see illustration, page 12), the angel Gabriel appeared to him. Zechariah was *"startled and gripped with fear"* (Luke 1:12). Every reference in Scripture to <u>Gabriel</u> follows with the fear factor (see GWDN, pages 222, 264; GWBI, page 166). I wonder if he discussed this with other angels: "Why are they so afraid? Is it my looks? My voice? What?"

Gabriel shared the good news that the prayers of Elizabeth and Zechariah would be answered—they would have a son, who should be named John. We know him as John the Baptist, who was the forerunner of Jesus Christ (see GWWB, pages 101–102, 293–294; GWBI, pages 168–170).

☞ **Check It Out:**

Luke 1:8–25, 39–45

priest: *mediator between God and others*

epitaph: *an inscription on a gravestone*

☞ **GO TO:**

Leviticus 21:1–7 (priest)

Luke 1:7 (childless)

Daniel 8:17; Luke 1:30 (Gabriel)

Zechariah probably used incense holders such as these when he performed his priestly duty of burning incense.

ACT OF GOD

the birth of John the Baptist

KEY POINT

Elizabeth was a woman of intimate faith who walked with God.

What Others are Saying:

Zechariah questioned and doubted Gabriel's message. The old priest wanted proof. That didn't sit too well with the angel. In modern terms Gabriel asked, "Don't you know who you are talking to?" Gabriel gave "proof" by striking the priest mute. Zechariah would not be able to speak until the birth of John.

After Zechariah went home to Elizabeth and wrote out his story of Gabriel's visit, she conceived and went into seclusion for five months. Scripture doesn't give her reasoning, but I think she secluded herself from the world to study, to pray, to praise God for answered prayer, and to prepare herself for raising a child who would bring the world one step closer to God. Jesus later said, *"I tell you the truth: Among those born of women there has not risen anyone greater than John the Baptist"* (Matthew 11:11).

Gien Karssen: People took what was happening to heart and said, "Watch that child. Wait and see what will become of him. God's hand is upon him in a special way." A new expectation broke loose. People began looking forward to what God was going to do. They were prepared for great things to come, for the Man who would come—Jesus, the Messiah. For all this God used Elizabeth, a woman of faith and remarkable character. What made her remarkable was that she was full of God.[4]

Today one out of five couples are infertile or have trouble conceiving. In Elizabeth's time, without modern medicine, I'm sure the numbers were even worse. We can learn from Elizabeth and her husband as they remained faithful in their service and prayers during their time of suffering and questioning. (We'll talk more on this subject in Chapter 2.)

God chose Elizabeth for a special blessing. She remained faithful to God during her entire life as she walked with him. What blessings and rewards he showers on the faithful! As you gain strength and stamina in the Lord, he will transform you from a wheezing jogger to a marathon runner. He can cause you to endure when you face life's challenges of heartache, grief, suffering, and change.

> **Matthew 4:4** Jesus answered, "It is written: 'Man does not live on bread alone, but on every word that comes from the mouth of God.'"

What's for Dinner? My Soul's Famished!

After the **baptism** of Jesus by **John the Baptist**, Jesus immediately went into the desert for forty days to pray and **fast** (see GWBI, pages 169–170; GWHN, pages 233–241). Baptism indicated the beginning of his ministry, and even God's son sought strength from his father, choosing the solitude of the desert.

There in the wilderness **Satan tempted** Christ, testing his inner spiritual strength during a time of physical weakness. Satan's first temptation dealt with Jesus' hunger by telling him to turn a stone into bread to prove he was the Son of God.

Jesus replied with an Old Testament story. When the Israelites wandered in the desert they survived on God's miraculous provision of **manna**, a bread from heaven. Jesus quoted Deuteronomy 8:3: "'Man does not live on bread alone but on every word that comes from the mouth of the Lord.'" The Israelites learned there was more to life than filling their stomachs. They needed God to satisfy their souls. The way Jesus broke the power of the temptation was by meeting it with God's truth from the Scriptures.

Think About It

REMEMBER THIS

☞ **GO TO:**

John 3:13–17 (baptism)

Isaiah 40:3–5 (John the Baptist)

Matthew 4:1–11 (tempted)

Exodus 16:31–32 (manna)

baptism: *a religious ceremony in which a spiritual leader uses water to show that a person belongs to God*

John the Baptist: *prophet who foretold the coming of the Messiah*

fast: *to willingly give up food for a time*

Satan: *"adversary," or enemy; Satan is the enemy of God and his people*

tempted: *to lure, entice, or coax to sin*

manna: *food God provided for Israelites in the desert*

What Others are Saying:

Bill Hybels: You can barely read a page in the Bible without encountering a situation where God is guiding someone. <u>Noah</u> was told to build a boat, and he was told exactly how to do it. <u>Abram</u> was instructed to leave his country and go to a land that God would show him. God guided Abraham's <u>servant</u> so that he could locate a wife for Isaac. Israelites were led on their <u>journey</u> out of Egypt by a pillar of cloud by day and a pillar of fire by night. The most productive, and most effective, way to receive God's guidance is the Bible. Almost all that we need to know is right there. Often the only things missing are the details. God has already told us in general terms how he wants us to live.[5]

Everyday Life

We are so confused by contradictory experts telling us what we can and can't eat that we're starving ourselves for fear of eating the wrong thing. We know we're to eat a proper diet, but what does it consist of? I recently read that years after the media blitz declaring bran the "cure all" food, it's been proven to have no major affect on cholesterol (see GWHN, pages 11–12). (That's okay by me. I wasn't real crazy about bran muffins anyway.)

☞ GO TO:

Genesis 6:11–22 (Noah)

Genesis 12:1 (Abram)

Genesis 24:1–27 (servant)

Exodus 12:40–14:18 (journey)

From now until eternity, experts will disagree on what our lips should or shouldn't touch for the overall health and fitness of our physical bodies. But nine out of ten religious experts would agree that the best diet for spiritual fitness is the Bible. The Scripture holds the answers to all of life's questions. It serves as our handbook to becoming faithfully fit.

KEY Outline:

Jesus Begins His Ministry
baptized by John
entered wilderness
for 40 days
fasted and prayed
tempted by Satan
overcame sin using
Scripture

KEY POINT

Scripture is food for the soul.

COFFEE BREAK
WITH GEORGIA

The Parable of the Squirrel

Suppose you were a squirrel. What would your Basic Survival Kit consist of? (If it took you more than two seconds to answer this, you're not cooperating with me.) Ask any local, run-of-the-mill, brown furry squirrel, and the answer is *nuts, nuts, and more nuts!*

Now, if you're wondering if *I've* gone nuts, just hang with me for a few more sentences.

The trees behind our house are filled with furry little critters scurrying here and there. Up the branches, down the branches, and dig, dig, dig. When we first moved into our house, one morning we watched from our kitchen window as a little brown squirrel dug and dug until his head disappeared. He popped back up, looked around cautiously to make sure there weren't any evil commando squirrels lurking in the woods, then quickly hid his stash of nuts. In a flash he filled in the hole and covered it, camouflaging it with leaves. He ran like lightning up the tree and out of sight.

His Basic Survival Kit consisted of nuts, nuts, and more nuts, hidden away for a future time of need. And sure enough, in winter we saw him (well, it *looked* like him) return to his nut stash for sustenance.

This story from Mr. Squirrel is a life lesson, or a **parable** (see GWBI, pages 191–192). Our Basic Survival Kit should consist of Scripture, Scripture, and more Scripture. The only truth we can rely upon is the Word of God. You might be battling poor health, mending relationships, facing grief, or seeking guidance in pressing decisions. Whatever it is, turn to your Basic Survival Kit and dig, dig, dig.

We have to constantly read God's Word and squirrel it away in our hearts, so in our time of need we have his help to survive. *"I have hidden your word in my heart that I might not sin against you"* (Psalm 119:11).

> **Proverbs 4:5–7** Get wisdom, get understanding; do not forget my words or swerve from them. Do not forsake wisdom, and she will protect you; love her, and she will watch over you. Wisdom is supreme, therefore get wisdom. Though it cost all you have, get understanding.

Supplement Boost

The Proverbs were wise sayings collected to train young men for leadership in governing Israel's **twelve** <u>tribes</u>. **Solomon**, the author and compiler of Proverbs, looked back on the guidance and **wisdom** he received as a young boy from his father, King David. He also recalled the tender loving care and <u>teaching</u> of his mother, **Bathsheba** (see GWWB, pages 214–218).

Wisdom and understanding provide the essential ingredients to succeed in everyday life as we overcome struggles, endure heartaches, and face life-changing decisions.

If we want wisdom, Proverbs says we need to start with a healthy intake of "the **fear** of the Lord" (Proverbs 1:7). God doesn't want us to dread him. Rather he wants us to seek his perspective about all areas of life.

parable: a story teaching a moral lesson

☞ **GO TO:**

Genesis 49:1–28 (tribes)

Proverbs 1:8 (teaching)

twelve tribes: descendants of the twelve sons of Jacob

Solomon: "peaceful" third king of Israel

wisdom: good sense; insight; understanding

Bathsheba: committed adultery with David; later married him

fear: reverence or worship

Think About It

Mankind has always searched for wisdom and truth. One prime-time TV show dramatizes that search by exploring spiritual themes every week, drawing millions of viewers. Am I talking about *Touched by an Angel*? Nope. I'm talking about the quirky hit, *The X-Files*. Searching for the reality behind bizarre cosmic happenings, FBI Agent Fox Mulder reassures himself, "The truth is out there." To find it, he needs the help of his partner, Dana Sculley.

Oprah Winfrey seems to be actively searching for wisdom. In recent months she was criticized for hosting on her daily TV show too many religious (and what I categorize as "not so religious") guests who claim they have answers to all of life's questions. Oprah's quest for wisdom has led her to inquire of others.

People were looking for wisdom two thousand years ago as well. Take Mary, for instance. When the mother of Jesus found out she would be pregnant with God's son she immediately <u>visited</u> her relative Elizabeth for guidance. There she found comfort, wisdom, and understanding of her divine calling as Elizabeth ministered to her.

☞ **GO TO:**

Luke 1:39 (visited)

Everyday Life

Laugh Out Loud

Like vitamin supplements that give our bodies an extra boost, we can add supplements to our daily Bible study by gaining wisdom from others who walk with God. You'll find a wealth of resources in this book's "What Others Are Saying" sections and in "Georgia's Bookshelf" at the end of each chapter. I encourage you to read devotional thoughts and dive into Christian women's magazines that are based on Scripture. To energize spiritually, I highly recommend that you attend a Christian women's conference. I always return home encouraged and renewed by the different perspectives and insights I find at such conferences. We are not meant to follow God alone. Hey, even the Lone Ranger wasn't really "lone"—he had Tonto!

KEY POINT

We can gain wisdom from others who have walked with God.

> **John 7:37–38** Jesus stood and said in a loud voice, "If anyone is thirsty, let him come to me and drink. Whoever believes in me, as the Scripture has said, streams of living water will flow from within him."

The Purest Water on the Market

During the last days of Jesus' ministry he faced opposition from the religious leaders. In the middle of the celebration of the **Feast of Tabernacles** Jesus went to the Temple courts and began to teach. The Jews were amazed at his knowledge and wondered if he was the Messiah (see GWRV, pages 269, 290–291, 318). Many believed and put their faith in him, but because of envy the **Pharisees** sent guards to arrest him. But no one laid a hand on him (see GWBI, pages 187–190).

Traditionally, on the last day of the feast the priest would draw water and take it to the Temple to be poured out. This represented the abundant supply of water God provided the Jews in the wilderness. Significantly, that was the day Jesus proclaimed that he was the Rock out of which the only water flowed that could quench the spiritual thirst of humanity.

Roger Frederickson: All through the Scriptures water has a rich and varied spiritual meaning, but always of life. It seems that the precious physical water, coming from well or river, bringing life and beauty to the barren land of Jesus, had become a symbol of that everlasting water which could quench and revive the parched, dying human spirit. So the teaching of Jesus, his words of wisdom and truth, is life, water for man dying of thirst.[6]

Water is a must for weight loss and weight management (see GWHN, pages 145–146). You can go without food for up to sixty days, but you can't live without water. It's life-giving, it replenishes, and it purifies. Water serves as an appetite **suppressant**. It helps eliminate waste and removes fat. It helps maintain proper muscle tone. Since water is natural, your body knows exactly what to do with it.

I had been out of town for a few days attending a conference, and when I got home wilted plants greeted me. I had forgotten to ask my husband to water the plants. My husband had to pass by one large plant every time he went in and out of our bedroom. I'm surprised he didn't hear the plant screaming "Water, water, I need water!" It looked like it wouldn't survive, but I watered it heavily. The next morning the plant looked so good that I suspected my guilt-ridden husband had run out in the middle of the night and replaced it with a new plant. (He hadn't.)

Like my poor neglected houseplant, when we go without being replenished and **purified** by the Living Water that Jesus gives, we become wilted and weary, barely hanging on to life.

☞ **GO TO:**

John 7:1 (opposition)

Leviticus 23:36 (Feast of Tabernacles)

Isaiah 53:1–12 (Messiah)

Exodus 17:7 (provided)

2 Corinthians 10:4–6 (Rock)

What Others are Saying:

Feast of Tabernacles: *an annual celebration of God's past care for his people*

Everyday Life

Messiah: *Hebrew word meaning "anointed one"*

Pharisees: *self-appointed Jewish leaders who often opposed Jesus*

suppressant: *subdue; restrain; conceal*

☞ **GO TO:**

James 4:8 (purified)

purified: *to make clean*

REMEMBER THIS

☞ **GO TO:**

Psalm 42:1–2 (thirst)

Psalm 51:1–2 (cleanses)

John 7:37–39 (Living Water)

cleanses: *make holy and pure*

☞ **Check It Out:**

John 4:4–26

KEY Outline:

The Samaritan Woman

was an empty vessel
was filled with Living Water
shared the message of Christ

KEY POINT

The Samaritan woman was filled with Living Water by believing Jesus.

When we drink the Living Water that Jesus gives, it quenches our <u>thirst</u> for righteousness. *"For he satisfies the thirsty, and fills the hungry with good things"* (Psalm 107:9). He **cleanses** and removes waste from our polluted souls. <u>Living Water</u> is a metaphor for God's Holy Spirit, who gives us strength and stamina to stretch ourselves beyond what we think is possible. Living Water is the purest, most natural ingredient our spirits know.

SNAPSHOTS OF WOMEN IN THE BIBLE

The Samaritan Woman

In the story of the Samaritan woman, we have a snapshot of an empty vessel being filled (see GWWB, page 46). Ordinarily, the daily task of drawing water from a well was a social event as women gathered in the cool of the morning for the chore. But the Samaritan woman was an outcast. Having failed at five previous marriages, she now settled for an illicit live-in partner. She either was not welcomed or chose not to endure the disapproving stares of the village women, forcing her to come in the dusty heat of the day to fill her pitcher.

Seeing a weary man seated at the well, she approached with caution. When he asked her for a drink, his accent gave him away. He was a Jew in Samaria. The Jews and the Samaritans hated one another, bitterly divided over religious issues that dated back centuries. She asked him why he would even speak to a woman, let alone an outcast Samaritan woman.

In their short conversation, not only did Jesus reveal the secret sins of her life and heart, but for the first time he revealed himself as Christ, the Messiah—the one who both the Samaritans and Jews had long awaited.

The meeting with Jesus transformed the woman. She ran back to the village, unashamed, telling everyone about him. Because of her enthusiastic testimony, Jesus and his disciples stayed in Samaria for two extra days. Many believed in him.

An empty vessel allowed herself to be filled with Living Water. A life, a village, and a world were changed forever as they quenched their spiritual thirst.

18   WHAT'S IN THE BIBLE FOR . . . WOMEN

> **Matthew 11:28** Come to me, all you who are weary and burdened, and I will give you rest. Take my yoke upon you and learn from me, for I am gentle and humble in heart, and you will find rest for your souls.

☞ **GO TO:**

Matthew 11:20 (miracles)

Matthew 23:1–5 (Pharisees)

Acts 15:10–11 (grace)

Get Some Rest

During this time in Jesus' ministry, even though he performed many **miracles** (see GWBI, pages 26–27, 86), the Jews rebelled against him. Still he held open the invitation to come rest in him. He knew how weary the people were.

The <u>Pharisees</u>, who had burdened the people with strict laws, did not practice what they preached. They knew the letter of the Law, but not the spirit behind it. The people felt they were saved by sheer obedience to the Law. They grew weary because keeping all of the Law as the Pharisees interpreted it was a hopeless task.

Jesus offered to lift their burdens, for only through the **grace** of Jesus are people saved. Only through resting in what Jesus has done for us will we find peace with God and man.

miracles: an act done by God's power

grace: the special favor of God; God's free gift of salvation

Everyday Life

What wakes you up in the morning? I have a new alarm clock that beeps at me. I liked the tone in the beginning. It wasn't as alarming as a fog horn blast. But sometimes when I wake, I have this sudden fear a garbage truck is backing over me, until I realize it's my alarm clock.

Earlier in my life, I didn't need an alarm. I had an internal clock that woke me up at the same time every morning, bright and early. Over the years, marriage, schedules, and childbirth seemed to change my internal clock forever. In fact, I think it broke.

I admit the real reason I have such a hard time getting up is quite simple: I'm not getting enough sleep!

Do you find yourself not only a physical but also a spiritual zombie? Are you not getting enough spiritual rest through prayer, scripture reading, and meditation? Maybe this is your wake-up call.

I promise I'll hit the pillow earlier and rest more in him. How 'bout you? *"Rest in the Lord, wait patiently for him"* (Psalm 37:7).

Evidently I'm not the only one lacking sleep. A recent cover story in *Life Magazine* read, "Why 70 Million of Us Are Sleepless in America." Did you know there are 3,000 sleep disorder clinics across America? According to the article, they've sprung up in response to a national nightmare—"an epidemic of sleeplessness."

Laugh Out Loud

KEY Outline:

Rest for the Weary
Jesus
- offers invitation
- lifts your spiritual burden
- his heart is gentle
- his heart is humble
- provides rest for your souls

One Congressional study determined we are a nation of zombies, and the cost to society is stunning. The article says nearly two thirds of Americans claim sleep deprivation affects their work, which translates into a $70 billion loss in productivity.[7]

The problem harks back to 1879, when a famous short-sleeper named Thomas Alva Edison perfected the light bulb. Over time, downtowns began to bustle after dark, shift work burgeoned, and reading into the night (later, listening to the radio, watching TV, and surfing the Internet) became part of American life.

Hey, it's Edison's fault! Actually, it's not his fault. It's our own choice. It's called responsibility. You *can* turn a light bulb off, you know.

Philippians 4:6–7 Do not be anxious about anything, but in everything, by prayer and petition, with thanksgiving, present your request to God. And the peace of God, which transcends all understanding, will guard your heart and your minds in Jesus Christ.

How Do You Spell Relief? I Spell It P-R-A-Y-E-R

The **Apostle Paul**'s (see GWBI, pages 220–225) simple message to the church at Philippi was don't **worry**. As we make our requests known to God through continual **prayer**, we experience the peace of God. As your heart and mind are torn in the struggles of living, God will guard your thoughts in Christ as you turn your worries over to him.

Charles R. Swindoll: I urge you to include in your schedule time to be alone with God. I am fortunate to live within ninety minutes of the mountains and less than forty-five minutes from the beach. Those are great places to commune with God. . . . The gentle breeze blowing through the forest is therapeutic. Sometimes just being alone out in God's marvelous creation is all that's needed for the scales to be removed from your eyes and for you to silence the harassment and the noise of your day and begin to hear from God. On those occasions the Lord ministers to us in a gentle whispering.[8]

Mother Teresa: If you are searching for God and do not know where to begin, learn to pray and take the trouble to pray every day. You can pray anytime, anywhere. Try speaking directly to God. Just speak. Tell everything to him. He is our father. We are all created by God, we are his children . . . . And if we pray, we will get all the answers we need.[9]

What Others are Saying:

"We Just Don't Talk Anymore"

Exercise is one of the greatest stress relievers. When we're stressed we often forget to exercise, even though that's when our body, mind, and soul need it the most. We can get so stressed out that we can't even sleep. Experts agree that the best exercise can be as simple as a stroll. Get as far away from the source of your stress as possible.

I would add to that stroll a more powerful solution: Make it a prayer walk. Prayer is a discipline that lets us escape this world and turn our stress over to God. Prayer nurtures your relationship with God. You <u>slow</u> down to meet him, <u>rest</u>, talk, and walk with him. The biggest complaint we women have in marriages is, "my husband won't talk to me." We don't want God to have the same complaint about us.

Even God's son took time away to be with him in prayer. If Jesus relied on its power, we should immerse ourselves in daily prayer.

KEY POINT

Prayer is a discipline that lets us escape this world and turn our stress over to God.

☞ **GO TO:**

Psalm 46:10 (slow)

Psalm 116:7 (rest)

EXAMPLES FROM THE BIBLE

Prayers of Bible Women

Old Testament

1 Samuel 2:2–10	Hannah, the mother of Samuel the prophet, prayed in the Temple.
Genesis 29:33	Leah, the wife of Jacob, bore six sons of the twelve tribes of Israel. She poured out her sorrows in prayer for she was unloved by her husband.
Judges 13:1–24	Samson's mother had a visit from an angel as she meditated and prayed in a field. The angel predicted Samson's birth and instructed her how to raise him.

Luke 2:36–38	Anna, an aged widow who lived and served in the Temple at Jerusalem, prayed both day and night. As Jesus' parents brought him to the Temple for consecration after his birth, Anna declared he was the promised Messiah.
Acts 16:14	Lydia, a wealthy businesswoman, met with women to pray. She opened her home as a house church.
Luke 1:46–55	Mary, the Mother of Jesus, prayed and praised God for the wondrous miracle virgin birth of Christ.

> **1 Timothy 1:12** I thank Christ Jesus our Lord, who has given me strength, that he considered me faithful, appointing me to his service.

What's My Goal?

In the letter the Apostle Paul wrote to Timothy, his co-laborer and unofficial son in Christ, Paul testifies of his personal relationship with Jesus and how God <u>changed</u> his life from a persecutor of Christians to a proclaimer of the Gospel of Christ. Through the Lord, Paul gained strength to carry out his mission.

There are two themes you read frequently in Scriptures: **faithfulness** and **endurance**. That's what it takes to know God intimately.

☞ **GO TO:**

Acts 9:1–42 (changed)

faithfulness: *loyal belief, trust*

endurance: *to continue, to remain firm*

EXAMPLES FROM THE BIBLE

Biblical Examples of Faith

"Now faith is being sure of what we hope for and certain of what we do not see" (Hebrews 11:1). By faith . . .

- . . . Abel obediently brought an offering that pleased God more than his brother Cain's offering. (Genesis 4:4)
- . . . Enoch trusted and walked with God so closely that God took him to heaven without an earthly death. (Genesis 5:21–24)

- . . . Noah trusted and believed God's warning of a flood, prepared an ark, and saved his family. (Genesis 6:13–22)
- . . . Abraham obeyed God's command to leave his homeland for land promised by God. He trusted that God would fulfill his promise of an inheritance. (Genesis 12:1–4, 7; Acts 7:2–4)
- . . . Sarah in her old age believed that God would make her a mother. A whole nation came from Sarah and Abraham as God blessed them with Isaac. (Genesis 17:19, 8:11–14, 21:2)
- . . . Isaac knew God would give future blessings to his two sons, Jacob and Esau. (Genesis 27:27–39)
- . . . Jacob blessed each of the sons of Joseph and prayed and worshiped God. (Genesis 48:1, 5, 16, 20)
- . . . Joseph, when he was dying, confidently spoke of God bringing the people of Israel out of Egypt. He was so sure he made them promise to carry his bones with them when they left. (Genesis 5:24; Exodus 13:19)
- . . . Moses' parents, when they saw God had given them a special child, hid him for three months, trusting that God would save him from the death the **Pharaoh** commanded. (Exodus 1:16, 22, 2:2)
- . . . Moses, when he grew up, chose to be mistreated along with God's people instead of living as the son of Pharaoh. By faith he left Egypt and did not fear Pharaoh. (Exodus 2:10, 11, 12:50; Hebrews 11:25)
- . . . Moses believed God's instructions and commanded his people to kill a lamb and sprinkle its blood on the door posts of their homes, so that God's Death Angel would not kill their oldest child. (Exodus 12:21–29)
- . . . Moses led the children of Israel out of Egypt and walked through the Red Sea on dry ground. (Exodus 14:22–29)

Earlier in this chapter, I told you a little about my weight loss. My battle is not over. In order to maintain my ideal fitness level, I cannot have a faddish or passing interest in proper exercise and diet. They have to be my way of life. It takes endurance. In the same way, our quest for spiritual fitness also takes a lifelong commitment.

KEY POINT

Faith is God's vehicle for bringing us closer to him.

Pharaoh: an Egyptian ruler

REMEMBER  THIS

Think About It

Ask yourself this question: "What do I want to accomplish with my spiritual fitness program?"

If you are spiritually healthy overall, you should raise your activity level. Dig deeper, aim higher, stretch yourself.

If you are just getting started, similar to the way fitness experts recommend light workouts for entry-level athletes, I recommend a moderate intensity of prayer and Bible reading for a total of 30 minutes a day. It will fortify your soul and help you attain your goal of being spiritually fit and drawing closer to God.

STUDY QUESTIONS

1. What is special about God's Word according to Psalm 19:7–11?
2. How did Sarah put her faith and trust in God?
3. What did Mary of Bethany surrender to Jesus?
4. As we exercise our way to spiritual fitness and commit to walking in God's truth, what three ingredients should be a part of our everyday life?
5. How did Elizabeth walk with God?
6. There is more to life than filling our stomach with food. What does God offer that satisfies our souls?
7. What did the Samaritan woman find at the well?
8. According to Romans 12:12, how does prayer make a difference in your life and the lives of others?

CHAPTER WRAP-UP

- On our quest to spiritual fitness, our first step is a regular check-up with the Great Physician. You must strive to develop an intimate relationship with him in order to become the woman he designed you to be.

- In order to stay in shape and remain healthy, spiritual fitness requires as much exercise, self-discipline, and good nourishment as physical fitness. You may have fallen out of the repetition of building your spiritual body. There's no time better than now to commit to doing prayer, worship, and Bible study.

- Our money-back guaranteed diet plan for spiritual fitness is: **ingest** the Scriptures. The Bible holds the answers to all of life's questions. It serves as our handbook to becoming faithfully fit. It's the only diet where you *should* eat as much as you can.

- Jesus offers Living Water. He invites us to come and rest in him. Through prayer, allow God to minister to you, to guide you, to

ingest: *to take into the body*

take away stress, and to quench your soul's thirst as you place your trust in him.

- Make it your goal to follow Jesus more closely.

GEORGIA'S BOOKSHELF

Some of Georgia's favorite books for strengthening your walk with God:

- *Come Walk with Me*, Carole Mayhall, WaterBrook Press
- *The God You're Looking For*, Bill Hybels, Thomas Nelson
- *Realizing the Presence of the Spirit*, Margaret Therkelsen, Revell
- *Strengthening Your Faith*, Women of Faith Bible Study Series, Zondervan
- *Something More*, Catherine Marshall, Chosen Books

2 RAINY DAYS AND MONDAYS

Loving God during Disappointments, Suffering, and Loss

Here We Go

Pick up a newspaper in Anytown, U.S.A. and you will find it filled with "rainy days and Mondays" stories any day of the week. (Even Monday.) "Rainy days and Mondays" stories tell of disappointments and suffering. Headlines bellow in bold print about murder, rape, violence, tragic accidents, death, bankruptcy, disease, and divorce. Behind the headlines are real people who are in the storm of suffering.

In the 1960s Dr. Elisabeth Kübler-Ross wrote a book called *On Death and Dying*. Dr. Ross wrote of the five emotional stages a terminal patient experiences once he knows he is going to die. She gained her knowledge by talking with over two hundred terminally ill patients. The first stage was denial, then anger, bargaining, depression, and finally acceptance.[1]

This chapter is not particularly about death; it's about living life during your suffering. But during our suffering we experience some of the same emotions Dr. Ross witnessed. We'll see what the Bible says about how we can handle our emotions when we suffer—and where to find recovery and the gift of hope.

KEY POINT

We must live life during our suffering.

EXAMPLES FROM THE BIBLE

Bad things do happen to good people, and the Bible is filled with "rainy days and Mondays" stories of men and women who encountered the storms of life and looked to God to calm the storm.

- Hannah was so distraught because of her infertility that she constantly wept and would not eat. (1 Samuel 1:7)
- When Michal helped her husband David escape the murderous wrath of her father, King Saul, she was separated from her husband because she went against her father. (1 Samuel 19:11–17)
- The Canaanite woman suffered over the condition of her child who was demon possessed. (Matthew 15:25–26)
- Jesus took pity on the mother who grieved over the death of her only son. (Luke 7:11–15)
- A sick diseased woman who had been crooked and suffered for 18 years came to Jesus for relief. (Luke 13:11–13)

How we respond to our rainy day disappointments determines whether we spot the silver lining among the storm clouds. If you look at life from the perspective that God is **sovereign** and will love and protect you in the hard times, you'll find that surviving the wind and rain can actually bring you closer to him.

> **Jeremiah 29:11** "For I know the plans I have for you," declares the Lord, "plans to prosper you and not to harm you, plans to give you hope and a future."

When It Rains, It Pours

Jeremiah was a **prophet** called by God to deliver a <u>message</u> to the Israelites. Because Israel's leaders began practicing **idolatry**, God allowed **Nebuchadnezzar** (see GWDN, pages 18–20, 39–42) to take the cream of Israel's society captive. Jeremiah wrote a letter to the captives, consoling those who were homesick and brokenhearted in exile. They may be suffering, he told them, but they shouldn't stop living. God wanted them to build houses, plant gardens, bear children, be good citizens, and not listen to false

---

KEY POINT

Rain falls on both good and bad people. Run to God for shelter.

REMEMBER THIS

☞ **GO TO:**

Psalm 141:8 (sovereign)

sovereign: *supreme authority*

☞ **GO TO:**

Jeremiah 29:1–32 (message)

prophet: *a person who speaks for God*

idolatry: *worshiping idols or false gods*

Nebuchadnezzar: *king of Babylonia, reigned from 605–562 B.C.*

WHAT'S IT THE BIBLE FOR . . . WOMEN

prophets. Speaking through Jeremiah, God promised that in seventy years he would free them, so they should be patient. They didn't know what the future held, but God did, and he knew they had a bright future—despite their current stormy times.

I'm sure disappointment has touched your life in some way. Like a crowd scattering to escape a downpour, we all get wet; but some get wetter than others. Suffering falls on the rich, the poor, the young, the old, the educated and uneducated, the saved and the unsaved.

I feel as though disappointments follow me. A few months ago during a thunderstorm in my life (complete with deafening thunderclaps and terrifying bolts of lightning to my soul), my sister Connie said, "Georgia, I'm going to give you a new name. You've been through so much. I'm going to call you the Energizer Rabbit. You just keep going, and going, and going."

I laughed and did my impersonation of the bunny marching around beating his drum. What else can you do but keep going? I use to ask God, "Why me?" Then as I suffered and grew closer to him with each storm, I now say, "Why not me?" Disappointment and suffering is another side of life. A painful side, yes, but one we all experience.

Joni Eareckson Tada: God's plan is specific. He doesn't say, "Into each life a little rain must fall," then aim a hose in earth's general direction and see who gets the wettest. He doesn't reach for a key, wind up nature with its sunny days and hurricanes, and sit back and watch the show. He doesn't let Satan prowl about totally unrestricted. He doesn't believe in a hands-off policy of governing. He's not our planet's absentee landlord. Rather, he screens the trials that come to each of us—allowing only those that accomplish his good plan, because he takes no joy in human agony.[2]

Like the Jewish exiles, we may feel as though we are trapped in a situation against our will. We can find hope in Jeremiah's message. Don't give up! Keep on living, for your God is the God of *"hope and a future."*

The Bible records many who did not give up when trials came their way. Jochobed was faced with the impending death of her baby boy, Moses, because Pharaoh had ordered all male Hebrew babies to be killed. Jochobed wove a basket boat, hid Moses in it, and trusted God to save Moses' life.

Everyday Life

KEY Outline:

Jeremiah's Message
keep living
be patient
wait on God
God has a bright future
for you

What Others
are Saying:

KEY POINT

Suffering is a part of life. God does not always remove suffering, but he fills it with his presence.

REMEMBER  THIS

The starving widow of **Zarepath** did not give up when she faced a famine. She gave her last food to the prophet Elijah. Because she followed Elijah's directions, she and her son survived.

☞ **Check It Out:**

1 Samuel 1:1–2:11

COFFEE BREAK
WITH GEORGIA

Remain Calm

The parting words of my physician as I left her examining room were, "Remain calm." I had already tried to "remain calm" days preceding my office visit when I discovered a lump during a breast self-examination. After I saw my doctor, she advised further evaluation and a mammogram to be done the following week.

During the week of waiting my mind echoed her words: "Remain calm. Remain calm." But that's hard to do when your mind races with all the worst-case scenarios. Knowing that breast cancer is the second leading cause of death in women, my greatest concern was: If I died, who would help raise my five-year-old son?

During my week of waiting, I spoke at a women's conference. My workshop title was, "Kids: Ya Gotta Love 'Em." I used 1 Samuel as my Scripture text, with Hannah as a model mother.

Hannah (see GWWB, pages 129–130) loved her son **Samuel** and trained him to know God, though she only had him for a short time. After he was weaned (which was three years or more, since the ancient East had no way to keep milk sweet), she had to release her son to Eli, the priest. She knew Samuel went to live in less-than-ideal circumstances, yet she offered beautiful worship as she released him to God.

☞ **GO TO:**

1 Samuel 1:1–2:21
(Hannah)

Hannah: *the mother of Samuel*

Samuel: *earliest of the great Hebrew prophets after Moses*

Hannah's example inspired me that day. As I led the workshop, I was supposed to be speaking to the audience, but I was actually speaking to myself. For the first time, I felt peaceful about my impending diagnosis. I knew that no matter what happened, I had trained our son to know and love God, and if I had to leave him before I wanted to, I was releasing him into God's hands. In fact, he had been in God's hands all along.

KEY POINT

Remain calm!

Visits with the radiologist, confirmed by biopsies, showed no sign of cancer, merely fibroid tumors. Praise God, it had been a false alarm. But even if it weren't, I still like my doctor's advice: "Remain calm." And in my times of waiting I will cling to the **exhortation**, *"Wait for the Lord; be strong and take heart and wait for the Lord"* (Psalm 27:14).

exhortation: *urgent encouragement*

> **Psalm 34:18** The Lord is close to the brokenhearted and saves those who are crushed in spirit.

If You Let a Smile Be Your Umbrella, You'll Get a Mouthful of Rain

Across the eons, heartbreak is heartbreak. The psalmist felt his pain as deeply as you or I do now. Yet across those same eons, God has been near and comes to his children in their brokenness. When we call out to him in our time of need, God hears and rushes to our side just as a loving mother rushes to the bedside of her sick child to love and comfort him.

Webster's definition for **denial** reads, "a refusal to believe or accept." In times of disappointment and suffering, denial serves as a buffer. We pop up the protective umbrella of denial, believing that since we have an umbrella, we won't get wet.

Denial can seem to help for a short period of time, but the strong winds of reality turn our would-be umbrella inside out. Eventually, we are forced to face the truth of our tempest. The first step to calming the storm is to move beyond denial by calling out for God.

Gerald L. Sittser: Denial puts off what should be faced. People in denial refuse to see loss for what it is: something terrible that cannot be reversed. They dodge pain rather than confront it. But their unwillingness to face pain comes at a price. Ultimately it diminishes the capacity of their souls to grow bigger in response to pain. They make the same mistake as patients who, following major surgery, refuse to get out of bed and put damaged muscles back to work. They pretend nothing is wrong and tell everyone that they are feeling wonderful. But denial of their problems causes muscles to atrophy until they cannot get out of bed at all. In the end denial leads to a greater loss.[3]

Homespun Wisdom: In her book *I'm Alive and the Doctor's Dead*, Sue Buchanan, a cancer survivor, recounts the time a doctor told her she would die from breast cancer. Fifteen years later, she had outlived him. In her humorous but honest narrative, Sue tells how her negative attitude toward chemotherapy had her fussing and stewing about the "yucky stuff." But after a couple of months of fighting against everything chemotherapy represented,

KEY POINT

When you are brokenhearted God loves you and is near.

denial: the refusal to believe or accept

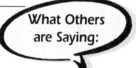

What Others are Saying:

KEY POINT

You must move beyond denial for healing to begin.

she forced herself to change her attitude. As she moved beyond denial, it dawned on her she shouldn't fight medical help. It was good. It could cure her. "I must accept this medicine into my body, be thankful for it, and trust it to work for me and make me well," she finally realized. At that point she raised her hands and prayed, "Dear God, take this medicine and put it where it will do the most good. Thank you. Thank you from the bottom of my heart." In Sue's case, moving beyond denial was literally the beginning of her healing.

> **1 Peter 4:1–2** Therefore, since Christ suffered in his body, arm yourselves also with the same attitude, because he who has suffered in his body is done with **sin**. As a result, he does not live the rest of his earthly life for evil human desires, but rather for the will of God.

I'm Drenched in Pain

The Apostle Peter wrote to the suffering church in **Asia Minor** (see GWBI, pages 304–308) with practical advice for their hardships. Persecution tested the believers, and they anticipated worse to come under Nero, the emperor of Rome.

Peter reminded the Church that Christ also <u>suffered</u> in the body, so we should put on the spiritual attitude of Christ. As we turn away from sin and turn toward Christ, we no longer live for our own <u>wants</u> and desires; instead, we follow him. We live as Christ would have us live according to his <u>Word</u>.

The isolation of our pain brings us to God. During Christ's suffering before his **crucifixion** (see illustration, page 33), he prayed to God. Though he had asked close friends for companionship, he prayed in isolation. Knowing what lay ahead, he asked God to "*take this cup from me*" (Matthew 26:39). God did not remove the pain and suffering, but allowed his son to suffer cruel death on a cross as a sacrifice for all humanity that we might have **eternal life**.

Our hope during suffering is in the intimate relationship we have with God. If we are <u>one</u> with him, we can enjoy life regardless of the suffering we experience.

---

sin: an act of wrongdoing; any violation of God's Law

☞ **GO TO:**

Matthew 27:1–66 (suffered)

2 Corinthians 5:14–17 (wants)

1 Peter 4:7–11 (Word)

John 3:14–15 (eternal life)

Romans 5:6–7 (one)

Asia Minor: *the peninsula between the Black and Mediterranean seas that includes most of Turkey*

crucifixion: *Roman execution where criminals were nailed to wooden crossbeams*

eternal life: *life forever in heaven with God*

The Crucifixion

Jesus was hung on a cross like a criminal or a runaway slave. Crucifixion was the most painful and degrading form of capital punishment.

EXAMPLES FROM THE BIBLE

Suffering was a common experience for many people in the Bible:

- Job, a wealthy man of God, lost his children, his possessions, and his health when Satan took them all away. Yet he stayed true to God and praised him during his suffering. (Job 1:1, 21)

- The Apostle Peter suffered the consequences and pain of his denying he knew Jesus. (Luke 22:55–62)

- Yet, he recognized his failures and turned back to Christ, as he was the first apostle to run to Jesus' empty tomb. (Luke 24:12)

- Priscilla and her husband, Aquila, suffered mistreatment and loneliness as they and other Jews were expelled from their home in Rome. They risked their own lives and faced persecution as they helped spread the **Gospel** with their coworker, the Apostle Paul. (Acts 18:2, Romans 16:3–4)

KEY POINT

Suffering and pain force our souls to grow.

Gospel: *"Good news";* *the Bible*

Think About It

The spiritual side of suffering is that pain can either turn you bitter or draw you closer to God. When mixed with patient faith, suffering can make your soul grow. Life-threatening events make our desires for earthly things vanish. The cars, the boat, the career—the trivial things of earth lose their luster. All you want is to feel God's ever-loving presence as he calms your soul, eases your pain, and renews your strength.

What Others are Saying:

magnitude: greatness; importance or influence

Jill Briscoe: Nobody knows what is around the corner of tomorrow. But one thing we can know: God will be waiting there for us. He is a God of comfort, a God well acquainted with grief and suffering. A God who knows what it is to have the forces of hell do their worst. Because God inhabits our future, he is never surprised by the **magnitude** of the troubles waiting for us. We may be surprised, but our heavenly Father never is.[4]

COFFEE BREAK WITH GEORGIA

Cradled in His Arms

The operating room was freezing. My body shook as nurses solemnly strapped me to the table for emergency surgery. With nowhere to look but up, I saw the brilliant lights form haloes as my vision moistened and blurred.

"Mrs. Ling, I need you to count backwards, starting with ten," instructed the anesthesiologist.

I begged the surgeon, "We want to have children. Please do whatever you can." His warm eyes assured me he would give me his best. Urgently, he repeated, "Mrs. Ling, please begin counting, now."

Swallowing hard, I began. "Ten, nine, eight . . ." My speech slurred. I silently prayed for God's protection. "Seven, six, five . . ." My thoughts spun like a whirlwind, reliving recent events as darkness veiled the room.

We were a statistic. One out of five couples have trouble conceiving or are infertile. After nine years of marriage, I had my first positive pregnancy test. We were elated. The nurse scheduled my first prenatal visit three long weeks away, but I knew our out-of-town vacation would make the time pass quickly. I could hardly wait to visit my physician.

During our vacation I experienced extreme abdominal pain, bleeding, and soaring fever. We made frantic phone calls, and upon

KEY Outline:

Peter's Message
suffering will come
Christ suffered
put on spiritual attitude
live for God

my doctor's instructions, I was rushed to an emergency room three hundred miles from home.

After several hours of examinations, ultrasounds, and concerned looks from attending physicians, we were finally informed I had lost the baby. My condition was life threatening, and I needed emergency surgery.

Even though a curtain was all that separated my husband and me from the emergency room full of patients and medical personnel, we found privacy in our little stall. We clung to each other and sobbed as our hopes and dreams of a little one were snatched from our very arms. Our grief for the one we would never cradle here on earth began that very moment.

My surgery was successful. We thanked God for that, and for the encouraging news that chances were good for another pregnancy. Our love grew deeper as we began to pick up the pieces. But nothing prepared me for the emotions that surfaced after the loss of our baby. Kind souls, trying to ease my pain with expressions like, "You're young, you can have more," "It was for the best," or "Just be thankful you were only a few months along," rubbed salt in my wounded heart. Days filled with silence but not understanding. Cards and phone calls were a wonderful blessing and comfort, but we grieved alone. Yet, God drew me closer to him through the isolation.

My sense of loneliness prompted me to ask God to never let me forget my grief. I wanted to remain sensitive to the grief of others and to help comfort them.

God answers prayers. Over the years, from that deep corner of my heart, pain and grief emerge when I hear about the loss of a child. I track down the family's address, write them an encouraging note, offer my sympathy and prayers, and send them one of my favorite books on the subject. I want them to know it is natural to grieve and they are not alone in their heart-wrenching journey.

When facing the lonely and tragic death of a dearly wanted unborn child, I knew I could turn to God because he has also experienced the pain of losing a son. He cradled me in his loving arms when I mourned over my empty arms—which God eventually filled. Two years later, I was in an operating room again, but this time I was able to cradle a scrunched-faced, squirming, healthy baby boy, my son Philip.

KEY POINT

When facing the lonely and tragic death of a dearly wanted unborn child, we can turn to God because he has also experienced the pain of losing a son.

Elijah: *a prophet to the Northern Kingdom of Israel; famous for his defeat of 400 false prophets at Mount Carmel*

☞ **Check It Out:**

1 Kings 17:1–24

King Ahab: *king over Israel in Samaria for twenty-two years*

Jezebel: *wife of King Ahab and enemy of Elijah*

Baal: *the main god of Canaanite people*

SNAPSHOTS OF WOMEN IN THE BIBLE

The Widow of Zarepath

The widow of Zarepath was no stranger to pain and suffering. But God rescued her from eternal suffering by showing her his power through the prophet Elijah.

Elijah had appeared with a message from an angry God to **King Ahab** and Queen **Jezebel** (see GWBI, pages 86–87; GWWB, pages 161–171). Ahab was described as one *"who did more to provoke the Lord, the God of Israel, to anger than did all the kings of Israel before him"* (1 Kings 16:33).

There were many reasons Ahab angered God, but one stood out: after he married Jezebel, a daughter of a king and priest of **Baal** (see illustration, this page), Ahab not only allowed her to build temples to this pagan god, but he joined her in worshiping the god of sex, nature, and war. Baal worship required the horrific practice of child sacrifice.

Elijah's simple yet bold message was a prophecy that no rain or dew would fall in Israel until he said it could. This was God's scornful way of saying to Ahab, "See what your god of nature can do now!"

Over two years later, the drought continued, and Ahab considered Elijah Public Enemy #1. God directed Elijah to go to Zarepath (see illustration, page 37), a great hiding place for him. It was Jezebel's hometown. No one would think Elijah stupid enough to go there.

At the city gate, Elijah saw the widow. I imagine her as a picture of suffering, an undernourished, hollow-eyed woman of skin and bones. I see her painstakingly bent over gathering sticks from the parched ground to cook her last meal for her son. Led by God, Elijah asked her for food and water.

Baal

A weather god associated with thunderstorms and fertility. Worship of Baal involved ritual prostitution and sometimes child sacrifice.

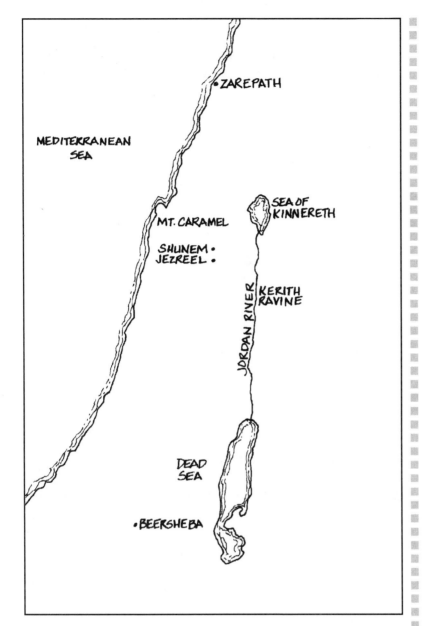

Elijah's Travels

Elijah ran from Queen Jezebel in Beersheba to the Kerith Ravine. Later he traveled to Zarepath where he met the widow.

The widow openly shared her struggles and fears, and her plans for one last meal. Soon her family's suffering would end in death.

Elijah told her not to be afraid. He had a message from God. If she followed his instructions, there would be food for her household until the drought ended and the rain returned.

What did the widow have to lose? She obeyed Elijah. And it worked! Day after day she went to the jug of oil and jar of flour

Canaanite: the ancient name of people living along the eastern shore of the Mediterranean

☞ **GO TO:**

Exodus 16:31–32 (manna)

manna: *Hebrew for "What is it?"; one of the foods God provided for the Israelites during the* **Exodus**

Exodus: *God's deliverance of the Hebrews from slavery in Egypt and their journey to a new land*

ACT OF GOD

First resurrection recorded

Think About It

☞ **GO TO:**

Exodus 3:7–10 (Exodus)

Psalm 4:5; Isaiah 26:4; Hebrews 2:13 (trust)

Psalm 103:21; Matthew 8:27; Acts 5:29; 1 Peter 1:2 (obey)

1 Timothy 5:15; Revelation 12:9 (devil)

devil: *Satan; "the adversary," enemy of God*

that she had emptied the day before. Day after day, jug and jar were again filled with enough to feed her household one more meal. It was just like the **manna** that God provided daily for the children of Israel in the wilderness. Her strength was renewed during her days of suffering.

Time wore on, and death surrounded her. Starvation swelled the bellies of children and claimed the lives of her neighbors. Her household was spared, until her son became ill and died. Her disappointment and doubt returned. In her suffering and anger she asked, as we do, "Why me? I've done what you asked. What have I done to deserve this?"

Elijah, through God, miraculously brought her son back to life. The widow of Zarepath proclaimed that Elijah truly was a man of God.

By accepting and following the instructions from God, a widow survived her days of suffering and loss.

The Bible is our message from God. Turn to it in times of disappointment and suffering. <u>Trust</u> and <u>obey</u> and God will be faithful to see you through, one day at a time.

Homespun Wisdom: I like to journal my experiences during life's thunderstorms. Later, the journal jogs my memory, for when Jesus the Son shines, I can look back and see that God truly helped in times of crisis. *"My God shall supply all your needs according to his riches in glory by Jesus Christ"* (Philippians 4:19).

> **Ephesians 4:26** In your anger do not sin. Do not let the sun go down while you are still angry, and do not give the **devil** a foothold.

Don't Pitch a Hissy Fit

The Apostle Paul wrote the church at Ephesus (see illustration, page 143; GWBI, pages 259–263) to give them guidance in their Christian walk. He advised them to control their anger. We can express our anger and frustration, but we are not to let anger turn to hatred and bitterness.

EXAMPLES FROM THE BIBLE

The Bible gives us pictures of men and women who allowed anger to control their emotions and actions in a negative way.

- Jonah, the Israelite prophet known for being swallowed by a big fish (see GWBI, pages 88–90), is also known for throwing a tantrum and pouting. Jonah's preaching in the city of **Ninevah** paid off—they repented and turned to God, so God showed his mercy. Jonah was mad and embarrassed, for he had preached ruin and destruction and God gave restoration and renewal. (Jonah 4:1–4)

- **Sarai**, **Abram**'s wife, had no children (Genesis 17:16). After waiting ten years for the Lord to fulfill his promise of blessing her with a child, she gave up. As was the custom, she devised a plan for her Egyptian maidservant, Hagar, to sleep with Abram. Hagar became pregnant. Sarai became jealous, then bitter, then hateful. In anger she mistreated Hagar, who fled the camp. (Genesis 16:1–3; see GWWB, pages 27–40)

- The children of Israel were led out of captivity into freedom. Instead of celebrating their deliverance, they seized upon every hardship as an excuse to grumble against their leaders Moses and Aaron. In anger they said they were better off as slaves in Egypt than starving in the desert. (Exodus 16:1–3)

Ninevah: *capital city of Assyria, east of Cilicia (see illustration in GWWB, page 28)*

Sarai: *the name Sarah had before God changed it*

Abram: *the name Abraham had before God changed it*

KEY Outline:

Destructive Anger Can Lead to

embarrassment
bitterness
resentment

Everyday Life

When things don't go our way, we regress back to the "terrible twos" and, as my mother would say, "throw a hissy fit" with God. You've seen the red-faced, clenched-fist little toddler stamping his feet, whining and crying because he didn't get his way. When we act the same way in our hearts, I'm sure God isn't surprised. Like parents who let those toddlers get it out of their system, and then love them back into reality, God does the same for us.

Gary Chapman, Ph.D.: Anger and depression are common human feelings. They certainly do not mean that we are bad persons. Anger arises inside when we perceive that we or someone else has been treated unfairly. Anger reveals our concern for righteousness and justice. Anger is not wrong. The Bible says of

What Others are Saying:

☞ **GO TO:**

Psalm 7:11 (angry)

Matthew 26:37 (depressed)

God that he is <u>angry</u> with the wicked every day. Jesus felt <u>depressed</u> hours before he went to the cross, but he did not allow his depression to control his behavior. Negative emotions are not sinful; they simply reveal that we are humans and when we encounter certain situations in life, we feel depressed or sad.

The important thing is that we do not allow our negative emotions to lead us to wrongful behavior. We process negative emotions by sharing them with a trusted friend. Emotions come and go. When we talk about them, they tend to go. When we hold them inside, they tend to stay.[5]

REMEMBER THIS

We can allow anger to be a road to recovery or a path to destruction. If you express your anger without losing control, it can help heal whatever is upsetting you. Communicating your feelings lets others know what you need from them and releases the stress of keeping your feelings silent. But if you give in to anger by allowing it to consume your thoughts and actions, it can destroy your relationships and build a wall around your heart. I hope you choose the road to recovery and let anger reveal truth, but not destruction.

What Others are Saying:

vestige: trace; sign; mark

redeemed: bought with a ransom

KEY POINT

Do not let anger destroy you. Let it go. Move on.

Joni Eareckson Tada: Unrighteous anger—anger that leads us away from God—sucks the last **vestige** of hope from our hearts. We stop caring, stop feeling. We commit a silent suicide of the soul, and sullen despair moves in like a terrible damp fog, deadening our heart to the hope that we will ever be rescued, **redeemed** and happy again.[6]

> **Psalm 42:1–5** As the deer pants for streams of water, so my soul pants for you, O God. My soul thirsts for God, for the living God. When can I go and meet with God? My tears have been my food day and night, while men say all day long, "Where is your God?" These things I remember as I pour out my soul; how I used to go with the multitude, leading the procession to the house of God, with shouts of joy and thanksgiving among the festive throng. Why are you so downcast, O my soul? Why so disturbed within me? Put your hope in God, for I will yet praise him, my Savior and my God.

When All Your Days Seem Like Mondays

In this passage, the psalmist is in misery. He's depressed. He can't eat and he cries both day and night. His soul thirsts for God. He wants relief from his suffering and heartache. His enemy seeks to destroy him and he wants God to deliver him.

In his loneliness and depression he reminisces about the good old days when he worshiped and rejoiced in the Temple. As he reflects on God he asks himself, "Why am I depressed and discouraged? I have hope in God, who will deliver me."

Stuart Briscoe: I have known some people who couldn't drag themselves out of depression if their lives depended on it. But I have known many more that could, if they would only tell themselves "put your hope in God." When people start looking at the Lord and his attributes and abilities instead of focusing on their own failings and situations, I believe they turn the corner toward emotional peace. But make no mistake; a definite act of the will is required.[7]

EXAMPLES FROM THE BIBLE

Bible women faced depression as they dealt with sorrow and pain, but they also found relief and happiness.

- Noah's wife spent over four months cooped up with her family and dozens of stinky, loud, hungry animals in the Ark. But finally the floodwater receded; they left the ark, built an **altar**, and praised God. (Genesis 8:20; Exodus 20:24–25)

- Hagar was mistreated and sent away by her mistress, Sarah. In the wilderness an angel comforted her and gave her strength and hope to carry on. (Genesis 16)

- Naomi grieved the deaths of her husband and two sons. She became bitter but stayed true to God as he blessed her with the company of her daughter-in-law Ruth (see GWWB, pages 195–204).

Did you ever hear that it rains all the time in Seattle? Well, guess what—it's true! And I have proof: as I write this book, under the dark cloudy skies of Seattle, it has rained a record of 91 straight days. Yes, 91 straight days of rain. Give me a break! **Noah** (see GWBI, pages 9–11) only had a downpour for <u>40 days</u>. What gives?

> **What Others are Saying:**

altar: a place for sacrifices; usually made from stones

Noah: built the famous Ark that survived the **Flood**

Flood: an ancient event when God judged humans by sending 40 days of rain to flood the earth

Everyday Life

☞ **GO TO:**

Genesis 7:17 (40 days)

I have to admit it's depressing. I now believe the statistic I heard that Prozac is prescribed more in Seattle than any other part of the country.

During times of disappointments and suffering, we feel as though all forecasts are for continuing gloom and every day feels like a Monday. But there is hope in dealing with depression.

Help, God! I'm Drowning!

The psalmist feels the waters of depression threatening his life. As the torment and pain increase, his misery is almost more than he can bear. He cries out in desperation, "Help, God! I'm drowning!"

Most people usually bounce back from disappointments. But when the sadness persists and you feel like you are drowning under dark skies, when everyday mundane things become too difficult, maybe your problem is deeper than a blue mood. If you're experiencing any of the following symptoms, you may be suffering from depression:

1. a sad, anxious or empty mood that lasts for two weeks or more
2. loss of interest or pleasure in most activities you once enjoyed
3. feeling of worthlessness, hopelessness, and quiet
4. significant change in weight or appetite
5. change in sleep habits
6. fatigue, loss of energy, agitation, and irritability
7. difficulty concentrating, making decisions
8. frequent thoughts of death or suicide

By informing you of these medical conditions I do not mean to frighten you. But if these symptoms describe you, I encourage you to seek medical advice.[8]

KEY POINT

Depression is nothing to be ashamed of. If necessary, seek professional help.

KEY Outline:

When You Suffer from Depression

go to God
seek counsel

The first step to receiving help is being honest with yourself and admitting you are depressed. Go to God and cry out to him in prayer. He has not forsaken you. He will help you; he will send a lifeline in your time of despair. Seek help from a doctor, minister, or professional counselor. He or she can give you support and advice. There's nothing to be ashamed of—depression is not a sign of weakness, and you are not alone. Statistics show that as many as one in five Americans will be affected by depression in their lifetime.

Gregory L. Jantz, Ph.D.: You can become strong again . . . You will have to start with honesty. When you are honest about your problem and your desire to change, you can go on to the next baby step, allowing for help. That can be followed by creating a plan. If you're in the fire now and you stay in the fire, you will be consumed. However, if you are willing to work through the challenges that face you, then the fire that seems to be singeing your soul will also have the power to purify and refine.[9]

What Others are Saying:

> **Isaiah 40:29** He gives strength to the weary and increases the power of the weak.

KEY Outline:

To Fight Depression
eat right
drink water
exercise

Get Out of the Rain

Isaiah the prophet addressed the children of **Judah** (see GWBI, pages 107–109) who were in exile. Gradually the captives had lost their hope of ever returning home. Discouragement and despair took over. Isaiah spoke of God's comfort and almighty power. He promised that God would renew their strength and give them the power they needed to walk the seven hundred miles back to their homeland.

Judah: one of the twelve tribes of Israel

Probably none of us will face a seven-hundred-mile walk home, but that doesn't mean Isaiah's message isn't for us. When we feel weary, whether from physical or emotional trials, God is always there, powerful beyond our understanding. When we seek his help, he gives us strength and renews our spirits for the journey ahead.

What does the Bible say about God's comfort and power?

Comfort

Psalm 23:4—*Even though I walk through the valley of the shadow of death, I will fear no evil, for you are with me; your rod and your staff, they comfort me.*

Isaiah 61:2—*He has sent me to proclaim the year of the Lord's favor and the day of vengeance of our God, to comfort all who mourn.*

Matthew 5:4—*Blessed are those who mourn, for they will be comforted.*

2 Corinthians 1:3–4—*Praise be to the God and Father of our Lord Jesus Christ, the Father of compassion and the God of all comfort, who comforts us in all our troubles, so that we can comfort those in any trouble with the comfort we ourselves have received from God.*

Almighty Power

1 Chronicles 29:11—*Yours, O Lord, is the greatness and the power and the glory and the majesty and the splendor, for everything in heaven and earth is yours. Yours, O Lord, is the kingdom; you are exalted above all the earth.*

Psalm 91:1—*He who dwells in the shelter of the Most High will rest in the shadow of the Almighty. I will say of the Lord, "He is my refuge and my fortress, my God, in whom I trust."*

Revelation 4:8—*Holy, holy, holy is the Lord God Almighty, who was, and is, and is to come.*

I remember Mom's advice when she sent us off to camp or college. She would always say, "Take care of yourself, eat right, and get plenty of rest." Let me be your mom and echo those words.

During struggles our whole life is turned upside down. Schedules change and our routine eludes us. Where calmness once ruled, chaos is now the order. We find ourselves so emotionally drained and weary we don't even want to *think* about eating, let alone actually take a bite. But in order to maintain strength, we must eat something, drink lots of water (tears and stress can cause **dehydration**), and try to sleep or at least nap.

I know there are days you can't imagine crawling out of bed, but I need to mention one more word: exercise. It doesn't have to be a workout. Start with baby steps: maybe

dehydration: *the excessive loss of water*

walk with a friend around the neighborhood, or play with the kids; anything to get you moving (see GWHN, pages 215–221).

What Others are Saying:

Verdell Davis: When a storm comes along of sufficient force to wipe out our livelihood, our health, our most treasured relationship, or perhaps our lifelong dreams, and we are left standing in the rubble of our shattered lives, we are in many ways reduced to infancy. So much has been lost and so much changed that we must essentially start over again. We must begin to walk before we can think about running or soaring. Indeed, we need help just to be able to stay on our feet.[10]

Physically, taking care of yourself during a time of crisis is crucial to maintaining a healthy attitude and gaining overall strength during your struggle. Spiritually, turn to Scripture for renewed strength as you place your trust in God.

REMEMBER THIS

> **Proverbs 17:22** A cheerful heart is good medicine, but a crushed spirit dries up the bones.

Laughing in the Rain

The book of Proverbs (see GWBI, pages 76–77) is a book of wisdom, with wisdom being the key to understanding life, emotions, and relationships. The author, believed to be Solomon, often uses sayings to describe truths about human experience.

Proverbs 17:22 speaks of the joy of wisdom. Joy is a prescription to lift the spirits. Even faced with struggles and pain, a cheerful heart is like medicine. As believers we can be the most joyful people on the planet, for we know the Creator of joy.

Joy from God and Joy for Believers

Joy from God

Psalm 16:11—*You have made known to me the path of life; you will fill me with joy in your presence, with eternal pleasures at your right hand.*

Philippians 4:4—*Rejoice in the Lord always, and again I say rejoice.*

KEY Outline:

Joy and Believers
joy is from God
sow tears and reap joy
rejoice always
be complete in Christ

KEY POINT

Laughter is a natural painkiller. Take large doses.

Romans 15:13—*May the God of hope fill you with all joy and peace as you trust in him, so that you may overflow with hope by the power of the Holy Spirit.*

Joy for Believers

Psalm 126:5—*Those who sow in tears will reap with songs of joy.*

John 15:11—*I have told you this so that my joy may be in you and that your joy may be complete.*

1 Thessalonians 5:16–18—*Be joyful always; pray continually; give thanks in all circumstances, for this is God's will for you in Christ Jesus.*

1 Peter 1:8—*Though you have not seen him, you love him; and even though you do not see him now, you believe in him and are filled with an inexpressible and glorious joy.*

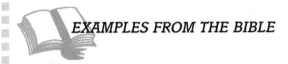 *EXAMPLES FROM THE BIBLE*

Even amidst times of trials, people in the Bible found reason for laughter.

- At the age of ninety-nine when Abraham and Sarah heard from God that they would have a son, Sarah must've bitten her tongue to keep from laughing, because the Scripture says she laughed on the inside (Genesis 18:12). In the midst of grief over her barrenness, she got a chuckle out of imagining herself pregnant.

- Paul encouraged the early church to rejoice even though they suffered, because God uses suffering to change and mold our character. (Romans 5:2)

- After a desperate escape through the Red Sea, Moses and Miriam joyfully led the multitude in a song service in the desert. (Exodus 15:1–21)

 Think About It

Patch Adams hit the movie screen this past year. Audiences laughed and cried as they watched Robin Williams portray a wacky, unusual doctor who touched hearts and made a difference in the lives of his patients with the medicine of laughter. The best part about the movie? Patch Adams is not just a fictional character, but a real doctor whose charitable health work is called the Gesundheit Institute.

We Laughed All the Way Home

In one of my days in the fog of despair, I made a quick trip to the grocery store with my sister Sherry. As we put the bags of food in the back of the van, I grabbed a banana to eat on the trip home. Before she unlocked the car doors, Sherry walked away to return our cart, so I waited in the parking lot clutching this banana. As a man walked by and smiled, I realized it looked like a gun, so I pointed my weapon at him and said, "I've got a banana and I'm not afraid to use it!" He immediately put up his hands and backed away laughing. He saw my sister as she headed back to the van and said, "Look out for that lady! She's got a banana and she's not afraid to use it." The joke surprised me as much as it did my "victim."

Laugh Out Loud

We may go through misery, trials, and difficulties on this earth, but remember the words of Jesus: *"Now is your time of grief, but I will see you again and you will rejoice, and no one will take away your joy"* (John 16:22). So laugh with a friend; watch an old *I Love Lucy* show; have your kids tell you some jokes; whatever . . . just have a good ol' belly laugh.

REMEMBER THIS

GEORGIA'S TIPS . . .

If life isn't so funny and you have to manufacture some laughs, try a few of these:

- Pick up a new humor book and read it when you're down.
- Pop in a funny video. (Liz Curtis Higgs and Chonda Pierce are two of my favorite comediennes. They always make me laugh, and you can buy their material as books or videos).
- Watch the old classics (*I Love Lucy*, *Arsenic and Old Lace*, Don Knotts in *The Ghost and Mr. Chicken*).
- Play a board game with your kids.
- Put on some music and dance with your kids.
- Try a new sport. (I took up in-line skating during a "not so funny" time in my life. My family got several great laughs, but probably not as many as my watchful neighbors.)
- Look for the absurdity in your situation. (Sometimes our difficulties pile so high, you can't help but laugh.)

> **1 Corinthians 12:25–26** So that there should be no division in the body, but that its parts should have equal concern for each other. If one part suffers, every part suffers with it; if one part is honored, every part rejoices with it.

Just Call My Name, I'll Be There

In the verses above, Paul compares the Church body to our physical bodies. To be whole, we need all the parts of our bodies. If you were one big eye, you wouldn't be able to hear. Just as our body depends upon all parts, to be whole we need to depend upon others.

When close friends offer help during your disappointment, learn to say yes. We were designed to help one another.

EXAMPLES FROM THE BIBLE

Friends in need and friends in deed in the Bible:

- When Job's friends Eliphaz, Bildad, and Zophar heard that Job was in the pit of despair, they immediately went to comfort him. (Job 2:11)
- Abram received the news that his nephew Lot had been taken captive in a battle. He rounded up a posse of 318 men and rescued Lot in his time of despair. (Genesis 14:14)
- Jonathan came to his friend David's aid and helped him run to safety away from the threatening hand of King Saul. (1 Samuel 20:4–42)
- Four friends of a paralytic heard Jesus was healing. They dug through a roof to lower their paralyzed friend down to where Jesus taught. Jesus took pity upon him and healed him. (Mark 2:1–12)

KEY POINT

Let others minister to you. It's their gift to you.

Everyday Life Our initial response to suffering is the oft-mistaken notion that we can handle it on our own. We think we can manage the house, manage the children, manage our marriage, manage the office, and manage our emotions all while our life is falling apart. I call it the Superwoman Syndrome. But the fact is, Superwoman usually can't find her cape during chaos. She needs help from her Superfriends and family.

Friends and family want to minister to you during your struggles. Allow them to help even in little ways, like grocery shopping or fixing meals. (Sometimes I almost look forward to being incapacitated, because two of my friends are such great cooks.) Each thing your friends do for you is that much unspent energy you can store in your reserve tank to use in days ahead when you *can* find your cape and face the world again.

Sue Buchanan: Gather up the gifts people offer one by one and put them in a big basket (figuratively speaking, of course). You'll find the gifts that are brought have a marvelous variety of intangible, indisputable qualities, such as humor, joy, acceptance, crying, listening, surprise, prayer, and perhaps the greatest gift of all—time. That basket, that source, will provide everything you need to get through an illness—or through life, for that matter.[11]

What Others are Saying:

> **KEY POINT**
>
> God's waiting room is a safe place to be.

> **Hebrews 10:23–24** Let us hold unswervingly to the hope we profess, for he who promised is faithful. And let us consider how we may spur one another on toward love and good deeds.

Somewhere over the Rainbow, Skies Are Blue

The teacher of Hebrews encourages the believers to hold tight, or fasten down, their hope. When trouble comes our way we are not to get off balance. We are to hold on, keeping our eyes fixed on Jesus and the hope he offers. If we grow weary and wavering, we are to encourage each other to hang in there and not give up.

> **KEY POINT**
>
> Biblical hope is inseparable from reliance upon God.

 *EXAMPLES FROM THE BIBLE*

Bible examples of hope and encouragement:

- While the children of Israel were in the wilderness, the Amalekites attacked them. The power of God was in Moses' **staff**. When he held the staff aloft, the Israelites were winning the battle. If Moses lowered his hands, the Amalekites were winning. When Moses grew weary, Aaron and Hur knew the hope of victory was in the raised staff, so they helped Moses hold up his arms. (Exodus 4:1–5; 17:8–13)

staff: a stick or rod used to guide sheep

- Deborah, Rebekah's maidservant and nurse, comforted and encouraged Rebekah as she waited in agony to deliver twins. Deborah helped raise the twins. Deborah must've encouraged not only Rebekah, but also her entire family, for when Deborah was buried they placed her under a tree and called it the "Oak of Weeping." (Genesis 24:59; 25:23–35:8; see GWWB, pages 126–127)

 Everyday Life

The hit TV show *Touched by an Angel* ranks most weeks as the second most watched drama series in the Nielsen ratings. It's been headlined as "TV's Heavenly Hit." It's really no surprise to me, because America is an audience filled with brokenness, looking for hope and comfort. I may disagree with the show's theology at times, but it gives me chills when one of the angels declares, "I am an angel, sent from God. He has a message. He loves you."

 **Think About It**

Hope is a necessity in surviving our disappointments. We cannot live in the land of hopelessness for very long—it will destroy us.

 GO TO:

Genesis 9:16 (covenant)

John 14:26 (Holy Spirit)

covenant: *a binding promise*

perseverance: *to keep trying despite difficulty*

Holy Spirit: *"the Paraclete," a Greek word translated as "Comforter" or "Helper"*

REMEMBER THIS

I'm no angel, but I have a message for you. God loves you. Your days may be rainy and dark, but don't lose hope. For as each day dawns, they will get brighter, the storm will let up and turn to a mist, the sun will shine, and you can look to the sky for the brilliant colors of the rainbow. Just as God made a **covenant** with Noah giving him hope for the future (see GWBI, page 10) and sealed it with a rainbow, God gives you hope in him, even through your suffering. *"We also rejoice in our sufferings, because we know that suffering produces **perseverance**; perseverance, character; and character, hope. And hope does not disappoint us, because God has poured out his love into our hearts by the **Holy Spirit**, whom he has given us"* (Romans 5:3–5).

Jesus knew his arrest and crucifixion were fast approaching, and he went to the garden of Gethsemane to pray. He was so distressed he said, *"My soul is overwhelmed with sorrow to the point of death"* (Mark 14:34). But Jesus didn't give up. He knew the resurrection awaited him.

Do not give up. The gift of hope is in God's Word and his son Jesus Christ. There truly are blue skies awaiting you beyond the rainbow, both here and in eternity. God has made a covenant with you just as he did with Noah, and he will not break his promise.

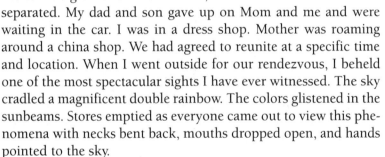
Verdell Davis: As time went on I began to be more and more aware of the ways God was bringing light into my dark days. Gradually, I found myself "cursing the darkness" less and moving toward the light more. I began to see rainbow colors in the hugs of friends, the offer of someone to help with a particular need, the unexpected phone call of encouragement when I thought I wouldn't make it through the night, the dawning of new insight into the ways of God with his hurting people.[12]

God's Business Card

Several years ago, my parents visited me and I wanted them to see the Pacific Northwest in all its splendor. Sometimes our beautiful snow-capped mountains outline the clear blue skies, but the weather didn't cooperate with my plans for my parents. Split, splat, drip, drop . . . sometime you should come on out for the Pacific Northwest Rain Festival, which runs from July 1 to June 30.

COFFEE BREAK
WITH GEORGIA

Now as you well know, you can't have your mom visit and not go shopping. So we donned our raincoats, grabbed our trusty umbrellas, and headed to a great outlet mall. There, we became separated. My dad and son gave up on Mom and me and were waiting in the car. I was in a dress shop. Mother was roaming around a china shop. We had agreed to reunite at a specific time and location. When I went outside for our rendezvous, I beheld one of the most spectacular sights I have ever witnessed. The sky cradled a magnificent double rainbow. The colors glistened in the sunbeams. Stores emptied as everyone came out to view this phenomena with necks bent back, mouths dropped open, and hands pointed to the sky.

As we drove home our conversation turned to the rainbow. Even though we were all in different locations, each of us witnessed this spectacular event. Mom commented that she was humored by the clerks who, moments before they saw the rainbow, acted as if it were a chore to assist you. But each clerk who had a turn viewing the magnificent rainbow returned to the store transformed and excited, making sure everyone she encountered, friends, and strangers alike, stepped outside to see the glory.

☞ **Check It Out:**

Genesis 15–21

KEY POINT

Never give up—there
is always hope. God
loves you.

Think About It

Whether they realized it or not, all who witnessed the rainbow had a close encounter with God (well, at least they were touched by his handiwork and saw his signature). I've always said that if God had a business card, it would have a rainbow insignia in the background.

When the hand of God touches you, your life is transformed, your personality is changed, and you have a new exciting outlook on life to share with friends and even strangers.

God has wonderful ways of reminding us of his eternal promises. Only he can turn gray skies into a rainbow, glowing like an opal. And only he can give hope and transform dark lonely lives into vibrant glowing personalities. *"I have placed my rainbow in the clouds as a sign of my promise until the end of time, to you and to all the earth"* (Genesis 9:13). Have a rainbow promise day!

> **Psalm 27:13–14** I am still confident of this: I will see the goodness of the Lord in the land of the living. Wait for the Lord; be strong and take heart and wait for the Lord.

Give Me Patience, Now!

As opposition surrounded David, he continually looked to God for deliverance. He wanted to learn God's ways. David had the faith and hope that he would see his rescue in the present "land of the living," not far off in the distant future. Even as David ran for his life when King Saul wanted to kill him, David took time to pray and wait on God. David learned patience as he waited for God to answer his prayers. In the lonely nights as David hid from Saul, I imagine he was glad he had practiced patience years earlier while tending his father's sheep.

Waiting is hard, especially when you're not sure what you're waiting for. And when we pray for relief from our sufferings, we're not sure if that relief will come immediately or much later. It's easy to become frustrated and anxious. That is why patience is a <u>virtue</u>. Take heart. Your patience will be rewarded in the future, when you see its effects in your life. *"No discipline seems pleasant at the time, but painful. Later on, however, it produces a harvest of righteousness and peace for those who have been trained by it. Therefore, strengthen your feeble arms and weak knees"* (Hebrews 12:11–12).

☞ **GO TO:**

Galatians 5:22 (virtue)

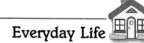

In our fast paced, fast-food, no wait, next day delivery society we are programmed to expect immediate attention to our wants and needs. It's no wonder when we shoot up a crisis prayer to God that we want him to answer immediately. We fail to realize that our rescue will come all in God's timing—not ours—and we can grow in our spiritual walk if we patiently wait on him.

When our son Philip was younger, he fell while running. I had to restrain him while the doctor inspected and cleaned a long, dirt-filled laceration. Philip's tears flowed down his cheeks, and his expression seemed to say, "How could you do this? How could you hold me still while they inflict pain?" It tore at my heart. I only hope he remembers the tears of love that welled up in my eyes as I held him. He didn't understand: despite his pain, I had to restrain him so he could receive the treatment he needed to get well.

Our heavenly Father weeps as he sees his children suffering, but he knows we gain faith in him, become stronger, and live closer to him if we cling to him during our time of waiting.

REMEMBER THIS

Sheila Walsh: Our impatience to have God move now, to act in ways that make sense to us, will drive us to take control of our lives. God is moving in ways that we cannot see or understand. This means we are left with the question, "Do I trust him?" We can choose to bow the knee now and ask him to forgive us for trying to squeeze the answer we want out of heaven, or we will bow the knee later in remorse at our foolishness in thinking that we knew better than God.[13]

What Others are Saying:

SNAPSHOTS OF WOMEN IN THE BIBLE

Sarah and Hagar

Sarai gave up a life of luxury to become a **nomad**, joining her husband as he followed God's command. But, obedience had its rewards.

Sarai and Abram were childless. God had promised heirs to them, but time was running out—the biological clock was ticking. A decade had passed since the promise, and Sarai was tired of waiting. She took matters into her own hands.

nomad: one who moves from place to place

☞ **GO TO:**

Genesis 2:24
(monogamy)

maidservants: *female slaves of wealthy families in Old Testament times*

monogamy: *the practice of marrying only once during life*

Sarah: *Hebrew for "princess"*

☞ **GO TO:**

Genesis 12:1–4
(promise)

ACT OF GOD

an angel appears to Hagar and brings hope

Hagar, an Egyptian slave girl, became a trusted servant to Sarai. The custom of the day allowed **maidservants** to bear children for a childless couple. Sarai thrust the responsibility of childbirth on her slave. Sarai departed from God's principle of **monogamy**, trusting her own wisdom over God's.

Abram went along with the plan. Hagar became pregnant. True to form, Sarai's ungodly acts bred seeds of discontentment as she watched Hagar's belly swell with life. Sarai suspected that Hagar now expected a share in Abram's wealth. In her jealousy, Sarai treated her slave so cruelly that Hagar ran for her life, into the wilderness.

In Hagar's suffering, loneliness, fear, and confusion, an angel of the Lord met her in her time of need. He called out her name. She must have been terrified at first, but then she was comforted to know that Abram's God knew her name. He knew her personally.

God gave her hope as he shared that her son would be called Ishmael, meaning "whom God hears." He promised a great nation would spring from Ishmael. She was able to return to Abram's camp with a renewed hope because she found God in the wilderness.

Time passed, and God fulfilled his promises to Sarai (now called **Sarah**) when she became pregnant and bore a son, Isaac. But when Sarah had her own son, once again she let the seeds of bitterness take control. She cast Hagar and Ishmael out into the desert.

Hagar found herself suffering in the wilderness once again, but this time she held the hand of her son—the son with which God had promised to make a great nation. Had God forgotten his promise? How could he fulfill it if Hagar and Ishmael perished in the desert?

As they came close to death she could not bear to watch her son die. She laid him under a bush, walked away, and began to sob. She must have thought she was delusional when she first heard her name. Then she remembered that familiar, comforting voice, the same voice she heard before in the wilderness.

God heard Hagar and her son cry for help and sent an angel that whispered her name and ministered to them. He provided a well of water and saved their lives, just as he promised. Scripture records, *"God was with the boy as he grew and lived in the wilderness"* (Genesis 21:20).

This snapshot is a study in contrasts. Sarah and Hagar, two different women who were forced to be in God's waiting room, both learned that God is always faithful. Neither behaved ideally, yet he kept his promises to them. *"Never will I leave you or forsake you"* (Hebrews 13:5).

> **Philippians 3:12–14** Not that I have already obtained all this, or have already been made perfect, but I press on to take hold of that for which Christ Jesus took hold of me. Brothers, I do not consider myself yet to have taken hold of it. But one thing I do: Forgetting what is behind and straining toward what is ahead I press on toward the goal to win the prize for which God has called me heavenward in Christ Jesus.

The Sun Will Come Out Tomorrow

The Apostle Paul wrote the Scripture above in his letter to the church at Philippi (see illustration, page 143). Imprisoned in a dark lonely cell, saturated in suffering, Paul found joy during misery—a ray of hope in Jesus. He uses the **metaphor** of a highly competitive athlete to illustrate that as Christians we should want to do all we can for God's kingdom. Paul said he was in no way <u>perfect</u>, yet he continued to strive toward the goal of doing God's <u>will</u>—his good, pleasing, and perfect will.

Paul forgot his past, his failures, his successes, and his suffering as he looked forward to his future of receiving heavenly <u>rewards</u> from God.

 *EXAMPLES FROM THE BIBLE*

Others who forgot the past and became what God wanted:

- Rahab, a **prostitute** in the city of **Jericho**, harbored two spies from Israel's army and saved her family from destruction. She left behind her immoral life and believed in God as she joined the Israelites. The New Testament commends her for her faith. (Joshua 2:1–21; 6:17; Hebrews 11:31)
- David rose above his moral failures of **adultery** and murder and became a **godly** king. (2 Samuel 11:1–16, 26)
- Joseph suffered the injustice of his brothers selling him as a slave, was wrongfully accused, and sent to prison. Yet he forgot the past, relied and waited on God, and became a ruler under the Egyptian Pharaoh and saved the nation during a famine. (Genesis 37:27; 39:1–23; 41:46–49)

☞ **GO TO:**

Matthew 5:44–48 (perfect)

Romans 12:1–2 (will)

Hebrews 11:6 (rewards)

metaphor: *symbolic story; image*

prostitute: *to sell oneself for sexual intercourse*

Jericho: *the first city taken by the Israelites during the conquest of Canaan*

adultery: *sexual intercourse between a married man and a woman that is not his wife*

godly: *devoted to God; holy; devout*

Think About It

Paul reminds us of what really matters: knowing Christ and forgetting the past that holds us back from becoming what God wants us to be. Forget your pain, hurt, bitterness, suffering. Look forward to a rewarding life today, and inner sunshine tomorrow—whatever the outward circumstance may be.

What Others are Saying:

Gregory L. Jantz, Ph.D.: Your ability to withstand the storms of your life will depend on your choice to never give up no matter what challenges may come your way. Re-igniting your passion for life requires that you be bold even when you are afraid and courageous even when you feel lost and despairing. As you move beyond your greatest fears to a willingness to allow God to give you the power to make the right decisions, you will find healing.[14]

KEY Outline:

What Really Matters
knowing Christ
forgetting the past
looking to the future

> **2 Corinthians 1:3–4** Praise be to the God and Father of our Lord Jesus Christ, the Father of compassion and the God of all comfort, who comforts us in all our troubles, so that we can comfort those in any trouble with the comfort we ourselves have received from God.

It's Your Turn

Instead of wallowing in his trials and sorrows Paul encourages the Christians in Corinth (see illustration, page 143) to comfort one another in their sufferings even as God has comforted them in their time of need.

consolation: comfort; relief

We don't have to walk in the same shoes of suffering in order to comfort, but those who've been there can offer great **consolation** to others. Paul alludes to *"the fellowship of sharing in [Christ's] suffering"* (Philippians 3:10). The "fellowship of suffering" is a club with a steep entrance fee. Yet it is no exclusive clique. Many of us are inducted despite our best efforts to stay out. Once you're in, though, no one can comfort you like a fellow member. This ability to help fellow sufferers adds great dignity and meaning to our anguish. In Christ, we never suffer for no reason.

Yes, your life has meaning. Your steps have led you down a road of hardships, yet through the power of God, you've survived. Your faith has been stretched. You have a new understanding of life. You know what's really important. You've weathered the storm. Now it's your turn to help others through their tempests; to share the comfort that Jesus ministered to you.

Kathy Lee Gifford's response thrilled my soul when reporters asked how she survived the year she was fodder for the tabloids. That year started with accusations that the factories manufacturing her line of clothing were child labor sweatshops. Then pictures of her husband in bed with another woman appeared in the papers. Kathy answered boldly that she survived only because she has a personal and intimate relationship with her Lord Jesus Christ. When asked "How did you do it?" she quietly answered, "<u>Faith</u> has played a key role in my life."[15]

That is probably part of the meaning and reason for her success and her suffering: so that she can be a <u>light</u> and **witness** to the world of what God has done in her life.

Everyday Life

☞ **GO TO:**

Luke 22:31–32 (faith)

Matthew 5:14 (light)

witness: *a person who gives evidence to support something*

REMEMBER THIS

God has plans for your life, far greater than you can imagine. Embrace him, embrace life, be a **testimony** of his unfailing love. Choose to trust him on the rainy days as well as when the sun is shining. The love and joy he gives you will shine through the clouds and draw others to the source of your hope.

What Others are Saying:

testimony: *any declaration that a thing is true*

Gerald Sittser: Suffering can lead to a simpler life, less cluttered with nonessentials. It is wonderfully clarifying. That is why many people who suffer sudden and severe loss often become different people. They spend more time with their children or spouses, express more affection and appreciation to their friends, show more concern for other wounded people, give more time to a worthy cause or enjoy more of the ordinariness of life.[16]

STUDY QUESTIONS

1. During the captivity of the children of Israel, what message of hope did Jeremiah deliver?
2. When drenched in pain, who can we turn to who knows our suffering? How does this change our approach to suffering?
3. How did the widow of Zarepath save herself and her son from starvation?
4. What advice on dealing with anger did the Apostle Paul give the church at Ephesus?
5. Bible women faced sorrow and pain, but also found relief and happiness. How did Noah's wife, Hagar, and Naomi find relief and happiness?

6. When depressed, what was the first step the psalmist took in receiving help?

7. According to Proverbs 17:22, how can you find relief for your heart when you are in the pit of despair?

8. The Apostle Paul compares the Church body to our physical body needing all its parts to be whole. When we suffer, how can we gain relief from others?

9. How did Rahab overcome her past and become what God wanted her to be?

CHAPTER WRAP-UP

- Life's storms of disappointment, suffering, and loss hit everyone. How we respond to the situation is what is important. After the initial shock, we must move beyond denial to calm the storm in our lives. If we run *to* God, rather than *away* from him, our soul will grow through the suffering.

- It makes sense to express anger rather than repress it. However, we cannot allow anger and bitterness to lead us into wrong behavior.

- Feeling down? Depression can be more than just the blues and may require treatment. God has provided Christian men and women who specialize in the field. Take the first step by crying out to God; then seek a Christian counselor who can give you emotional, mental, and spiritual support and advice. Take care of yourself during this time. Maintain your strength by eating, remembering to drink water, and trying to get physical exercise. Allow your friends and family to help out during your crisis, and find something to laugh about.

- God has not forgotten you. Do not give up! Be patient. Turn to Scripture and prayer for comfort, guidance, and strength. God loves you. Cling to him during your time of waiting.

- Your life has meaning, though it may not be the meaning you expected. There is a rewarding life available to you today and tomorrow. Live life to its fullest one day at a time and share with other suffering souls how God has helped you survive your struggle. Your life will be a comfort and blessing to others.

GEORGIA'S  BOOKSHELF

Some of Georgia's favorite books on the subject of suffering:

- *When God Weeps*, Joni Eareckson Tada, Zondervan Publishing
- *A Grace Disguised*, Gerald L. Sittser, Zondervan Publishing
- *God's Vitamin C for the Hurting Spirit*, Kathy Collard Miller, Starburst Publishers
- *Becoming Strong Again*, Gregory L. Jantz, Ph.D., Revell
- *It Had to Be a Monday*, Jill Briscoe, Tyndale House

Part Two

FAMILY TIES

REVEREND FUN

"Honestly Adam, if you crack one more joke about me 'raising Cain' I'm going to invent the doghouse this very instant and you'll be sleeping in it tonight."

3 "YOU'RE NOT A WOMAN . . . YOU'RE A MOMMY!"

Realizing the Blessings, Power, and Responsibility of a Mother's Love

Here We Go

The tide has slowly turned since the 70s and it now seems back in vogue to be a mom. We no longer need to hide the fact; we can wear the "Mom Badge" with great pride. The problem is that between the *Leave It to Beaver* mom of the 60s and the *Home Improvement* mom of the 90s, there was a huge void for mom role models. Today's mom needs a full time coach to help "*train up a child in the way he should go*" (Proverbs 22:6).

Sometimes we spend too much time and effort searching for the right books, psychologists, and experts to teach us how to be perfect parents. God designed women with a unique heart of love that not only opens to let her children in, but longs, yearns, and pulls her to be with her children. That God-designed "mother's heart" can take you a long way if you simply listen to it.

In addition, God gave us all the child-rearing principles we need in his Word. He gives us direction that helps us develop an everlasting love for our children while we focus on teaching them values, heritage, Scripture, and the simplicity of life without undue stress.

As we gain better understanding of our children and discover the unique way each child learns, we can encourage, build confidence, and bring out the best in them. Let's see what the Bible has to say to moms.

> ***KEY POINT***
>
> Listen to your "mother's heart." It will bring you a lot closer to your children.

KEY Outline:

Teach Your Children
values
their heritage
Scripture
simplicity of life

☞ **Check It Out:**

Luke 2:41–52

☞ **GO TO:**

Leviticus 23:1–4 (Feast)

Luke 2:41–51 (return)

Luke 2:19 (memory)

Mary: *the mother of Jesus by a miraculous virgin birth*

Jesus: *Hebrew for "the Lord saves"*

Joseph: *Mary's husband and the earthly father to Jesus*

Feast of the Passover: *an annual celebration of God's delivering the Jews from Egypt*

Temple: *God's "house"; a place of worship*

Think About It

Jerusalem: *capital of the Jewish nation*

Nazareth: *a town in Galilee among the southern hills of Lebanon where Jesus grew up*

> **Luke 2:51–52** [Jesus'] mother treasured all these things in her heart. And Jesus kept increasing in wisdom and stature, and in favor with God and men.

The Miracle of a Mother's Heart

Mary, the mother of **Jesus,** and her husband, **Joseph**, had just celebrated the **Feast of the Passover** at the **Temple** in **Jerusalem**. They were on their <u>return</u> trip home to **Nazareth** traveling with a group of friends and family. During the long hike to and from Jerusalem, the women usually walked along and talked in one group as the men trailed behind in another informal cluster. The children ran back and forth between the groups just enjoying the trip, so it wasn't unusual for your child to be out of view for lengthy periods. Still, it came as a shock when, at the end of the first day's journey, Mary and Joseph could not find their twelve-year-old son, Jesus.

Mary and Joseph returned to Jerusalem and searched for three days. They finally found Jesus in the Temple (see illustration, page 65) sitting among the teachers, listening and asking questions. As frantic parents would, they scolded Jesus and asked, "Where on earth have you been? We've been worried sick! What got into you? Why did you do this?"

Jesus said he was about his father's business. As an adolescent, he suggested to his parents that their business may not coincide with God his Father's business. Yet, Jesus submitted to his parents and went home.

I think Mary knew that day that Jesus was separating himself from them. She may have sighed as she added another <u>memory</u> and new experience of motherhood to the treasury in her heart.

A mother's heart is a treasure box that gives splendid gifts *to* a child and is filled with joyful gifts *from* a child. Some mothers find their new heart as soon as their baby is born. Others discover this heart after they surrender to it. Sadly, some never discover this heart, or the God who designed it.

A mother's heart:

1. is a treasure box of love
2. loves beyond measure
3. is created to have the same capacity of love that God has for his children

KEY Outline:

A Mother's Heart Is God Designed
*a treasure box of love
a miracle*

transforms: *changes the condition, nature, or function*

4. loves, gives, disciplines, protects, separates, heals, laughs, teaches, grieves, builds, shares, and suffers with a child

5. not only **transforms** a mother, but transforms her child as well

6. is a miracle

I'd heard about this thing called "mother love" for years. I thought it was the longing, the desire to be a mother. I yearned for years to fill my empty arms, but until I felt that first "butterfly" movement and heard the heartbeat of the life within me, I never knew the transforming power of mother love. Its primal strength took me by surprise. The surgeon said he had only performed a **C-section.** But I'd swear a heart surgeon must have worked alongside him, too, because when they wheeled me out of surgery and laid that little bundle on my chest, my heart was different— larger. It was large enough to lodge this child for the rest of my life.

We all know that men and women are different (thank

Flashback

C-section: *Caesarian section; a surgical operation for delivering a baby by cutting through the mother's abdominal and uterine wall*

goodness!). God gave women a special gift, a special design, a Designer Label Heart. The same heart that served as a lifeline to the child in the womb, is still a lifeline to the child outside the womb.

What Others are Saying:

Brenda Hunter, Ph.D.: Ah, the power of mother love. How it stretches and swells across generations, uniting mother and child, fleshing out the expectant mother's identity and femininity, shaping the personality and life of her child, and changing society in ways our culture has chosen to ignore. Mother love is ultimately a love song, a siren's call, luring women to new ways of being . . . to sacrifice and being turned inside out . . . to fulfillment.[1]

> **Psalm 127:3** Children are a gift of the Lord. The fruit of the womb is a reward.

☞ **GO TO:**

Genesis 1:1, 28
(creation)

contingencies: uncertain conditions

The Face Only a Mother Could Love

God created life, and children are the continuation of life. Our name is passed down from generation to generation as children are born and new life continues. God blessed us, his <u>creation</u>, with the gift of children. Children are not a burden. They are a blessing.

Everyday Life

A recent headline read, "Kate Mulgrew Plans to Abandon 'Voyager' Ship for Her Family." Kate may be better known to all Trekkies as Captain Janeway of the Federation Starship *Voyager*. The article quoted her as saying, "I'm so privileged and happy I had this job. But we're talking about a block of time that I've missed now with them; years in which nurturing was crucial to them, to their self-esteem, the kind of nurturing that comes without conditions or **contingencies**, the kind of nurturing that is so simple and basic to human nature regarding the relationship between mother and son. We missed it." The story told how her two teenage sons wanted her to come home, and how she wanted to make up for lost time with her boys before they finished growing and left home.

KEY Outline:

A Heart That Loves
 gives
 disciplines
 protects
 separates
 heals
 laughs
 teaches
 grieves
 builds
 shares
 suffers

Homespun Wisdom: A young mother wrote me a thank you note for some hand-me-down clothes I passed along to her son. The card read, "Your generosity comes at a great time. The at-home business I've been involved in hasn't made us the money we thought we would make, and going back to work began to look like our only alternative. But, as the Lord has done so many times in my life, he **humbled** me and brought me to my senses. What price can I put on those tiny faces and innocent eyes? Suddenly a larger house, new toys, and self-indulgence just didn't seem that important to me anymore."

This is the mystery of motherhood: the mystical pull; the longing, yearning, loving heart that pulls you to the face only a mother could love—your children.

Deloris Jordan (Michael Jordan's mom): Whenever I held one of my newborn children, I was struck by the infant's total helplessness. I remember the sobering realization that this child will know only what I as a parent provide for him. Who and what he becomes will be decided by the foundation I lay.[2]

"You're Not a Woman . . . You're a Mommy!"

One afternoon years ago while on kitchen duty, I was in suds and dirty dishes up to my elbows when our two-year-old son, Philip, asked to play our "You're not a . . . " game. It went something like this: Philip would make an elephant noise and say, "I'm an elephant." Then I would say, "You're not an elephant! You're a little boy." He would giggle and go on to the next sound and animal. I was happy to keep him occupied this way while I scrubbed pots and pans.

COFFEE BREAK
WITH GEORGIA

After we played a few rounds of our game, he decided that Mommy should take a turn. He said, "You're a mermaid."

I replied properly, "I'm not a mermaid! I'm a woman."

To my surprise he responded, "You're not a woman . . . you're a Mommy!"

Ouch! Out of the mouth of babes! He was on to something. I decided he was a baby genius, a two-year-old psychiatrist, because his response showed me why it's so hard to leave a career and be a stay-at-home mom. It feels as if everyone is secretly thinking you're no longer a real woman. You've changed into some lesser creature, a Mommy.

I always said I would leave my career and raise my children until they were in school, and then maybe work part-time. I had

☞ **GO TO:**

Luke 8:41–46 (humbled)

humbled: not proud; to make meek

What Others are Saying:

waited eleven long years before Philip was born and I was determined to stay home. Over the years I struggled to remain content with that decision. I even tried running a consulting business out of my home that first year. But it was hard to make phone contacts between diaper changes and screams, so I decided to *"learn to be content in every situation"* (Philippians 4:11) and become the best mom I could be.

After some self-analysis, I think I know why I struggled at first with my decision. I am a very goal-oriented person and have always felt driven to be successful. I guess you could say I'm competitive. In business I seem to have the golden touch, and I enjoyed the praise and the perks that went along with it.

But as ever, if we are open to his sculpting, God uses every situation to help us grow and create something new. Over the years, I've learned some valuable lessons since I've been at home. For example: I really don't need adulation or a big paycheck to motivate me. I found out before Philip entered school that we really could survive without a second car. I don't have to have a closet full of the latest designer clothes or a house full of new furniture. I learned to enjoy the solitude of being at home, to slow down and get back in touch with God, and to appreciate what he blessed me with. I learned a new gratefulness for the "bread winner" in our family and stopped taking him for granted. I reflected on my childhood and reached a whole new perspective on my mother and the years of sacrifice, love, and nurturing she gave her children.

But the most valuable treasure I received from deciding to stay home was the gift of time—the time spent with our son. I'm glad I didn't miss any of his firsts: his first hugs, first kiss, first step, and first words. What a blessing.

According to Barna Research, 78 percent of women work outside the home. I don't think any less of full-time working moms. In fact, I pray for them to be the best they can be at work and home, because they have a hard row to hoe (that's a Kentucky gardening phrase).

There's not a clear-cut commandment to spend twenty-four hours a day with your children. Each woman has to make her own decisions and ask God for his guidance in her life. (See Chapter 6, "All I Do Is Work, Work, Work," for helpful hints for the full-time working mom.) But we are instructed to love, honor, and raise our children in the Lord. *"Love the Lord your God with all your heart and with all your soul and with all your strength. These commandments that I give you today are to be upon your hearts. Impress them on your children"* (Deuteronomy 6: 5–7).

KEY POINT

Time with your kids is a treasure.

KEY Outline:

God Wants Us to
love our children
honor our children
raise our children in the Lord

Nine years have flown by and now as our son spends his days at school, I spend my time writing from my home office. I thank God for allowing me to be a stay-at-home mom with Philip. And I thank God for the gift of joy Philip brings me and the never-ending love I have for him. In the end, I'm proud to say I'm no mere woman. I'm a Mommy.

> **Titus 2:3–4** Teach the older women to be **reverent** in the way they live, not to be **slanderers** or addicted to much wine, but to teach what is <u>good</u>. Then they can train the younger women to love their husbands and love their children.

Kids: Ya Gotta Love 'Em

In this passage **Titus**, a <u>coworker</u> of the Apostle Paul, is now on his own in a ministry in **Crete**. Paul is writing to give him specific guidelines on how to set up the new church.

As examples, or **mentors**, older women were instructed to teach the younger women. After living long lives, and learning by trial and error, older women were not to let their "wise old age" go to waste. No matter what age we are, God has a special plan and purpose for each of us!

Paul specifically instructed older women (you know who you are) to teach younger women to love their husbands and love their children.

The journey of parenthood is a wild ride. Put God in the driver's seat, put love in the passenger seat, and the bumps in the road will seem much smoother.

EXAMPLES FROM THE BIBLE

There are many good models of parenting in the Bible:

- Though Samson's parents objected to his marriage, they still loved him. They were disappointed, yet they showed their love by attending his wedding. (Judges 14:3–5)
- Solomon knew his mother, Bathsheba, loved him, but she feared her son Solomon would not succeed King David on the throne. So she exposed a plot by Adhonijah, David's

☞ **GO TO:**

Romans 12:1 (reverent)

Philippians 4:4–9 (good)

reverent: live as if worshiping God

slanderers: gossipers; spread stories that hurt

☞ **GO TO:**

Galatians 2:1 (coworker)

Acts 27:12–13 (Crete)

REMEMBER THIS

Titus: coworker of Paul; church leader

Crete: a large island in the Mediterranean Sea

mentor: a wise, loyal adviser

KEY Outline:

**Older Women Should
Teach Younger
Women to**

love their husbands

love their children

prodigal: *one who
spends recklessly*

KEY POINT

Find the language of
love your child under-
stands and use it.

languages of love: *a
person's preferred way to
receive affection—a word,
a touch, a present, a
service*

son by Haggith, another wife, to become king. In her
wisdom she pled her son's case before the dying King
David, and Solomon was named the new King of Israel.
(1 Kings 1:11–31; Matthew 1:6)

- The blind boy's mother and father brought him to Jesus in
  hopes of healing. They faithfully stood beside their son
  and watched as Jesus spat on the ground and placed the
  mud over the boy's eyes. Then they led the boy to the Pool
  of Siloam to wash away the clay just as Jesus instructed.
  The parents went home with a boy who could see their
  loving faces for the very first time. (John 9:2)

- One of Jesus' parables portrayed God's love for us by
  describing an ungrateful, insulting, **prodigal** son who
  demanded what was in his father's will before the father
  had died. The son wasted the money, but when he returned
  home, his father ran to him, kissed and hugged him, and
  celebrated his return, for his *"son was dead and is alive
  again; he was lost and is found"* (Luke 15:13–24). Implicitly,
  these stories commend parents who love their kids. It
  shows that they are acting like God.

Everyday Life

As moms, we can't give up. We must keep on loving our children
through the good and bad times, relying on God's instruction and
help.

Years ago I was asked to conduct a workshop on loving your
children. I went straight to the source and asked our five-year-old
son, "When do you feel the most loved?" Without hesitation he
answered, "When you give me hugs and kisses and when Dad
wrestles me."

With age, his answer to that question will change. Later I'll
probably hear answers like "When you let me do my own thing,"
or "When you give me my own credit card." But whatever stage
you are in with your children, they need to know your love through
word and action. We must balance the tender side of love and the
tough side of love. We must learn our children's personalities and
which of the **languages of love** each responds to. What makes
them feel loved? How do they communicate their love? How do
we communicate our love to them?

James Dobson: I should warn those who have not yet assumed the responsibilities of parenthood; the game of raising kids is more difficult than it looks. Parenthood is costly and complex. Am I suggesting, then, that newly married couples should remain childless? Certainly not! The family that loves children and wants to experience the thrill of **procreation** should not be frightened by the challenge of parenthood. Speaking from my own perspective as a father, there has been no greater moment in my life than when I gazed into the eyes of my infant daughter, and five years later, my son. What could be more exciting than seeing those tiny human beings begin to blossom and grow and learn and love? And what reward could be more meaningful than having my little boy or girl climb onto my lap as I sit by the fire, hug my neck, and whisper, "I love you, Dad." Oh, yes children are expensive, but they're worth the price. Besides, nothing worth having comes cheap.[3]

Stitching Prayers

I have a confession to make. I have a favorite blankie. Yes, I'm a closet cuddler. When I married, I had to give up my teddy bear. But I kept my blankie **incognito**, as an ordinary blanket at the foot of the bed, just in case it got too cold.

It's a special, one-of-a-kind blanket. It's a quilt, handcrafted by my Granny Curtis and my great-grandmother, Mommy Duck (she waddled like a duck—hence, the nickname). It was a family tradition to make each grandchild a quilt when they were born. Their kids kept them busy with fourteen grandchildren.

To me, it's not just a quilt; it is a patchwork treasure chest filled with wonderful memories.

Both of these godly women are gone now, yet seem close as I cuddle my soft, worn blankie. I can visualize them around the quilting hoop, hard at work as they chat about their family and the latest grandchild. Dreaming of what the future would hold for their grandchildren, and hoping to share many years with them, they said little prayers as they stitched away, stitch by stitch by stitch.

It reminds me of <u>Hannah</u> (see GWWB, pages 129–130), a godly childless woman, who year after year went to the Temple and prayed for a son. In making deals with God, she vowed if God blessed her, she would give up her son, and commit him to be a **Nazirite**. At one Temple visit, her downcast soul was lifted when the priest pronounced God's blessing upon her. Later, Hannah

What Others are Saying:

procreation: producing offspring

incognito: with identity disguised

☞ **GO TO:**

1 Samuel 1 and 2 (Hannah)

Nazirite: a person who devoted his life to God; would not drink wine or cut his hair

and her husband conceived a child. True to her vow, Hannah gave her son Samuel to the priest, to serve in the Temple. Year after year, she made a special cloak for her son and journeyed to the Temple to present it to him. You can imagine Hannah designing this coat in her mind, then spending long hours clipping the sheep, brushing the wool clean, crushing and boiling root and berries to create brilliant colors, dyeing the wool, and then weaving the yarn so tightly. Perhaps with each stitch, she prayed for her son, stitch by stitch by stitch . . . stitching prayers, if you will, asking God's blessing on her son in her absence. With the help of his mother's prayers, Samuel grew to be the greatest Hebrew prophet since Moses.

☞ **GO TO:**

Jeremiah 15:1 (prophet)

Luke 15:4, 7 (99)

Do we pray stitching prayers for our children and those we love? Anything we do needs to be stitched in prayer. It's the thread that holds our lives together. Prayer strengthens, comforts, encourages, heals, and gives us peace of mind, as we give everything to God. If a stitch in time saves nine, perhaps stitching prayers can save even the one in 99.

☞ **GO TO:**

Exodus 20:1–17; Joshua 23:6 (Law of Moses)

> **1 Kings 2:2–3** "I am about to go the way of all the earth," he said. "So be strong, show yourself a man, and observe what the Lord your God requires: Walk in his ways, and keep his **decrees** and **commands**, his **laws** and requirements as written in the **Law of Moses**, so that you may prosper in all you do and wherever you go."

decrees: *laws that are declared publicly*

commands: *rules given by God applying to all people*

laws: *commands by God that tell people what they should or should not do*

Law of Moses: *the Ten Commandments and all related laws*

I Never Wanted to Be a Teacher

One of my favorite parental scenes in the Bible is in 1 Kings 2:2–4. Solomon is at his father's deathbed as King David is giving his final instruction to his son. Don't you find it interesting that David didn't dwell on the "Ten Management Tips for Running the Kingdom"? With his last breath, David was still teaching his son. I'm sure the charge to *"walk in his ways"* lingering in Solomon's ears was the key to his success as he ruled the kingdom.

"Walk in his ways." Those same words can be key to the success of our children in life, too.

☞ **GO TO:**

1 Kings 10:1 (success)

How many times have you heard little girls say, "I want to be a teacher when I grow up"? I don't think I ever said those words. When she was in grade school, my sister Sherry already knew she wanted to teach. She kept to her goal, and over the years she's taught them all—elementary through college. My sister Connie is a fabulous preschool teacher as well. She loves it!

Little did I know that parenting is all about teaching.

I am a researcher, by nature. I don't go into anything without knowing a little bit about the subject first. I remember when I was pregnant I read everything I could get my hands on about pregnancy. Then when our son was born I lived by the book, *What to Expect the First Year*. But even with all the books and advice on the library shelves, we must always thank God for his instruction manual, the Bible, where we can find out how to raise our children the way God wants us to.

GEORGIA'S TIPS . . .

As David taught Solomon, what do we teach our children about walking with God?

- Walk in INTEGRITY. If we walk in God's ways, we will be surefooted and will not slip and fall into sin. *"The man of integrity walks securely, but he who takes crooked paths will be found out"* (Proverbs 10:9).

- Walk in NEWNESS. Don't live the way unbelievers live. They are far away from God. Your attitudes and thoughts must be different from theirs. Walk in goodness and holiness. *"You were taught, with regard to your former way of life, to put off your old self, which is being corrupted by its deceitful desires; to be made new in the attitude of your minds; and to put on the new self, created to be like God in true righteousness and holiness"* (Ephesians 4:22–24).

- Walk by FAITH. Trust that God's ways and teachings are true. *"We live by faith not by sight"* (2 Corinthians 5:7).

- Walk in LOVE. As a child imitates his father, we are to follow the example of our heavenly father and walk in love, just as Christ loved us. *"Be imitators of God, therefore,*

KEY POINT

The most important aspect of this teaching profession called parenting is to instill in our children the Word of God.

KEY Outline:

Teach Your Children to Walk in

integrity
newness
faith
love
Jesus

KEY POINT

Our main responsibility is to help develop our children's inner lives and instruct them in the way of the Lord.

Think About It

as dearly loved children and live a life of love, just as Christ loved us and gave himself up for us as a fragrant offering and sacrifice to God" (Ephesians 5:1–2).

- Walk in JESUS. Just as you trusted Christ and made him Lord of your life, now walk in him, gain strength and truth from him. Just as a plant is nourished and rooted deep within the ground, you can build life on Christ's teachings. *"So then, just as you received Christ Jesus as Lord, continue to live in him, rooted and built up in him, strengthened in the faith as you were taught, and overflowing with thankfulness"* (Colossians 2:6).

The task of raising children is not so overwhelming when we realize that success in life will come when we teach them to walk in God's ways. We need not consume ourselves with dreams of having our children become rocket scientists or Nobel Prize winners. Our main responsibility is to help develop their inner lives and instruct them in the way of the Lord.

> **2 Timothy 1:6–7** For this reason, I remind you to fan into flame the gift of God, which is in you through the laying on of my hands. For God did not give us a spirit of timidity, but a spirit of power, of love and of self-discipline.

I Only Want the Best for My Child

☞ **GO TO:**

Exodus 28:41
(ordained)

Philippians 2:19–20
(encouragement)

1 Corinthians 16:10–11
(timid)

ordained: *set apart*

In 2 Timothy, Paul writes his farewell letter from prison to Timothy, who had been his faithful partner in ministry for over fifteen years. Paul encourages Timothy to *"fan into flame the gift of God."* This was the very gift Paul had prayed over and blessed when he laid his hands on Timothy and **ordained** him into ministry. Paul was reminding and encouraging Timothy to use his God-given gifts of <u>encouragement</u> and a sensitive heart. As we read between the lines of 1 and 2 Timothy, it appears Timothy may have been shy or <u>timid</u>. Paul exhorted him to carry on his mission in confidence (see GWBI, pages 273–280).

We can use Paul's encouragement to Timothy as a model. As parents, we too want to encourage our children to discover their unique gifts and carry out their own special mission in life.

Every child is different. Every child has unique gifts. You don't have to be a psychologist to notice that your child has his own individual quirks and is gifted in a certain area. But you do have to be a wise mother to understand your child and bring out the best in him or her.

In our son's class, each child has a different bent or gift. Lindsay loves ballet and excels in dance. Aubrey tries to take care of everyone's needs, always remembering to pray for them. Philip is a talented artist who sees life in intricate details. Jason is a math whiz and can build a Lego town in a flash. The world awaits this class of 2010 filled with Olympic medal winners, missionaries, artists, and inventors. I wonder how their lives will impact the world.

I highly recommend a fabulous author, Cynthia Tobias, who is an expert on the subject of **learning styles**. I became a fan of hers when Philip entered preschool. She has made a world of difference in how I appreciate, respond to, and nurture our son's special gifts and learning styles. She cuts through all the technical mumbo jumbo and helps you appreciate the different ways in which children receive, process, and respond to information. She can help you remove a lot of unnecessary frustration at home and at school while helping your kids achieve greater self-esteem.

As mothers we need to plant seeds of confidence and fan the flame in our children. We need to encourage our children in their area of giftedness. God has great plans for your child, just as he did for Timothy. He created each of us one of a kind. A child raised in an environment of encouragement and confidence may change the world.

Cynthia Tobias: Often the characteristics and behaviors that annoy us most about our children will be the qualities that make them successful as adults. You may feel your child talks too much or moves too much or takes too many chances, and yet those are some of the traits that are consistently found in successful entrepreneurs and business leaders. Although you must maintain bottom-line accountability and discipline, remember that the children who may be most inconvenient for you now may, when they grow up, turn out to be the best thing that ever happened to this world![4]

KEY Outline:

Mothers Plant Seeds of
faith
confidence
encouragement

learning styles: *ways that diverse personalities learn*

REMEMBER THIS

What Others are Saying:

KEY POINT

You can bring out the best in your children when you understand their unique giftedness.

ACT OF GOD

angel appears

☞ **GO TO:**

Judges 13:9 (quiet)

Judges 13:6 (reverent)

Judges 13:23 (faithful)

KEY POINT

Manoah's wife honored God's commands and raised her son as he instructed.

kosher: clean according to Jewish dietetic law

☞ **GO TO:**

Judges 14:3
  (confronted)

KEY Outline:

Delilah
  sinful, deceitful

**Manoah's Wife
  (Samson's mother)**
  faithful to God

SNAPSHOTS OF WOMEN IN THE BIBLE

Samson's Mom

The scripture gives her no name. She is only referred to as someone's wife and someone's mother. But there was a time when she felt no one would even call her mother. In her story, a barren faithful woman and a barren fallen nation come face to face.

An angel of the Lord appeared to Manoah's wife. It's not recorded where this first revelation took place. But in the glimpses Scripture gives us, I see a woman of character; a quiet, obedient, and reverent woman who remained faithful to God's commandments while, in the sinking nation around her, *"everyone did as he saw fit"* (Judges 12:25). I believe she may have been alone in prayer, praising the Creator and calling on him to save the nation that now lived under the control of the Philistines.

The angel's message brought joy and hope. Her empty arms would be filled and her son Samson would begin to deliver Israel out of the hands of the Philistines. Her son had a religious mission, and thus was to be set apart as a lifetime Nazirite. The angel instructed her even in pregnancy not to drink wine or anything from the fruit of the vine and not to eat anything that was not **kosher**, so as not to defile the child in her womb.

Samson was born, and the Lord blessed him and his mother. She dedicated herself to God and raised her son for his mission.

Parenting didn't stop when Samson was grown and making choices on his own. When he chose to go against God's command by marrying a woman who worshiped other gods, Manoah and his wife confronted him and protested his choice. They reminded him of his vows.

I'm sure the heart of Samson's mother grieved as she watched her son, a miracle baby, a man with God-given strength, cave in to moral weakness. He gave himself over to passion, lust, and sin—sin that eventually ended his potential for becoming a great judge.

During Samson's last stand, when he was blinded and tied to the pillars (see illustration, page 77), I wonder if he reflected on the women in his life. What sharp contrasts! Delilah (see GWWB, page 224), a sinful, deceitful woman he forsook all to have, betrayed him for silver. His mother, a woman of character, loved, understood, encouraged, and remained faithful to God. He must have thought of his mother, or at least remembered his mother's teachings; for he repented of his selfishness, and God gave him his strength enough to bring down the building onto the Philis-

Samson at the Pillars

Samson destroyed himself along with his Philistine captors when he knocked down the pillars that supported the temple.

tines—and himself. Though his life was cut short, he did begin the deliverance of Israel, just as the Lord foretold to his mother before his birth.

As mothers we don't know how our kids will turn out. We are not called to be enforcers of the faith, but like Samson's mother, we are called to be obedient to the faith—to love, pray for, encourage, and instruct our children in the way of the Lord.

Think About It

> **Matthew 6:25–27** Therefore I tell you, do not worry about your life, what you will eat or drink, or about your body, what you will wear. Is not life more important than food, and the body more important than clothes? Look at the birds of the air; they do not sow or reap or store away in barns and yet your heavenly Father feeds them. Are you not much more valuable than they are? Who of you by worrying can add a single hour to his life?

I Want a Simple, Stress-Free Life

Jesus taught his disciples to trust in God. As the song goes, "Don't worry, be happy!" He wanted them to let go and let God be in control of the driver's seat (or chariot seat).

Worrying is a waste of time and energy and causes stress as it complicates our lives. We think we are in control, but we really can't control what happens from day to day. So Jesus gives us a simple stress-free plan: live one day at a time in him.

Everyday Life

Around spring of 1997, I stepped back and looked at my juggling act called life. I accepted the fact that my life was too busy, my child's life was too cluttered, and life in general was way out of balance. I worried where I would find the time to squeeze in *just one more thing*. I was stressed out! I longed for a good night's rest, a cup of tea with a friend, and a night alone with my husband. I wanted a simple, stress-free life.

KEY Outline:

Life's Priorities
God
family
self

Maybe it had something to do with my impending fortieth birthday as I reflected on what was important in life, but I made some changes. We even went so far as to sell the 3,200-square-foot house that took me five hours to clean. In its place we bought a 1,400-square-foot little cottage that I can whip through in minutes. I yanked the smothering unwanted weeds of overcommitment out of my schedule, slowed down, and limited our son's extracurricular activities (i.e., sports) to one per season. I actually began to breathe as I slowed my pace, turned everything back over to God, and put him back where he belonged: first.

☞ **GO TO:**

Luke 11:39–42
(worried)

When Martha complained to Jesus that her sister Mary was too busy listening and not helping her serve his dinner, Jesus told her she was <u>worried</u> about too many secondary things. She was caught up in the things of least importance while Mary had chosen the thing of most importance: spending time with Jesus.

Think About It

A simple life has its advantages. It has less stress, it's more rewarding, it makes room for God and family. Paradoxically, if you leave more empty spaces in your schedule, your life can fill with simple pleasures.

 GEORGIA'S TIPS . . .

Tips to simplify your life:

- Slow down for prayer and Scripture reading.
- Sit down and clock out how you spend your day, week, and month.
- Evaluate and prioritize your life in this order:
  God
  family
  self
  career
  extracurricular activities
- Learn to say yes to top priorities and no to low priorities.
- Enjoy the simple pleasures with your children like taking walks, skating, gardening, flying a kite, and cooking.

Lynda Hunter: Ask yourself, What will it matter in five years? Do I need it? Can I simplify it? This will help you prioritize, decide what not to do, and discern which things are worth the effort or are not worth doing.[5]

> **Mark 6:30–32** The apostles gathered around Jesus and reported to him all they had done and taught. Then, because so many people were coming and going that they did not even have a chance to eat, he said to them, "Come with me by yourselves to a quiet place and get some rest." So they went away by themselves in a boat to a solitary place.

Stress—a Childhood Disease?

As word spread about Jesus' teachings and miracles, people were always following him, some just watching, others pressing for a miracle. When the crowds grew so large that Jesus and the disciples couldn't even eat, Jesus knew what to do. Despite all the demands of the crowd, he took his apostles away to a "solitary place."

We can learn from Jesus. When our children's lives get too stressed, we need to help them find stress relief. Take a good long look and evaluate their schedules. Simplify them. If necessary, make your child slow down, step back, and get some rest.

 *KEY Outline:*

Advantages of Living a Simple Life
more rewarding
less stress
makes room for God
leaves room for family
allows you to enjoy simple pleasures

 **What Others are Saying:**

KEY POINT

What's important in your life? Set priorities to balance and simplify life.

 *KEY Outline:*

Remember
slow down
get rest
less stress

Everyday Life

Our son has a new nickname. My husband calls him "Mr. Homebody." Every time we ask him what he wants to do, or where he wants to go out to eat, nine times out of ten he will say, "Let's just stay home."

That tells me he doesn't really want to go, go, go. He wants to slow down and enjoy the peace and quiet of his own home, his own kitchen table, and his own back yard.

Being **"stressed out"** is not reserved for adults only. This fast-paced world we live in is filled with a million and one things to do: nonstop Nintendo games to play, organized sports for toddlers on up, pressure to excel in school, an avalanche of media. Result: kids don't have much down time. When I see kids on edge and angry, with dark circles under their glazed eyes, they have the look of stress. Physicians tell us we're growing our kids into unhealthy adults, giving them a head start on health-related problems such as ulcers, heart failure, and depression. Doctors advise us to look at our children's schedules and simplify their load.

stressed out: tired, nervous, or depressed from overwork or mental pressure

Think About It

Dr. Archibald Hart, author of *Stress and Your Child*, offers the following tips for helping your child ease the anxiety of excess stress at school:

- Don't put undue pressure on your child to make better grades than he or she is capable of making. Arrange for tutoring or counseling if your child seems unduly stressed about grades.
- Monitor the number of extracurricular activities your child is involved in.
- Let your child talk about anxiety. Sharing one's worries helps relieve them.
- Watch for signs that a very young child is under stress at day care. Typical symptoms: "clingy" behavior, an increase in temper tantrums, and other stress-related behavior.
- Be alert to security problems and be prepared to work with the school and other parents to solve these problems.[6]

KEY POINT

Do you understand your child's stressful world? Try simplifying it to relieve stress.

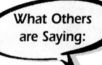

What Others are Saying:

Dr. Archibald D. Hart: To help our children protect themselves from stress disease and to prevent the establishment of the habits that will lead to stress-related illness, we must teach our children how to control their level of arousal and literally switch off their adrenaline when it is no longer needed. They must learn how to moderate and control their use of adrenaline and become less dependent on being "psyched up."[7]

> **Romans 5:5** Hope does not disappoint us, because God has poured out his love into our hearts by the Holy Spirit, whom he has given us.

The Stress of Flying Solo

As women of faith we can have confidence and hope in God. We have a free gift from God, the Holy Spirit, which fills our hearts when we accept Jesus as Lord of our lives. The Holy Spirit fills us with hope, confidence, and safety in God. No matter how bad the circumstance, no matter how much life has disappointed us, no matter how much we suffer we can place our hope and trust in God to see us through. You may be stressed out from raising your children as a single mother. Perhaps a man has hurt you deeply. Remember that God is never a disappointment and he can heal the hurt.

☞ **GO TO:**

1 Corinthians 13:8, 13 (Holy Spirit)

When you are parenting on your own, stress knocks on your door—and brings along some friends: loneliness, isolation, doubt, and a mountainload of other emotions.

Whether you have been divorced, widowed, or simply abandoned, don't lose **hope**. As we discussed in Chapter 2, God is a God of hope. This is a solo flight you never asked to pilot, but with God's help and a hope for a better tomorrow, you can land you and your children safely.

Everyday Life

hope: trust, reliance

Your solo flight of parenting may be different than the family's next door, but prioritizing, reducing stress, and finding balance in your own world will smooth out the turbulence you encounter along the way.

REMEMBER THIS

Tips for Juggling Career and Family

Quality living takes balance. Try these tips: (1) Set priorities. Decide what you can and cannot live without. Eliminate the activities that don't fit with what is important to your family; (2) Ask your children to take responsibility for some household chores; and (3) Learn to say, "No." When you are asked to do things that don't fit with your family's priorities, decline the request.

KEY Outline:

Remember
don't lose hope
you are not alone
God is with you
find ways to relieve stress

☞ **Check It Out:**

2 Timothy 1:1–6

☞ **GO TO:**

Acts 16:1 (father)

spiritual father: adopted father of the faith

KEY Outline:

Paul
  spiritual father

Timothy
  spiritual son

☞ **GO TO:**

Philippians 2:19–20 (sensitive)

1 Corinthians 16:10–11 (reserved)

missionary: a person sent out to spread a religion

Gospel: the good news of Jesus Christ

SNAPSHOTS OF WOMEN IN THE BIBLE

Eunice

Eunice's heart must have swelled with pride when her son Timothy shared the Apostle Paul's letter with her. What relief they felt to know that Paul had not yet been executed by the Romans.

Paul was like a father to Timothy. Timothy's own <u>father</u> was not known to be a Christian. In fact, scholars believe he died and Eunice raised Timothy alone. Timothy adopted Paul as his **spiritual father** and close companion. Between his travels with Paul and his pastoring a church Paul founded, Timothy ministered with Paul for over 15 years.

I imagine Eunice and Timothy this way:

Following in the footsteps of her mother Lois, Eunice passed her faith along to Timothy. Daily they studied the commandments and principles God set forth for his people. As she raised her son, she didn't know if he would ever share her faith, but day after day she continued to teach, encourage, and love him.

Eunice worried, at first, about Timothy's timidity. But she saw a boy who loved to learn—why, he drove her crazy with his meticulous details!—and she loved his tender heart. He was so <u>sensitive</u> to the needs of others. She had known God would use him in a special way; still, it surprised her when Paul asked young Timothy to join him on his **missionary** journey to spread the **Gospel**. They were so opposite—Paul was bold and daring, while Timothy was quiet and <u>reserved</u>. She had wondered how they would work together, but Timothy had proven to be the support, the detail man, and the strong right arm Paul needed to accomplish his mission.

Now, all these years later, tears trickled down her cheek as she read Paul's words: *"I have been reminded of your sincere faith, which first lived in your grandmother Lois and in your mother Eunice and, I am persuaded, now lives in you also."* Her life had meaning. She had raised her son alone but had remained faithful to God. As a result, she and her mother had influenced not only her son, but now were instrumental in establishing the church and spreading the good news of Jesus.

> **1 Thessalonians 5:11** Therefore encourage one another and build each other up, just as in fact you are doing.

M-O-M-S (Moms Offering Moms Support)

In Paul's letter to the believers in Thessalonica, he deals with the questions concerning the Second Coming of Jesus (see GWRV, pages 285–292). They wanted to know: What happens to those who die before Jesus returns? When will he return? And in the meantime, how should we live?

Paul answers in verse 11 how we should live in the Christian community while we wait. As people belonging to God, we are to encourage one another in our daily lives. In our everyday walk as moms, we learn from both Paul and women of the Bible to encourage one another.

 *EXAMPLES FROM THE BIBLE*

Women who offered support:

- After **Mary** the mother of Jesus found out she was pregnant, she spent three months with her cousin, Elizabeth (who was pregnant with John the Baptist). They ministered to each other during her stay. (Luke 1:39–56)
- Lydia, a businesswoman of Philippi, encouraged and met with other women at the riverbank to pray and worship. (Acts 16:13)
- Mary, the mother of **John Mark**, supported her friends and the establishing of the Church by opening her home for others to come and pray. (Acts 12:12, 25)
- Mary, the Mother of Jesus met with other women and the apostles in the **Upper Room** in Jerusalem. They came together to pray, encourage, and comfort one another after Jesus had ascended into heaven. (Acts 1:14)

My roots run deep in the foothills of the Appalachian Mountains in Kentucky. The area is known for its heritage in mountain crafts such as cane bottom chairs, handcrafted dolls, and beautiful quilts. During the Depression, mountain moms made little corn shuck dolls and hand-stitched quilts from colorful rags and sold them in New York City craft stores. That was how they provided desperately needed income for their families.

☞ **GO TO:**

John 14:2–3 (Second Coming)

Luke 23:43 (What)

1 Thessalonians 5:2 (When)

1 Peter 2:1–10 (belonging)

Mary: *the mother of John Mark, and relative of* **Barnabas**

John Mark: *an apostle of Christ; assisted Paul and Peter*

Barnabas: *"son of encouragement;" a leader in the early Church*

Upper Room: *the room where Jesus had the Last Supper with his disciples*

Isolation helped create these world-renowned mountain crafts. You didn't get out much in the back hills and hollows of the mountains, and the necessities of life were either not available or you had no funds to acquire them. So you made them.

In museums around Kentucky you can see black-and-white photos of women gathered around a quilting hoop, or groups of gals churning butter or clustering around a hot stove or canning food while little kids play around their feet. Any of these tasks could have been accomplished at home, alone. But they knew that work was made easier when accomplished with a friend. In fact, *life* was made easier when lived and shared with a friend. Woes were shared, emotions were mended, and prayers lifted up as traditions and values were passed around the quilting hoop.

Times haven't changed that much. Isolation is still a big factor with moms. We're a mobile society and move thousands of miles away from the support of our own mothers, grandmothers, and extended family.

Moms can feel isolated in their own four walls, and need support. I encourage you to get that support through a local church group or through an organization like MOPS (Mothers of Preschoolers). I recently came across a great ministry for moms called Hearts at Home, founded by Jill Savage. If you are online you can check them out on the Web at www.hearts-at-home.org. You'll find challenging articles, a bulletin board, secular and Christian networking opportunities for moms at home, and information on their regional conferences designed to encourage mothers at home (and those who want to be stay-at-home moms).

As you involve yourself in your Christian community of moms, you won't feel so alone. Sharing the common bond of motherhood will develop long lasting friendships, renew hearts, convey truths, and lift up prayers. You'll return home refreshed and ready to meet the needs of your family.

Think About It

KEY POINT

Moms need support from other moms. Don't go it alone.

Donna Partow: Young mothers today rarely have the ready-made support system offered by nearby family members, the kind of support that our mothers and grandmothers could take for granted. That's why it is so important for you to take the initiative to join an organization like MOPS (Mothers of Preschoolers) or similar mothers' group. Chances are the other mothers in the group struggle with the exact same issues you face. Don't wait for someone to reach out to you, take the initiative and set the pace.[8]

The Lasting Impressions of a Mother's Love

COFFEE BREAK
WITH GEORGIA

In the summer of 1997 a nation mourned the loss of their princess. The world grieved as Princess Diana, the most watched woman in the world, was buried.

I confess I'm a news junkie—and during that week, I wrestled the channel changer out of the King of the Remote's hands and watched countless news shows covering the story. Daily, I read local and national newspapers and magazines to keep up on breaking news. Through the tragedy, what impressed me most about this fairy tale princess was a thread that reporters wove into all the coverage. From dignitaries to lowly ordinary citizens, the people spoke of the love Princess Diana had for her sons.

A *Newsweek* headline read, "A Mother Before All Else." The subtitle said, "Even Diana's critics praise the way she raised her boys. How will they cope in the years ahead?"

That same summer I attended the funerals of two mothers. The first was a 38-year-old wife and mother of two young sons. All who mourned with the family had concern for the children left behind and silently wondered how they would cope.

A few weeks later I attended the funeral of a 62-year-old wife and mother of nine children. Even though these children were adults, their mother seemed to be the glue that held their extended family together. I had concern for the children left behind and silently wondered how they would cope.

If you asked the children left behind how they cope now, I'm sure they would say they cling to memories. Memories of a gentle touch. A loving gesture. An infectious smile. Memories of a loving mother.

Mary, the mother of Jesus, met in the Upper Room with the

other believers after Jesus had ascended back to heaven (John 20:17). I imagine the women gathered around Mary, offering the encouragement and support she so desperately needed. She held memories in her heart not only of a smiling son, but of a sacrificial Savior pouring out his blood. Memories of a powerless mother watching in helpless agony as they crucified her son. An angel's message thirty-three years earlier made her spirit rejoice, yet a prophet warned her that a sword would pierce her heart. Scripture records three times that Mary *"treasured all these things in her heart."*

Whether we must watch the death of a child, as Mary did, or stand helplessly by and watch one dear to us destroy himself or herself with bad choices, we have a Savior who knows what suffering is. He can comfort us in our own suffering. One way he sends strength and encouragement is through other women who cross our path, offering their friendships in our time of need.

Jesus knows what suffering is, so he can comfort us in our suffering. Look for strength and encouragement from others as part of his comfort.

STUDY QUESTIONS

1. Children are a gift from God. According to Deuteronomy 6:5–7, what are we to impress upon our children?
2. The Apostle Paul instructed older women to teach younger women. What were they to teach them to do?
3. How did Hannah help her son, Samuel, grow to be one of the greatest Hebrew prophets?
4. Based on the example of King David giving instructions to his son Solomon, what instruction can we parents give our children that is key to their success in life?
5. As parents, what can we learn from Samson's mother?
6. In Matthew 6:25–27, what simple stress-free plan did Jesus give us?
7. What gift did God give believers that fills us with hope, confidence, and safety?
8. As Eunice raised her son Timothy alone, what did she do that had the most important influence on his life?
9. What encouraging words can we learn from 1 Thessalonians 5:11 as moms try to find support?

- A mother has the blessing of loving and being loved by her children. She has the power to create, sustain, and shape another life; and the responsibility to carry out her mission in God's way. Look to his Word for wisdom in fulfilling this role of mothering.

- Children are a gift from God. He delights in his children and provides mothers with a special gift—a heart transformed into a treasure box filled with an abundance of love. This loving heart pulls you to be with your children.

- Get a better understanding of your children by discovering their learning styles. As much as possible, accept who they are. Major in developing their strengths.

- If you long for a simple life, you can do much more than merely pine for it. It's out there waiting for you. Evaluate, prioritize, and look to God for guidance and wisdom in your life and the lives of your children. Jesus gave us a simple plan for living one day at a time in him. Keep your eyes focused on the important things in life—an intimate relationship with God and your family. Enjoy a life filled with simple pleasures.

- Motherhood can be lonely and a time of isolation as you spend most of your waking hours with your children. Look to other moms for support. You will find encouragement from other women as you travel down this road together.

GEORGIA'S  BOOKSHELF

Some of Georgia's favorite books on the subject of mothering:

- *The Power of Mother Love*, Brenda Hunter, WaterBrook Press
- *Every Child Can Succeed*, Cynthia Tobias, Focus on the Family
- *Stress and Your Child*, Dr. Archibald Hart, Word
- *Mothers and Sons*, Jean Lush, Revell

4 HOME FRONT OR BATTLEFRONT?

Developing Meaningful Relationships within Your Family

Here We Go

I've always said I could get along with my family if it just weren't for the people involved. Too many times the home front slowly turns into a battlefront where the family fights a daily war. The arsenal is filled with the ammunition of hurtful words fired back and forth at one another. Children get caught in the crossfire and suffer battle fatigue. The home becomes less of a collection of adjoining rooms, and more like separate barracks in various occupied territories. Individuals don't unite and support one another; to survive, they hunker in their bunkers.

As fitness guru Susan Powters put it, "Stop the madness!" Strong loving families raise children who build strong loving relationships, inside and outside the fort called home.

We want to raise strong children because, among other reasons, they are the **foundation** for our future. In turn, God is the foundation we build our children upon, for *"unless the Lord builds the house, its builders labor in vain"* (Psalm 127:1).

How we get along with one another will determine if we live in a war zone or live in peace. The heartbeat of the family is the woman, who somehow holds it together. She may be a mom, wife, sister, or daughter, but she seems to most often be the peacekeeper.

foundation: the fundamental principle on which something is founded

Think About It

John C. Maxwell: The best thing you can do to strengthen your family is to build your marriage relationship. It's certainly the best thing you can do for your spouse, but it also has an incredibly positive impact on your children. My friend Josh McDowell wisely stated, "The greatest thing a father can do for his children is to love their mother." And the greatest thing a mother can do for her children is to love their father.[1]

☞ **Check It Out:**

Genesis 3

> **Genesis 1:27, 31** So God created man in his own image, in the image of God he created him; male and female he created them. God saw all that he had made, and it was very good.

Polar Opposites, or Polar Attraction?

sin: an offense against God

Adam and Eve lived in paradise until **sin** entered the Garden of Eden. Then everything changed. First they fell into the blame game. Then their blind love eroded as they saw each other's imperfections and felt the need to cover their once seemingly perfect bodies (see GWWB, pages 3–26; GWBI, pages 3–8). Then they hid from their friend and Creator, God: the one they knew they had disappointed, the one who gave them life, the one who had the answers to all of their confusion.

temptation: an inward pull to do wrong

Think About It

When the **temptation** of discontentment, bitterness, an unforgiving spirit, or countless other versions of strife and loneliness enters your garden of marriage, look to God for help and healing. When he made men and women different from one another, he did not make a mistake. God created Eve as a **helpmate** to Adam. The poor guy was lonely. That's why opposites attract—men need help. For balance, they need a different perspective. As much as men hate to admit it, woman completes man.

☞ **GO TO:**

Genesis 2:18
  (helpmate)

Think of two magnets. Their strong repulsion to one another can turn into equally strong magnetism if one of them will turn around. Our differences can drive us apart, or, like complementary halves, they can help us become more whole.

helpmate: a suitable partner; a being like Adam

Gary Chapman, Ph.D.: Love is the most powerful weapon for good not only in the world but in a troubled marriage. When we choose to reach out with a loving attitude and loving actions toward our spouse in spite of past failures, we are creating a climate where conflicts can be resolved, wrongs can be confessed, and a marriage can be reborn.[2]

SNAPSHOTS OF WOMEN IN THE BIBLE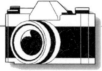

Rebekah

She knew when they looked at her they envisioned beautiful grandchildren to carry on their names. She heard them bartering with her father, trying to arrange for their sons to marry her, but her father always waited and never agreed to any price, no matter how high. Father told her he'd know when the situation was right. Until then, she would have to be patient.

Rebekah didn't know why he waited. She wondered how she could get him to change his mind and arrange her marriage. There were more than enough suitable men in her region. She should know—her beauty attracted them like bees to a beautiful flower. But she knew she must wait and trust her father.

With a pitcher on her shoulder in the cool of the evening, Rebekah made her way down the dusty path to the well. It was crowded with villagers gathering to water their animals. Near the well she noticed a weary stranger sitting among his camels. As with most men, when his eyes fell on her, they brightened. She glanced his way but went about her business drawing water—although she did wonder why he had not watered his thirsty camels. As she turned to make her way back up the path, the stranger asked her for a drink. He had kind eyes, and she gladly quenched his thirst. Seeing the man had no pitcher with which to draw water for his animals, Rebekah graciously asked if she could water his herd (see illustration, page 92). She knew it would be a long hard task; ten camels would lap up gallons of water, but she was willing. Rebekah was known for her enthusiastic spirit, her kindness to strangers and always going the extra mile. Other village ladies shook their heads and went about their own business.

Rebekah expected nothing in return for watering the camels, but this man, Eliezer, not only gave her gifts of gold, but he stopped and praised the **Lord** for making their paths cross.

They arranged for Eliezer to lodge with her family. She ran ahead to tell her parents who was coming for dinner. Rebekah loved the

What Others are Saying:

☞ **Check It Out:**

Genesis 24:1–67

KEY Outline:

Man Needed
a helpmate
balance
a different perspective
a woman

Lord: "Lord" in the Old Testament referred to the essence of God, his power over his people and the earth

Well and Water Jug

Rebekah probably drew water from a well like this one and carried the heavy jugs by balancing them on her head. She would have had to draw approximately 250 gallons of water to satisfy Eliezer's camels, because each camel would drink up to 25 gallons of water.

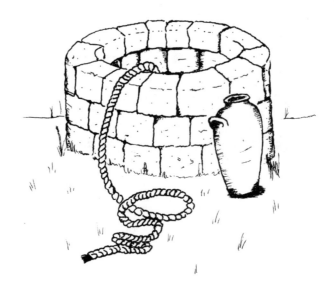

kinsmen: *relatives or family members*

covenant: *a special binding promise, like a treaty*

☞ **GO TO:**

Genesis 15:18
(covenant)

Genesis 12:1–3
(mother)

Think About It

rhythmic jingle her new bright gold bracelets made as she hurried home. Her pace grew with each clink of the metal.

Eliezer praised the Lord as he rounded up his camels. The Lord had answered his prayer. He had been sent to his master Abraham's **kinsmen** on an important mission to find a wife for Abraham's son, Isaac. God had made a **covenant** promise to Abraham that he would be the father of many nations (see GWBI, pages 15–16; GWWB, page 36). Abraham said the Lord would guide Eliezer and so he had.

There was no negotiation regarding Rebekah. Her father, Bethuel, sat in awe of Eliezer's story. He knew the Lord led Eliezer to Rebekah and that God's hand would be on this marriage. Bethuel would not go against the Lord. He told Eliezer to take her and go. Knowing she may never return to her homeland, Rebekah's mother and brother wanted more time to say good-bye, but Eliezer insisted they must depart quickly. The family asked Rebekah if this was what she wanted. It was. She wanted to be married. This man promised her she would be a mother of nations. She, too, perceived the hand of God leading Eliezer. She said she would go.

Scripture says the servant told Isaac the whole story. Isaac was probably still breathless not only from her beauty, but from seeing the Lord's hand in his life. He took her to be his wife, and he loved her.

In a time of marriage negotiations, God made the final arrangement as he led his servant to Rebekah, a woman willing to see and believe the sign of God. This woman's faith was so strong that she was willing to commit to a man she had never seen.

Rebekah exhibited two important qualities in a strong marriage:

1. The willingness to leave all that is familiar behind. She left her family, friends, and homeland to follow God's lead.

2. She trusted God and made a lifelong commitment to her marriage. In a culture where love was not a prerequisite for marriage, God rewarded her with a man who truly loved her all of her days. The children of their union, Jacob's descendants, are called Israel, God's chosen people.

> **Genesis 2:23–24** The man said, "This is now bone of my bones and flesh of my flesh: she shall be called 'woman,' for she was taken out of man." For this reason a man will leave his father and mother and be united to his wife, and they will become one flesh.

The Love Triangle

For every two couples who get married there is one divorce. Because of this, churches around the country are encouraging a form of marriage covenant called the Community Marriage Agreement. Some states offer this strict agreement as an alternative to a regular marriage license. In a nutshell, under this agreement divorce is no option—you commit to a covenant of faithfulness.

Covenants are standing contracts between two partners. This unique relationship called marriage is between a husband and wife, where a man and woman can live in a sexual relationship within the approval and laws of their social group. A Christian union takes it one step further. It is a covenant between a man, a woman, and God—a love triangle. If that triangle is kept intact, a lifelong commitment to faithfulness can stand the test of time as two become one.

Bob Russell: Almost always when I counsel with a couple before I perform their marriage ceremony, I will draw a triangle on a piece of paper (see illustration, page 94) and write at the top, "God," and at the lower corners, "husband" and "wife." Then, tracing the ascending lines of the triangle, I will point out how the closer you get to God, the closer you will be to each other.[3]

KEY Outline:

Eliezer
trusted God
prayed for guidance
experienced blessing and success

Rebekah
trusted God
recognized his leading
took a leap of faith
experienced blessing and love

ACT OF GOD

Eliezer's prayers were answered

KEY POINT

Love is not merely emotion. Love is primarily choice and action.

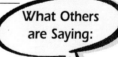

What Others are Saying:

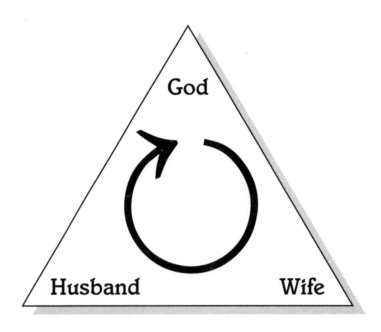

God

Husband   Wife

GEORGIA'S TIPS . . .

Five Little Things You Can Do to Strengthen Your Marriage:

1. Love your spouse as you wish to be loved.

2. Do an unexpected act of kindness. "Sweet nothings" can mean everything in the midst of a hurried and harried day.

3. Find something to praise your spouse for: a personal quality, a nice outfit, a recent accomplishment.

4. Make a date with your spouse. Husbands and wives need time alone together. Set a date and time tonight.

5. Forgive your spouse for anything he may have done to upset you. Let him know immediately that he is forgiven.[4]

Tough Times in a Troubled Marriage

I love weddings, and it's guaranteed I'll cry at every one I attend. I used to be a wedding photographer and I loved every moment of it. The only problem was, photographers aren't suppose to cry. Blurred vision while looking through a lens is not a good thing.

I loved snapping away and capturing on film the excitement of the day, the tenderness and love in the newlyweds' eyes, and the anticipation of living a life happily ever after. Never in a million years would newlyweds think that their dreamy romance would turn into a troubled marriage and nightmare. It breaks my heart when I hear of a happy couple I photographed years ago now broken by tough times and a troubled marriage.

Scripture offers encouragement and solutions to broken relationships. With God's help and the advice and wisdom from a professional Christian counselor, a marriage that may look like it's over can have a new beginning, a healing, and a true restoration.

If the reality of divorce or separation has landed on your doorstep, God has not abandoned you. When you turn to him in your loneliness and despair he will walk beside you—or even carry you—each step of the way.

Let's see what the Bible says about tough times in a troubled marriage.

> **Matthew 7:24** Therefore everyone who hears these words of mine and puts them into practice is like a wise man who built his house on the rock. The rain came down, the streams rose, and the winds blew and beat against that house; yet it did not fall, because it had its foundation on the rock.

S.O.S.!

If you cling to the promise that a house built on a strong foundation (the foundation of God) will withstand the storms of life, you can hold on and stand firm for your marriage. The life of your family may depend on lonely you, equipped with little more than your S.O.S. distress call—and God's transforming power.

 ## EXAMPLES FROM THE BIBLE

A mended relationship is shown in the story of Gomer, the unfaithful wife of **Hosea** (Hosea 2–3). She became a slave in prostitution. It is believed other men fathered two of her three children. To reconcile their marriage relationship, Hosea sought out Gomer, bought her out of slavery, and forgave his straying wife. This also is an illustration of how God sought and redeemed his nation Israel despite the unfaithfulness of his people.

Hosea: a prophet, spoke message of reconciliation

Think About It

KEY Outline:

Seek Help
*first from God
second from a
professional
counselor*

peace: *harmony or calm
feelings*

forsake: *leave, abandon,
or give up on*

REMEMBER THIS

☞ GO TO:

John 14:27 (peace)

Joshua 1:5 (forsake)

Think About It

Your ship is sinking and you're screaming for help. The fierce gale stings you with relentless wind and rain. You're sending out the S.O.S. signal, but there is no response. You feel that if a few more waves crash in, your marriage will be lost in a sea of despair.

Don't give up. Don't lose hope. Your problem is you're sending the signal to the wrong person—your spouse. Chances are, he's lost that loving feeling and can't find the lifeline. Remember, most men won't stop and ask for directions after driving around lost for hours. Why do we then expect them to jump in headfirst and ask for help on deep personal issues? You need help first from God and his Word, then from a professional counselor.

Homespun Wisdom: Successful relationships are all about getting along and understanding people. If we try to understand the motives behind our own behavior and our spouse's behavior, we may be better armed to confront and resolve issues. I make no claims to being a counselor, but I have benefited from the advice and guidance of a counselor in hanging on to my commitment to marriage when the storm raged against us.

There are no quick fixes to mending marriages, but there are solutions. Making a commitment to God and your spouse to stay together and to work toward resolving your differences is the first step to a successful marriage. Hang on to your beliefs, anchored to the truths found in the Bible. You may not know what the future holds, but you can find **peace** in knowing that God will not **forsake** you. He is with you every step of the way.

During a time of strife in my marriage, I found that when I looked inward there were things I needed to change. I began to make those changes, but it was hard. I'm a "take charge" kind of gal, but I had to realize that I can only take charge of me. As much as I would like to be Queen of the World, I'm responsible for my actions, alone. I needed to leave the rest up to God.

Forgiveness is a stepping stone to **reconciliation**. Forgiveness means letting go of **anger** and **bitterness**. It does not mean that you approve of the behavior you're forgiving. It means you give up the notion that you have the right to hurt someone back. On a daily basis I have to surrender everything over to God, allowing him to work in my life and marriage.

My sea of despair has slowly calmed, but there are still occasional squalls that pop up out of nowhere. Even in these moments of discouragement, the Bible and help from my counselor has turned me back into a seafaring voyager.

Peter was able to <u>walk on stormy water</u> as long as he kept his eyes fixed on Jesus. Similarly, take your eyes off the storm and look to the one who can calm the seas. This is the surest way to find days ahead that will be smooth sailing.

GEORGIA'S TIPS . . .

Stepping stones to reconciliation:

1. Forgive: *"Be kind and compassionate to one another, forgiving each other, just as in Christ God forgave you"* (Ephesians 4:32). *"For if you forgive men when they sin against you, your heavenly Father will also forgive you. But if you do not forgive men their sins, your Father will not forgive your sins"* (Matthew 6:14–15).

2. Let go of anger and bitterness: *"Everyone should be quick to listen, slow to speak and slow to become angry, for man's anger does not bring about the righteous life that God desires"* (James 1:19). *"God has called us to live in peace"* (1 Corinthians 7:15). *"See to it that no one misses the grace of God and that no bitter root grows up to cause trouble and defile many"* (Hebrews 12:15).

Connie Neal: It may be the desire to get out of your marriage altogether . . . or a longing to have an affair with someone who appreciates you; or the urge to treat your husband as poorly as he treats you. There's no shortage of ways you can do your will when the Father's will seems too hard a road to walk. That's why you need to settle this issue up front: Are you willing to do the will of your Father in heaven?[5]

---

forgiveness: a decision not to punish or seek revenge for an offense against you

reconciliation: the making of peace between people, a settling of differences

anger: a desire to fight back

bitterness: feelings of hatred and resentment

☞ **GO TO:**

Matthew 14:22–31 (walk on stormy water)

KEY POINT

Stand by your commitment to marriage—if necessary, get help.

What Others are Saying:

All the Queen's Horses . . .

The buzzing alarm woke me from a sound sleep at 3:00 A.M. I jumped out of bed, headed downstairs and switched on the TV to join millions of worldwide viewers gazing starry-eyed at the wedding of the century. That was years ago, and my newlywed husband thought I was nuts for getting up in the middle of the night to watch Princess Diana and Prince Charles say "I do." But of course he couldn't understand. Cinderella hadn't been his childhood idol. But she had been mine, and this was definitely a twentieth-century Cinderella Wedding, with horsedrawn carriage and all. I wasn't about to miss it.

The years since then flew by for me, but judging by all the front cover tabloids, I'm sure those same years seemed like eternity to the royal couple. Di was suppose to be like Cinderella: move to the palace, marry the prince, and live happily ever after. But as the world watched, the magic ended. Di's sparkling eyes turned dark and empty when she glanced at Charles. Her heart-melting, shy smile was reserved only for the camera, and her shattered emotions became tabloid talk.

I never wanted this fairy tale romance to end. I always hoped they would come to their senses, renew their commitment, give in to the Queen's persistence and give it another try. But it was official in September of 1996 when the clerk's red rubber stamp stained the divorce papers—the marriage was over. Another fairy tale romance ended. All the Queen's horses and all the Queen's men couldn't put Charles and Di back together again.

Wouldn't it be nice if Cinderella's fairy godmother could say "Bibbidi-Bobbidi-Boo!" and instantly make your marriage perfect? We all know it takes a lot more than that to turn romance into a lifelong marriage. What's needed is not a fairy godmother; it's God the Father being the central focus of the union.

Over the past 20 years of marriage I have to admit my husband and I have not had a fairy tale romance. But with Christ as the head of our home, my house is my castle, my husband is my prince, and God is our King.

Though all the Queen's horses and all the Queen's men could never put life back together for Di and Charles (or anyone else, for that matter), the King of Kings can put all the shattered pieces back together again. But first we have to pick up those pieces and

KEY POINT

What's needed is not a fairy godmother; it's God the Father being the central focus of the union.

put them in his hands. That may seem hard, but it shouldn't be, for *"He healeth the broken in heart and bindeth up their wounds"* (Psalm 147:3).

> **James 1:5** If any of you lacks wisdom, he should ask God, who gives generously to all without finding fault, and it will be given to him.

Decisions, Decisions: In or Out?

James, the brother of Jesus, is writing to the new believers who were scattered about the Roman world (see GWBI, pages 301–304) when they fled from persecution. James knows that godly wisdom is a great gift. He gives a simple plan to get it: If you need wisdom, ask for it. God will give it to us.

Up 'til now we've concentrated on finding the wind for the sails of your drifting marriage and overcoming marital problems. But you may be the reader who is shaking her head, thinking that I just don't understand what you're going through. Maybe you are in a physically abusive relationship; you've forgiven the **infidelity** time after time; and in order for you and your children to survive, you see no alternative but divorce.

So let me make this clear: In no way am I saying to allow your husband to abuse you or your children. Get to safety and seek professional help immediately. Do not keep the abuse secret. Physical abuse is not only damaging to you; it is also harmful to your children's physical and emotional state.

If you are being emotionally abused, turn to God and ask him for wisdom in your situation. Repeated, prolonged attacks on your worth as a person hurt deeply. Seek help from a professional counselor or your pastor. Then follow James' advice, and ask God what he wants you to do.

Leaving a physically abusive marriage is an important decision. It is more difficult to decide if you should leave an emotionally abusive marriage. In extreme cases, divorce or separation may be your only options. These should be your last resort.

> When you feel you've depleted all of your options, continue to ask God for wisdom in order to have the knowledge to make the **right** decisions. Wise women seek God. God is the source of wisdom and wisdom is found in Christ and the Word.

KEY Outline:

God
source of all wisdom

Wisdom
found in Christ and his word

infidelity: sexual unfaithfulness of a spouse

☞ **GO TO:**

Colossians 1:9–12 (right decisions)

Psalm 111:10 (source)

Colossians 2:2–5 (Christ)

REMEMBER THIS

right: correct action

Decision Making

always seek God's
wisdom

then seek professional
help

**If Physical Abuse Is
Involved**

get out

then seek professional
help immediately

☞ **GO TO:**

Malachi 2:16 (divorce)

divorce: legal and formal
dissolution of a marriage

KEY POINT

Always seek God's
wisdom first for
decision making.

Gary Chapman, Ph.D.: Is there hope for women who suffer physical abuse from their husbands? Does reality living offer any genuine hope? I believe the answer to those questions is yes. An abused wife can become a positive change agent in the marriage, but I do not believe that she can do it alone. She will need the help of a trained counselor, the support of family or friends, and she will need to draw upon her spiritual resources. I urge you if you are in an abusive marriage to seek counseling immediately. It will be worth the time, effort, and money you spend, and offers the greatest potential for a positive outcome in what has become a destructive marriage.[6]

> **Matthew 19:8** Jesus replied, "Moses permitted you to divorce your wives because your hearts were hard. But it was not this way from the beginning. I tell you that anyone who divorces his wife, except for marital unfaithfulness, and marries another woman commits adultery."

Separation or Divorce?

Separation or **divorce** was not part of God's original plan. But when sin entered the Garden of Eden human hearts hardened and Adam and Eve turned their backs on God's original design (see GWWB, pages 10–16).

In Old Testament times, the family was structured with the husband as the head of the household. Wives and children were sometimes treated like property. But God gave laws for the people of Israel to live by. God's Law described what types of marriages were forbidden, and gave other guidelines for marriage so that God's people could have clean, healthy, blessed relationships.

No-No's for Marriage

Leviticus 18:1–29 (unlawful sexual relations)

- no sexual relations with close relatives
- no sexual relations with your neighbor's wife
- no sexual relations with the same sex
- no sexual relations with an animal

Exodus 20:14 (one of the Ten Commandments)

- You shall not commit adultery

Deuteronomy 22 (laws and guidelines for marriage violations)

- no cross dressing
- no falsely trashing a woman's reputation
- no sleeping around
- no marrying your stepparent

We don't live in ancient Bible times, but we shouldn't ignore the wisdom in these guidelines. You can see in the Old Testament Law and in Jesus' words in Matthew 5:31 (*"Anyone who divorces his wife must give her a certificate of divorce."*) that divorce is permissible when a spouse is sexually unfaithful. However, there never seems to be a win/win ending to divorce, so it should be held as the last resort.

Gary Chapman, Ph.D.: There are no "and they lived happily ever after" divorces. The effects of divorce linger for a lifetime. This is not to say that there is no life after divorce. It is to say that life after divorce is always **impacted** by life before the divorce. Because the marriage relationship is unique among human relationships and involves deep emotional ties on the part of the husband and wife, there is no walking away without pain.[7]

impacted: affected, influenced

EXAMPLES FROM THE BIBLE

The Bible speaks of men whose hearts were **hardened** as they turned away from God's commands. Tough consequences always resulted from their actions.

hardened: made tougher or more cruel and unfeeling

- In the days of Noah, humanity's heart turned from God. The earth was corrupt and full of violence and God destroyed the earth with a flood. Noah, a righteous man who walked with God, preached the impending destruction, but only he and his family were saved. (Genesis 6:10–22)
- At Sodom and Gomorrah, humanity's heart turned from God. The wickedness and sin of these cities was so great that God destroyed the cities with brimstone and fire from heaven. (Genesis 18:20; 19:24)

- King Saul's heart turned from God as he disobeyed God's commands. Saul was replaced by David, a man after God's own heart. (1 Samuel 15:11; 13:14)

- Pharaoh's heart was hardened so that he would not listen to Moses in order that God could do many more signs and wonders. The children of Israel would see that God's hand was against Egypt. (Exodus 7:3–5)

- The children of Israel's hearts were hardened as they grumbled and complained and tested God because of their thirst for water in the wilderness at the place called Meribah. (Psalm 95:7; Exodus 17:7)

- The writer of Hebrews encouraged believers to keep from allowing their hearts to be hardened by sin's deceitfulness. (Hebrews 3:13)

 **REMEMBER THIS**

Seek counsel before you make the final decision on divorce. Know that while God hates divorce, he loves you and will never turn his back on you.

> **1 Corinthians 7:10–11** To the married I give this command (not I, but the Lord): A wife must not separate from her husband. But if she does, she must remain unmarried or else be reconciled to her husband.

Separation

Paul wrote to the church at Corinth (see illustration, page 143) to bring help to their relationships. Early Christians apparently wondered if they could serve Christ better by being single. They wanted to know if marriage was a stumbling block to their service. Paul encouraged them to stay in their marriages, but if for any reason they separated they should work toward reconciliation.

So even if infidelity is not involved, but you cannot withstand the physical abuse or extreme emotional battering from your spouse, Scripture implies you are permitted to separate. This is not intended as a trial run for divorce, but as a **separation** with the intent to reconcile. It is a time to get relief, a time to seek counsel, a time for prayer, and a time for positive behavior change.

separation: agreement by which a man and wife live apart temporarily

Reconciliation is the making of peace between people. Christ gave us the supreme example of reconciliation as he brought reconciliation between God and humanity.

Romans 5:11—"*But we also rejoice in God through our Lord Jesus Christ, through whom we have now received reconciliation.*"

2 Corinthians 5:18–19—"*All this is from God, who reconciled us to himself through Christ and gave us the ministry of reconciliation: that God was reconciling the world to himself in Christ, not counting men's sins against them. And he has committed to us the message of reconciliation.*"

Colossians 1:19–20—"*For God was pleased to have all his fullness dwell in him, and through him to reconcile to himself all things, whether things on earth or things in heaven, by making peace through his blood, shed on the cross.*"

EXAMPLES FROM THE BIBLE

The Bible mentions at least two marriage separations neither of which were because of mistreatment:

- Moses and his wife Zipporah separated for a time. Moses left Midian for Egypt with Zipporah and their two sons as God commanded. Zipporah eventually returned to Midian with their children. There is no mention of her until after Moses led the Israelites out of Egypt. Then his father-in-law brought Zipporah and their sons to reunite and reconcile with Moses. (Exodus 4:18–19; 18:5)

- David and Michal were separated due to the attempts of King Saul, Michal's father, upon David's life. Michal heard of her father's plan to kill her husband and she helped David escape. Years passed as David hid in the hills. King Saul gave Michal in marriage to another man, named Paltiel. Seven years later, after Saul was dead and David became king, he sent for Michal and they reunited. Yet, Michal's love and adoration for David turned to bitterness. True reconciliation did not occur in their marriage, for Michal chose bitterness over love and forgiveness. (1 Samuel 18, 2 Samuel 3–6)

Think About It

KEY Outline:

Divorce or Separation?

Divorce
- God hates it
- allowed if spouse is sexually unfaithful

Separation
- provides relief from mistreatment
- done with intent to reconcile
- seek counsel
- strive and look for positive behavior change
- reconcile or remain unmarried

If you choose separation, the Bible clearly states that you must remain unmarried. During this time your spouse may decide that he doesn't want to reconcile. He may end up divorcing you, but I encourage you to stay true to God's Word and trust that God will not abandon you.

What Others
are Saying:

Jan Silvious: This final **caveat**, "remain unmarried," is a good test for you personally. Are you willing to face the fact that your mate may not reconcile, may never marry anyone else, and may not die for a long time? Are you willing to live without a mate and still be content? I have found that this is a good personal litmus test for an individual bound to a fool through marriage when things are stressful and strife is at a high pitch. Ask yourself, Am I willing to separate, remain unmarried, or be reconciled? If not, then "**detachment**" is the option that will allow you to remain married, to hope in God, and to maintain a sense of peace in the midst of your circumstances.[8]

caveat: a notice; warning

detachment: withdrawal

> **Proverbs 3:13–18** Blessed is the man who finds wisdom, the man who gains understanding, for she is more profitable than silver and yields better returns than gold. She is more precious than rubies; nothing you desire can compare with her. Long life is in her right hand; in her left hand are riches and honor. Her ways are pleasant ways, and all her paths are peace. She is a tree of life to those who embrace her; those who lay hold of her will be blessed.

What Family Tree Did You Fall Out Of?

The book of Proverbs is like an Idiot's Guide to Finding Wisdom. There is no treasure or jewel greater than wisdom. Wisdom is knowledge and understanding applied to life. Solomon, author of Proverbs, compares wisdom to a life-giving tree, and those who are nourished by this tree and the ways of God will live a blessed and happier life. In the next few pages, we'll consider how we can apply wisdom (the tree of life) to our relations (the family tree).

Laugh
Out
Loud

There are times you wonder what tree this relative fell out of. You're sure there's no way in the world it is grounded in *your* family roots. You may even be tempted to just chop it down and feed it into the chipper. But we all know we need to resolve problems, not destroy, deny, or run from them—even if family is your problem. *Especially* if family is your problem.

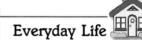

One of the most difficult battles in developing meaningful connections with relatives is handling troublesome relationships within your extended family. Remember how the press dug up embarrassing information about President Jimmy Carter's brother, Billy, and President Clinton's brother, Roger? The Carters and the Clintons are really no different than most of our families, they are just in the limelight and their family tree is exposed for all the world to see. But also remember President Carter and President Clinton love their brothers.

Your problem may be with a sibling, a parent, or in-laws, but like it or not you are related and you will have to deal with your family sooner or later. You may want to go into the Witness Protection Program, but the Feds don't make that available just for the asking.

> **Psalm 1:1–3** Blessed is the man who does not walk in the counsel of the wicked or stand in the way of the sinner or sit in the seat of mockers. But his delight is in the law of the Lord, and on his law he meditates day and night. He is like a tree planted by streams of water, which yields its fruit in season and whose leaf does not wither. Whatever he does prospers.

My Mama Didn't Raise No Fool

If we are to be like a *"tree planted by streams of water, which yields its fruit in season and whose leaves do not wither"* (Psalm 1:3), we will be constantly watered and nourished by the Word and bear **fruit** as we live in Jesus. By using the fruit of the Spirit we can deal with our most difficult relationships. *"But the fruit of the Spirit is love, joy, peace, patience, kindness, goodness, faithfulness, gentleness, and self-control. Against such things there is no law"* (Galatians 5:22–23).

It should come as no suprise that love heads the list, because *"God is Love"* (1 John 4:8), and the greatest of Christian qualities is love (1 Corinthians 13:13).

fruit: the result, product, or consequences of something

REMEMBER THIS

Think About It

The fruit of the Spirit is the outward expression of Christ's love in us. Below is a table of the fruit of the Spirit with descriptions of each aspect.

- LOVE: the love of Christ that unites man with God and man to man. (John 15:12–13)
- JOY: the celebration of God's love. (John 15:11)
- PEACE: the ability to live in harmony with God and man. (John 14:27)
- PATIENCE: calmness under **provocation** or strain. Applies both to God's patience toward us and our patience toward others. (1 Corinthians 13:4)
- KINDNESS: the outward expressions of godly affection as we grow in Christ. (Colossians 3:12)
- GOODNESS: love in action, as in "acts of goodness." (2 Thessalonians 1:11)
- FAITHFULNESS: enduring, reliable loyalty. (Hebrews 10:23)
- GENTLENESS: free of harshness, like the kind spirit of Christ. (1 Corinthians 4:20–21)
- SELF-CONTROL: discipline in heart and actions as we follow God's teachings. (Acts 24:25)

provocation: to bring something about

Everyday Life

personality types: individual **temperaments** and behavior

temperaments: one's customary frame of mind or natural disposition

Several years ago while attending a conference on **personality types**, I sat in amazement as Florence Littauer took attributes of each personality and connected all the strengths and weaknesses piece by piece, like a puzzle. Before my very ears she described members of my family. A light went off in my head and I suddenly understood not only my family better, but just about everyone else, too.

The four basic personality types that Florence describes are listed on page 107.[9]

Think About It

In all of our personality profiles we have major weaknesses. To live in harmony with others, we can't just say, "Well, that's me; take it or leave it." We each have certain specific traits that usually are the cause of difficulties in our relationships. Since my mama didn't raise no fool, I knew I had to take a good look in the mirror and face whatever foolish behavior I found before I could jump headfirst into understanding those around me.

Personality	Characteristics
Popular Sanguine	Outgoing
	Desires fun
	Emotional
	Outspoken
	Relationship oriented
Perfect Melancholy	Introverted
	Desires perfection
	Organized
	Pessimistic
	Task-oriented
Peaceful Phlegmatic	Introverted
	Desires peace
	Unemotional
	Pessimistic
	Relationship-oriented
Powerful Choleric	Outgoing
	Desires power or control
	Outspoken
	Strong-willed
	Optimistic

pessimistic: *a tendency to focus on whatever is gloomy or bad*

optimistic: *a tendency to focus on whatever is cheerful or good*

Alice and Mildred, two sisters, kept up a feud for thirty years. On Mildred's seventieth birthday, Alice, who was seventy-five, felt a pang of remorse, but it passed. Yet later, when she heard Mildred was ill, she felt compelled to visit.

From her sickbed, Mildred looked sternly at her sister. At last she said in a faint voice, "The doctors say I'm seriously ill, Alice. If I pass away, I want you to know you're forgiven. But if I pull through, things stay as they are!"[10]

Laugh Out Loud

EXAMPLES FROM THE BIBLE

From character traits of individuals described in the Bible, listed below are examples of personality types:

- Popular Sanguine: Jezebel, the wicked queen who persecuted the prophets and worshiped the false god Baal was a materialistic woman who loved living in the lap of luxury. She loved being the center of attention and partying with her sensuous cult. Jezebel displayed traits of the Popular Sanguine who is outgoing, desires fun, and is outspoken and emotional (1 Kings 16:1–2 Kings 11:37). And don't worry—just because a person has a Popular Sanguine personality, that doesn't necessarily mean they're as evil as Jezebel!

- Perfect Melancholy: Martha, the sister of Lazarus and Mary, was very task-oriented and had to have everything perfect as she prepared and served a meal for Jesus and his followers. Martha displayed traits of the Perfect Melancholy as she desired organized perfection and was pessimistic. (John 11:1–12:2)

- Peaceful Phlegmatic: Thomas, a disciple of Christ, was pessimistic and doubtful. When the other disciples told him that they had seen the risen Jesus, he doubted and would not believe unless he saw for himself. Thomas displayed traits of the Peaceful Phlegmatic. (John 20:24–29)

- Powerful Choleric: Simon Peter, an apostle of Christ, was ready to fight and go to prison or death with Jesus. He drew his sword and cut off the ear of a servant when men came to arrest Jesus. He displayed traits of a Powerful Choleric with his strong will, impulsive outspokenness, and optimism. (Luke 22:33, 50)

KEY Outline:

Personality Types
Popular Sanguine
Perfect Melancholy
Peaceful Phlegmatic
Powerful Choleric

What Others are Saying:

personality puzzle: the whole picture of your personality and how it fits with other personality types

Marita and Florence Littauer: While we cannot force others to change—although we may try—and we can't make them adore us, we can learn to get along with them. . . . When you understand the emotional needs of the **personality puzzle** you can give others what they need instead of what you need. When we can change our perspective and do unto others as they would like and not as we wish to do according to our own personality, we can transform relationships.[11]

SNAPSHOTS OF WOMEN IN THE BIBLE

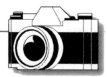

Abigail

Abigail's heart raced when she saw a servant running toward her. Chest heaving breathlessly, he collapsed at her feet. His garment was drenched with sweat. Fearing bad news, she grabbed a pitcher of water to quench his thirst so she could hear his urgent message. She knew her foolish husband Nabal must have done something terrible again.

The servant described how David and his warriors had protected Nabal's flocks both day and night during sheep shearing. When David sent his men to ask for gifts of food, Nabal insulted David and refused him. Upon hearing the insults, David armed four hundred of his men and swore to kill Nabal's household. The warriors were on their way, and the servant rushed to Abigail because Nabal would listen to no man.

Abigail had no time to pity her foolish husband. She had been the recipient of Nabal's mean spirit. The servant was right; she knew what Nabal was capable of and knew he would not listen to reason. But this time he had gone too far. His folly could bring immediate death upon her entire household. She paced anxiously, concocting a plan she hoped would save them.

She instructed her faithful servant to gather gifts of loaves, wine, sheep, corn, raisins, and figs. She ordered him to go ahead of her, meet David and his warriors, and present her gifts. Abigail then quickly dressed in her most beautiful clothes to meet the man who held her life in his hands.

She mounted her donkey and prodded it to the path David and his men were traveling on. Her hands trembled as she saw the dust cloud of four hundred warriors drawing closer. At last they came into view ahead, marching around a bend. Asking God for courage, she ran and fell at David's feet in a gesture of honor and humility. In her wisdom she took full responsibility for not knowing that his men guarded their workers.

If she could deflect David's heart of revenge away from Nabal toward her, perhaps he would see a beautiful woman and stop long enough to listen. She knew of this David who as a boy stood against the giant Philistine, Goliath, with only a sling. She begged him to let God have revenge, assuring him that *"the lives of your enemies [God] will hurl away, as from the pocket of a sling."* She begged him not to let a vengeful act haunt him later, when he would be king.

The beauty, wisdom, and courage of this woman took David by

☞ **Check It Out:**

1 Samuel 25:2–44

☞ **GO TO:**

1 Samuel 17:1–51 (Goliath)

ACT OF GOD

Nabal's death

surprise. He blessed her, blessed God, and changed his attack plans. Their lives were spared.

Abigail returned home to a drunken husband and decided to wait until morning to tell him of her actions. Upon hearing of his narrow escape Nabal immediately suffered a heart failure and ten days later died at the hand of God.

Upon hearing the news of this newly widowed woman, David sent a messenger to ask Abigail to marry him. Abigail accepted. David gained political status in the area, and a beautiful, intelligent, and wealthy wife who took care of his financial needs. Abigail married the man who would be the second king of Israel (see GWWB, pages 193–194).

Think About It

In this snapshot of Abigail we see that she lived in a less than ideal circumstance with her mean-spirited, foolish husband. But she did not stand idly by and watch when his behavior nearly destroyed the household. She looked to God for wisdom, she accepted the reality and truth of the situation, and she took immediate action, mustering up the courage and the plan that saved her family.

> **Proverbs 23:24–25** The father of a righteous man has great joy; he who has a wise son delights in him. May your father and mother be glad; may she who gave you birth rejoice.

In-Laws or Outlaws?

Proverbs calls our attention to the wisdom of our parents. We are to honor, respect, and appreciate them for giving us life, and treasure their teachings. If we grow to live righteous lives, we bring great joy to our parents.

Everyday Life

Sometimes when you reflect on your marriage vows, "for better, for worse," you feel the "worse" part is dealing with in-laws. Getting along with difficult personalities can be stressful, but it is not impossible. You can have meaningful relationships with the ones who raised your husband. If we heed their advice, there are some instances where we gain wisdom from our out-laws. I mean, in-laws. Let's see what the Bible says about in-laws.

EXAMPLES FROM THE BIBLE

- Isaac and Rebekah grieved over their new daughters-in-law Judith and Bashemath. Their son Esau had married these foreign women who worshiped foreign idols. (Genesis 26:34)

- King Saul, David's father-in-law, became jealous and feared his countrymen would want David as king. Saul attempted to kill David and became his persistent enemy. (1 Samuel 18:6–29)

- Peter was so concerned about his sick mother-in-law he immediately spoke to Jesus about her illness. Jesus came and healed her. After she was healed she got up and fixed them a meal. (Mark 1:30–31)

- Laban was Jacob's father-in-law. He tricked Jacob into marrying his daughter Leah, when he originally agreed to let Jacob marry Rachel. Jacob worked seven more years to marry Rachel because of his love for her. (Genesis 28:10–30)

- Ruth, a widow, was so devoted to her grieving mother-in-law Naomi that she left her country to follow Naomi and adopt Naomi's God. (Ruth 1:16)

> **Exodus 18:7–9** So Moses went out to meet his father-in-law and bowed down and kissed him. They greeted each other and then went into the tent. Moses told his father-in-law about everything the Lord had done to Pharaoh and the Egyptians for Israel's sake and about the hardships they had met along the way and how the Lord had saved them. Jethro was delighted to hear all the good things the Lord had done for Israel in rescuing them from the hand of the Egyptians.

Honor His Father and Mother

As a young man, when Moses fled Egypt to Midian, he married Zipporah (see GWWB, pages 222–223). There he tended sheep for his father-in-law Jethro for forty years. It was while Moses was out in the fields with the sheep, doing an ordinary day's work, that he encountered God in the burning <u>bush</u> and realized the **calling** upon his life.

☞ **GO TO:**

Exodus 3:2 (bush)

calling: God's direction or purpose for your life

☞ **GO TO:**

Exodus 12:31–13:22
(Egypt)

burnt offering sacrifice:
*ritual of burning a
sacrifice to honor and
thank God*

KEY POINT

Moses benefited from
heeding his father-in-
law's advice.

Think About It

Moses knew that God's call required him to return to Egypt. He wanted to bring his wife and sons with him. Out of respect for his father-in-law, and probably wanting his approval, Moses requested Jethro's permission to leave. Jethro gave Moses his blessing and Moses embarked upon one of the greatest journeys recorded in history as he led the Jews out of Egypt.

Somewhere along the way, Zipporah and Moses' sons were sent back to Jethro. Exodus 18 describes when the family reunited. Jethro was overjoyed with the deliverance, brought Moses' family to him, and declared a new belief that the Lord was greater than any other gods. Jethro then offered a **burnt offering sacrifice** to God.

The next day, Moses sat as judge, trying to resolve everyone's problems. It took all day and dragged on into the night. Jethro saw that Moses had a micro-managing problem. Others were capable of dealing with most of these problems, so Jethro suggested that Moses handle only the hardest cases and reminded his son-in-law that Moses needed to be pursuing his real calling: *"teach them statues and the law, and show them the way in which they must walk and the work they must do"* (Exodus 18:20). Moses immediately turned Jethro's idea into policy, more evidence of Moses' special respect for his father-in-law.

Moses' workday became easier, allowing him to focus less on the urgent and more on the important, because he listened to his father-in-law. Jethro found an enthusiastic faith in the true God, because he listened to his son-in-law. This is how family is meant to work.

The infamous Hatfields and McCoys are known throughout the nation for the longest and bloodiest family feud in American history. How did this feud ever begin? No one knows for sure! But one theory attributes it to a forbidden marriage between sweethearts in the families. It became in-laws against in-laws, and eventually when the in-laws broke the local law, they became outlaws against outlaws. My husband Phil can trace his ancestors back to the feud's stomping grounds in Logan County, West Virginia. His family was not related to these two fighting families, but his great-grandfather, Moses Alley, was the next-door neighbor of the Hatfields. In fact, Moses Alley's farm adjoined the Hatfield farm.

Moses Alley was born the year after the first shot of the feud rang out. Yet over the next thirty years of this blood war, he never sided with either family. He was a peaceful farmer, a carpenter and, like his father before him, a circuit riding preacher. His children remembered him building coffins for victims of the feud, but never taking part. Unlike his rowdy neighbors, Moses Alley enjoyed a peaceful relationship with his in-laws on the very same West Virginian mountaintop known for a family feud. Family peace can be your legacy, too.

We are instructed in the **Ten Commandments** (see GWBI, pages 28–30) to **honor** our fathers and mothers. In marriage, husband and wife become one. If you are one with your husband, then his parents are your parents. That means you are to honor them. Our relationships don't have to be family feuds.

Think About It

What Others are Saying:

Susan Alexander Yates: God has called us to serve our mates and to honor our parents. These two foundational principles are vital in building friendships within the family. It will not always be easy. It may be inconvenient and costly to honor your parents. And you will not be able to please everyone. Your ultimate job is not to keep everyone happy, but to be faithful to God's calling, which is to love your spouse, to nurture your children, and to care for your parents.[12]

☞ **GO TO:**

Exodus 20:1–17 (Ten Commandments)

Ten Commandments: *God's laws given to Moses for the Israelites*

honor: *to show great respect or high regard for*

GEORGIA'S TIPS . . .

How do we honor our in-laws? Five little tips:

1. When we talk about them, accentuate the positive, not the negative.
2. Listen with an open mind and heart. Be open to their wisdom and advice.
3. Keep close contact with them, unless the relationship is causing problems. If so, defuse the possible explosion by detaching physically until you and your husband can confront and handle the problem together.
4. Care for them when they are sick.
5. Encourage your children to call or write. (If we want our children to honor us, they must see how we respect and honor our own parents.)

KEY Outline:

Two Principles
serve your mate
honor your parents and your mate's parents

> **Proverbs 17:6** Children's children are a crown to the aged, and parents are the pride of their children.

I Wish My Mama Lived in My Village

KEY Outline:

God's Calling
love your spouse
nurture your children
care for your parents

In Bible times, headdresses and garlands were worn to show honor and respect. They were given by those who loved and admired the one who was crowned. Likewise grandchildren are the crown of grandparents' lives, their pride and joy. Grandparents love to admire the new generation of life from their own children.

Unlike today, in Bible times the whole extended family lived together, worked side by side, and shared daily in each other's lives. Sometimes one "household" could constitute an entire village of family and relatives, a true clan.

Flashback

As I raise my own children, living three thousand miles from my mom and dad is a heartbreak for me. I reflect on growing up with my grandmother and the wonderful impact she had on my life. Granny Curtis was a quiet wallflower, yet spirited and fun. She could have been Sophia's twin on the TV series *The Golden Girls*. She was small in stature, but a giant in faith; uneducated, yet filled with godly wisdom. Her life was long and every life she touched was blessed. She will live in our hearts forever. Yet my children won't know their grandparents, as I knew mine.

Make every effort to include the rest of your clan in your life. Your children will experience confidence and stability if they have a deep sense of who and where they spring from.

Homespun Wisdom: We as adults need the support, wisdom, and love of our parents and grandparents. But it is also a privilege to be a grandparent—and a great responsibility.

<u>Lois</u>, a grandmother, is mentioned in the Bible as playing a vital role in planting seeds of faithfulness in her grandson, Timothy. Those tiny seeds of faithfulness grew into full bloom, because Timothy played a vital role in establishing the first church.

☞ **GO TO:**

2 Timothy 1:5 (Lois)

GEORGIA'S TIPS . . .

Five little things that grandparents can do to help plant the seeds of faith in their grandchildren:

1. Pray for them daily.

2. If you don't live close, send cards, call, write, or e-mail. Let them know that you love them.

3. Tell them stories. Make it an adventure. They'll be amazed how well you got along without color TV and computers. Let them get to know how God walked with you during your struggles, joys, and successes.

4. Take an interest in your grandchildren's special gifts and hobbies. Work alongside them and encourage their giftedness.

5. When the opportunity arises, share your faith. Grandparents have a way of accepting and loving grandchildren that sometimes gets them to listen when they turn a deaf ear to their parents.

If your grandmother doesn't live in your village you can still be close even though many rivers and woods separate you. Take time to go through photo albums and tell your children about the images captured on film. My father-in-law Papa Ling died before our son Philip was born; yet Philip is well acquainted with Papa Ling. He even knows the traits and habits he inherited from Papa Ling because we keep grandfather's memory alive in our hearts.

Charles R. Swindoll: God's **patriarchs** have always been among his choicest possessions. Abraham was far more effective once he grew old and mellow. Moses wasn't used with any measure of success until he turned eighty. Samuel was old when the God of Israel led him to establish the "school of the prophets," an institution that had a lasting influence for spirituality and godliness in the centuries to come.[13]

KEY POINT

Grandparents are a blessing . . . tap into their resource.

REMEMBER THIS

What Others are Saying:

patriarchs: the founders of the Hebrew families in the Bible

COFFEE BREAK
WITH GEORGIA

Laugh
Out
Loud

☞ GO TO:

Matthew 1:5
(ancestors)

Heritage Drives

An old song goes, "Gonna take a sentimental journey . . ." I remember laughing when I heard a radio disc jockey who had just played the song announce, "And that was, 'Gonna Take a Semi-Mental Journey'!"

Well, all this talk of heritage brings back some memories for me. If you'll indulge me, I'll take you on my semi-mental journey, back to the Sunday afternoon drives my Dad always imposed upon us as kids.

There were four of us siblings: Sherry, Connie, David, and me. Add one station wagon (naturally . . . this was way before mini-vans), Mom, Dad, and even the family dog, and you've got the cast of characters. On Sunday afternoons Dad would pile four grumbling, reluctant kids in the wagon and go for a "drive." None of us kids were thrilled about the journey, but we knew that at the end we would pull into the ice cream shop. So the hour or so spent driving had a pretty good payoff. Besides, that way we had plenty of time to reflect and decide which of the many ice cream flavors we wanted: vanilla or chocolate. (This was also before anybody'd ever conceived of 31 flavors.)

My Dad cruised the countryside, pointing out to us the one-room schoolhouse he attended, or the swimming hole where he spent countless hours playing with his buddies, or the cemeteries that held our <u>ancestors</u>. All these years later, I now realize I've had a longer-lasting payoff than merely ice cream. Because all those places are etched in my mind, I have heritage. Little did I know as we peered out the windows of that station wagon we were actually looking into the windows of our past.

Dad's Sunday afternoon "heritage drives" helped me understand my dad, his way of thinking, his vision and dreams for his children. Through those places I saw his undying love for God and his family of the past, present, and future. To my surprise, the blessings were well worth the trip.

> **Colossians 3:12–14** Therefore, as God's chosen people, holy and dearly loved, clothe yourselves with compassion, kindness, humility, gentleness and patience. Bear with each other and forgive whatever grievances you may have against one another. Forgive as the Lord forgave you. And over all these virtues put on love, which binds them all together in perfect unity.

Your Turn to Care for Your Caregiver

Paul addresses the believers in Colossae (see illustration, page 143) in their new life as God's children. In these few verses he gives us a wonderful depiction of love and a recipe for a caregiver. He gives ingredients for not only a successful walk in life, but also ingredients needed in our hearts and actions to care for our parents in their time of need.

Now that I'm forty-something and my parents are in their late sixties I've given more thought about caring for them later if they grow disabled. My dad is a big planner, so he already has special insurance in case the need arises for long-term care. But what if his plans don't come off as intended, or what if I don't think the care facility is adequate? What if he and Mom are treated like just another number, unloved, or wanted just for the income they bring?

I was privileged to see love in action when both of my grandmothers needed special long-term care. My parents sacrificed time, energy, and finances to be with their mothers when needed most. My parents were there to help bathe them, feed them nibbles of food, read favorite passages of Scripture, and pray with them. My grandmothers knew they were loved.

A person's greatest need is to know that he or she is loved. Our expression of love and gratitude to our parents needs to surface when the caregiver role changes. The ones who gave us life and provided for our every need, now need to be cared for. As their children, and as people of faith, we must do right by them.

KEY Outline:

Loving Caregivers Show

compassion
kindness
humility
gentleness
patience

Everyday Life

Think About It

Joni Eareckson Tada: The attitude of reverence and acknowledgment of God's authority and power must be present with you in every circumstance: at the deathbed, in the waiting room, and in the nursing home. At every point of decision and every expression of hope, we must acknowledge his sovereign will. God is the giver and sustainer of life, and he is holy. Our dependence upon him for wisdom must be accompanied by the knowledge that we are accountable to him for how we apply that wisdom. When he shows us something through wisdom and his word, we have to agree not to second-guess, manipulate, or misconstrue.[14]

EXAMPLES FROM THE BIBLE

KEY POINT

A person's greatest
need is to know that
he or she is loved.

- Joseph, the ruler of Egypt under Pharaoh, showed compassion when he sent for his family to save them from the famine. His aged father came to Egypt with all of his sons, their wives, and children, their livestock, and property (Genesis 46:1–48:10). Joseph provided for his father until his death. Scripture records his loving relationship and acts of kindness. *"Now Jacob's eyes were failing because of old age, and he could hardly see. So Joseph brought his sons close to him, and his father kissed them and embraced them"* (Genesis 48:10–11).

- Ruth, a young widow, left her homeland to accompany her widowed mother-in-law Naomi. She provided for both of them by gleaning from the barley fields (see illustration, page 120). Ruth's commitment to Naomi is a famous quote from the Bible: *"Where you go I will go, and where you stay I will stay. Your people will be my people and your God my God"* (Ruth 1:16).

- Peter's mother-in-law lay in the bed with a fever. Out of love for her, Peter asked Jesus to help her. Jesus healed her and she got up and waited on them. (Luke 4:38–39)

SNAPSHOTS OF WOMEN IN THE BIBLE

Ruth and Naomi

When famine hit the area surrounding Bethlehem, Naomi and Elimelech tried to escape its results by moving from Judah to Moab. The **Moabites** were enemies of the Jews, and God had warned the Jews not to have anything to do with them. While in Moab, Elimelech died, leaving Naomi a widow. Then, contrary to God's command, her two sons married Moabite women. The sons died, too, leaving Naomi in a foreign land with no relations except two "forbidden" daughters-in-law.

Eventually the famine in Judah ended. Since Naomi had few ties in Moab, she decided to move back to her homeland and her own extended family. In a selfless gesture, she released her daughters-in-law from any commitment to her. She encouraged them to remain with their own people and find new husbands. One daughter-in-law, Orpah, took Naomi's advice. But the other, Ruth, could not be dissuaded. In one of the most stirring speeches of commitment in the Bible, she told her mother-in-law, *"Don't urge me to leave you or to turn back from you. Where you go I will go, and where you stay I will stay. Your people will be my people and your God my God. Where you die I will die, and there I will be buried. May the Lord deal with me, be it ever so severely, if anything but death separates you and me"* (Ruth 1:16).

Naomi and Ruth made it back to Bethlehem. Naomi had left there relatively wealthy, only to return empty, poor, and bitter. But she didn't stay that way for long, because God had an extraordinary plan of deliverance for Naomi and her "forbidden" daughter-in-law.

Ruth did the only thing she could and began **gleaning** in the grain fields so the two women would have food (see illustration, page 120). It was hard physical labor in the hot sun, but each morning she went back to the fields.

One day, she unwittingly began gleaning in fields belonging to Boaz, a relative of Elimelech, Naomi's dead husband. Through the family grapevine, Boaz had heard about Ruth's kindness and loyalty to Elimelech's widow. Apparently Ruth was beautiful enough for Boaz to notice her in the field. After making inquiries and finding out who she was, Boaz offered her his protection and told her not to go into any other fields. He even made sure she had extra grain. When Ruth came home and told Naomi about Boaz, Naomi praised God. Because Boaz was a relative, in Jewish law he

☞ **Check It Out:**

Ruth 1–4

Moabites: descendants of Moab, the son of Lot by incestuous union with his daughter

☞ **GO TO:**

Leviticus 19:9–10 (gleaning)

gleaning: gathering leftover grains after harvest

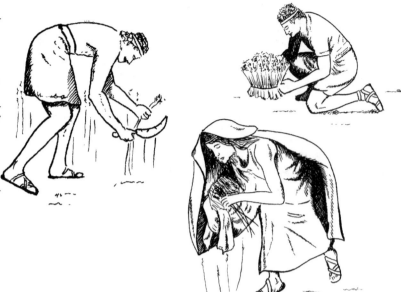

Man Using Sickle

Harvesters would use sickles to cut the wheat stalks.

Man Gathering Wheat into Sheaves

After the stalks were cut, they were gathered into "sheaves."

Gleaning

Old Testament Law allowed the poor to follow the harvesters and gather the grain that fell to the ground during harvesting. This is what Ruth did.

☞ **GO TO:**

Deuteronomy 25:5–10;
Ruth 4:14 (Kinsman Redeemer)

Kinsman Redeemer: a person who takes responsibility for a deceased relative's property and family

Think About It

could potentially be a **Kinsman Redeemer** (see GWRV, pages 75–76), take Ruth as his wife, and redeem Naomi's property.

In the end, Boaz married Ruth. (I'm leaving out a few plot twists, so you might want to read the story yourself.) God had provided for both the old widow and the young widow. But the story was larger than their lives. Boaz and Ruth produced a son, Obed, who was the grandfather of King David; and ultimately, David's lineage produced the Messiah.

In this snapshot of in-laws we see love in action. Naomi and Ruth clung to each other and first did everything they could to survive, then surrendered and let God do the rest while they patiently waited on him. God turned a funeral filled with grief and sorrow into a wedding celebration complete with joy and new life.

God's plans are often far better and grander in scope than we can imagine. Who would have guessed that God wanted the Messiah to have a Moabite woman as his ancestor? But there she is (Matthew 1:5–6). After Naomi lost all the men in her life, and before God's redemption came, she must have had days of despair. Just as God surprised her with blessing upon blessing, he may have similar surprises in store for you. God truly redeems those he loves and he still works through those who love him and *"walk by faith, not by sight"* (2 Corinthians 5:7).

In Naomi's time, a childless widow became the responsibility of her dead husbands' brother, who would marry her, buy back the property of the deceased, and provide for the widow. Naomi gained redemption of her property through the marriage of Ruth and Boaz. Then Boaz gave her lineage through Obed. God offers us redemption through our "kinsman-redeemer," Jesus Christ. Through his death on the cross Christ paid the price for man's redemption and salvation (see GWBI, pages 55–56). In effect, he bought us back. And he has made us part of an eternal lineage. *"In him we have redemption through his blood, the forgiveness of sins, in accordance with the riches of God's grace that he lavished on us with all wisdom and understanding"* (Ephesians 1:7).

REMEMBER THIS

STUDY QUESTIONS

1. What foundation must our families and marriages be built upon?
2. What important elements needed in marriage did Rebekah exhibit? How did God reward Rebekah when she followed his lead?
3. Has anything broken your love triangle between God, your husband, and you? What can you do to reconnect the triangle?
4. When is divorce permissible according to the Bible? What is the intended goal of separation?
5. What personality type would the Apostle Peter fit?
6. How did Jethro encourage his son-in-law Moses?
7. The snapshot of Ruth and Naomi was a story of love that can brighten the soul of even a bitter mother-in-law. Naomi and Ruth's love overcame suffering and grief and endured. How did Ruth show her love and commitment to Naomi?

CHAPTER WRAP-UP

- The love that works in a marriage is a Christ-centered love that overcomes anger, bitterness, and resentment. A love that changes hearts and renews relationships is built like a triangle with God as the head of the family joining husband and wife as one.

- Contrary to the naysayers, you can get along with almost anybody—it just takes tons of effort, research, wisdom, and understanding on your part. Family will always be a part of our lives. They may bless us or haunt us, but it is up to you to decide how you will respond. Be willing to forgive.

- Maintain healthy communication with the ones you call family. Discovering your own personality and temperament will help you understand yourself and others as you strive to live in harmony.

- You can cultivate rewarding relationships with your in-laws. You have the power and wisdom from the Bible to transform the feud into friendship, and gain perspective and wisdom from your in-laws.

- Grandparents can play a vital role in nurturing, supporting, and building faith in our families. Grandchildren are their pride and joy. Take the effort to build upon their foundations and include them in your lives.

- Open your heart and eyes to the physical needs of your parents. As you become the caregiver of your aged parents, love them with your whole heart during this last passage of their lives.

GEORGIA'S  BOOKSHELF

Some of Georgia's favorite books on the subject of developing loving relationships:

- *Loving Solutions*, Gary Chapman, Northfield Publisher
- *Holding On to Heaven while Your Husband Goes through Hell*, Connie Neal, Word
- *When Love Dies: How to Save a Hopeless Marriage*, Judy Bodmer, Word
- *Foolproofing Your Life*, Jan Silvious, WaterBrook Press
- *Healing the Scars of Emotional Abuse*, Greg Jantz, Revell
- *Getting Along with Almost Anybody*, Florence Littauer, Revell

Part Three

BREAD, BREADWINNERS, AND BREAD BAKERS

REVEREND FUN

At the first supper.

5 MONEY, MONEY, MONEY

Discovering Smart Ways to Handle Money and Overcome Financial Failures

Here We Go

"It's my money and I'll do with it what I want!" Whoa! How many times have you either heard that statement or proclaimed it yourself? Well, contrary to popular belief, it's not your money. It's mine. (Just kidding. I wanted to see if you were paying attention.) Actually, it's God's money. He has graciously loaned it to us. How we view and use his money will not only affect the quality of our life in the physical realm, but also in the spiritual.

God created the universe and owns everything in it. He doesn't need our money. If he wants money, he can whip up a solid gold planet. But he uses money as a meter. God can monitor our heart's condition when he watches how we manage, spend, save, and let go of our money. He can look deep into our hearts and see the motivation that lies behind our actions, *"for where your treasure is, there your heart will be also"* (Matthew 6:21).

"How-to" money books have always been on the top of the *New York Times* Best-sellers List. The topics range from quick and dirty ways to make money, to how to safeguard your finances, how to invest, how to buy insurance, and how to plan for college, retirement, and death.

Think About It

KEY POINT

Money: It's not yours. It's God's!

What Others are Saying:

☞ **GO TO:**

Psalm 24:1 (owns)

The Bible itself is a fantastic "How to" book and has a great deal to say about money. Rest assured you're not the only financially challenged woman on the planet. With a little encouragement and guidance from the Word, you can discover smart ways to handle money and overcome financial failures.

Jerry and Ramona Tuma: The first step in making godly financial decisions is to realize that God doesn't own just 10 percent but everything—100 percent of our paychecks, our homes, our household goods, our cars, our jobs, our retirement plans, our mates, and even our kids. And since he <u>owns</u> everything and we are his property, our job is to be caretakers or stewards over his property.[1]

> **Proverbs 22:7** The borrower is servant to the lender.

The Platinum Path to the Poor House

The book of Proverbs has a lot to say about wealth. Scholars believe the sayings in Proverbs were compiled as a collection of instructions for the young men and future leaders of Israel, so we presume most of these guys came from wealthy families. And as we all know, just because Papa knew how to handle and accumulate wealth doesn't mean that little Hilkiah got the wealth gene. So in order to lead, Israel's finest young men were taught how to handle money.

In Bible times if you were unable to pay back a loan, you could be forced to be the lender's slave until the loan was paid in full. Likewise, today, through our bad spending habits and the mentality of "buy now, pay later," we can easily become slaves to the lender as we work ourselves to death trying to pay off our debts.

 Everyday Life

I just received another one in the mail. The letter read, "Congratulations, Georgia Curtis Ling, you've been preapproved for a Platinum Card with a credit line up to $100,000. Platinum is more than a status symbol. . . ."

You know the rest of the story. You feel flattered until you find out credit card companies issue cards to just about anybody, including the dead and occasionally man's best friend. Due to living on credit our nation now has more individuals filing for bankruptcy than ever. We live from paycheck to paycheck as our financial lives spin out of control. You start out with the regular old credit card, move on up to flashing that Gold Card, and after the Gold has lost its luster, you covet the shine and prestige of the Platinum. Before you know it you've gone from Platinum to the poor house in no time. If the next letter from the credit company were honest, it would read, "Congratulations! You are a slave to your lender!"

Homespun Wisdom: One of the best Bible-based books I've read on wising up financially is the best-seller *Financial Peace* by Dave Ramsey, a financial consultant and popular radio talk show host. He experienced devastating financial ruin after getting too far into debt and nearly losing everything he owned.

Tips from Dave Ramsey on credit card debt and payoff:

1. Throw a "plastic surgery party" with your family. That's right, cut the credit cards up.

2. Quit borrowing more money.

3. Start your debt reduction immediately.

4. Prioritize your debts in ascending order with the smallest remaining balance first and the largest last. Do this regardless of interest rate or payment.

5. Pay the debts off in this new order.

6. As you pay off the first debt, take the amount you used on that payment and add it to the next payment on the list.[2]

KEY Outline:

Smart Money Management
no more plastic
stop borrowing
reduce your debt now

KEY POINT

Wise up. Get out of debt and stay out.

What Others are Saying:

Dave Ramsey: I know that suggesting you stay out of debt is radical and may seem utterly ridiculous, but I am tired of seeing grown adults on the brink of suicide, widows left with a legacy of debt, and children who are taught by example that if I want it I get it now. Dump debt. If you don't, remember you are instantly the servant to the lender.[3]

Richard Carlson, Ph.D.: In over a dozen years as a stress consultant, one of the most pervasive and destructive mental tendencies I've seen is that of focusing on what we *want* instead of what we *have*. It doesn't seem to make any difference how much we have; we just keep expanding our list of desires, which guarantees we will remain dissatisfied. The mind-set that says "I'll be happy when this desire is fulfilled" is the same mind-set that will repeat itself once that desire is met.[4]

Check It Out:

2 Kings 4:1–7

GO TO:

1 Kings 17:1 (Elijah)

1 Kings 19:19–21
(Elisha)

Leviticus 25:39–42
(Law)

Nehemiah 5:1–4
(slaves)

Genesis 37:37
(sackcloth)

Luke 7:44–50
(anointing)

prophet: a holy man with
a specific, personal
mission from God

sackcloth: a coarse black
cloth, usually made of
goat's hair, worn as a sign
of mourning

anointing: persons and
things were anointed
with oil to signify
separation unto God

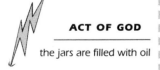

ACT OF GOD

the jars are filled with oil

SNAPSHOTS OF WOMEN IN THE BIBLE

The Prophet's Widow

The widow sat alone on the dusty floor in her little empty house and wept bitterly. She rocked back and forth, clutching her own arms for comfort. The one who once held her in his arms was dead. She grieved for the loss of the man she loved, but now she faced a greater threat: the loss of her sons.

Her husband died and left them with nothing. She could have coped with that loss for her husband was a man of God, a junior **prophet** in training under Elijah and Elisha (see GWBI, pages 86–88). They lived in a small community of loving, caring, and godly people. She knew she could rely on them in her time of need. But her husband had left them in debt and under the Law, her creditors had the right to take her children as slaves to repay the debt. She couldn't bear to lose her sons. Even with her mind paralyzed with fear, she knew she must go to the only man she could turn to.

She drew her scarf of mourning over her face, and in her black **sackcloth** she ran to Elisha, the prophet. She hoped this man of miracles had one for her. The widow fell at his feet and told her story. Elisha, too, mourned for the loss of one of his students and listened to her with compassion and wisdom.

Elisha asked what she had in her home. Did she have nothing of value? The widow said she only had a jar of oil (see illustration, page 129) her husband had used for **anointing**.

Elisha nodded his head in contemplation. Finally, he instructed her to go to her neighbors and to borrow as many empty vessels as she could find. Then she was to take her sons into the house, shut the door, and pour the jar of oil into the vessels.

It made no sense. The contents of one little jar would only moisten the bottom of one empty vessel; why assemble a house full of them? But instead of questioning the illogical instructions, she quickly obeyed. A glimmer of hope lit in her heart as she ran home, called her sons, and went from house to house gathering vessels.

When they had done as Elisha instructed, they closed the door and huddled around the first vessel. She held the tiny bottle of oil and looked into the questioning eyes of her sons. Then she began carefully pouring the oil.

Her heart beat faster as she saw the oil well up in the first jar. The boys smiled in puzzlement. A new light danced in their hollow eyes as they grabbed another container and watched it fill.

Then another, and another, and another until all were filled! Their miracle had come! Sunbeams shone through the cracks in the roof onto the full containers, and the oil glistened like gold as the widow wrapped her arms around her sons and wept tears of joy.

The widow told the boys to stay inside the house with the door shut, as she had to go learn what to do next.

She ran through the community to Elisha and excitedly told him what happened. She requested his further <u>guidance</u>.

Elisha told her to go, sell the oil, pay her debts, and live on the rest.

The prophet's widow trusted this man of God, received a miracle, and her mourning was turned to joy. Now her sons would not be taken as slaves to repay her husband's debt.

This widow's snapshot reveals a woman who knew she must take action even though life had taken a horrific turn for the worse. She turned to a wise, trustworthy man. She followed his advice by using what little she had to get out of debt. In his wisdom, Elisha knew she and her family needed to experience this miracle together. Facing adversity, then experiencing God's grace and deliverance together as a family, would bond them as one.

Olive Oil Press

Oil was used to prepare food, fuel lamps, and as an ingredient in medicine and in cosmetic ointments. Olive oil was also used in religious observances, such as offerings, and in the consecration of priests. With so many purposes, the widow's oil would have sold immediately, providing plenty of money to pay her debts and live comfortably.

☞ **GO TO:**

Proverbs 12:15
(guidance)

Think About It

If you've become a slave to your debtor, first pray for wisdom, then seek advice from a godly person you can trust. Take action and use what you have before going to others for help. Involve your family in this challenge. Empty your heart of pride, anger, and resentment and let God pour himself into you, for *"he is able to do immeasurably more than all we ask or imagine, according to his power that is at work within us"* (Ephesians 3:20).

KEY POINT

Godliness with contentment is the key that unlocks the plastic prison.

> **1 Timothy 6:6–10** But godliness with contentment is great gain. For we brought nothing into the world, and we can take nothing out of it. But if we have food and clothing, we will be content with that. People who want to get rich fall into temptation and a trap, and into many foolish and harmful desires that plunge men into ruin and destruction. For the love of money is a root of all kinds of evil. Some people, eager for money, have wandered from the faith and pierced themselves with many griefs.

I Want It and I Want It Now!

The Apostle Paul hit the nail on the head. Godliness with contentment is the key to life. It is the key that unlocks the door of the plastic prison of credit card debt, and the key that opens the heart to a new way of life.

When we focus on wanting more things, we are saying that God has not given us enough. His gifts to us are endless—the ability to see new buds on the trees, smell garden roses, feel crisp fall air against our skin, taste fresh apple cider, hear snow crunch beneath our boots. The love of money gets our eyes off God's greatness and makes us dissatisfied with what we have.

There is nothing inherently wrong with wealth. Wealth and poverty are both litmus tests of our character. Contrary to misquoted Scripture, money is not the root of all evil. The *love* of money, also known as greed, is the root of all evil. Greed can become an all-consuming drive that can throw you off balance and even lead you into physical and spiritual bankruptcy.

EXAMPLES FROM THE BIBLE

If greed had a face, it would look like one of these:

- **Delilah** is known throughout history as the one who betrayed her lover **Samson**. The Philistines were enemies of Samson and they wanted him dead. They approached Delilah and offered her a huge sum of money to find the secret of Samson's strength. Her greed motivated her acts of betrayal. (Judges 16:5)

- **Judas Iscariot**, one of the twelve disciples of Jesus, was not content with the direction of Jesus' ministry. Judas betrayed Jesus for thirty pieces of silver and turned him over to Jesus' enemies to be crucified. (Mark 14:10, 43)

- Simon the Sorcerer amazed the people of Samaria with his sorcerous power. Philip, an evangelist, came to town and preached about Jesus. Simon became one of his converts. When Simon saw the miracles the apostles were able to do, he offered them money to purchase the secrets of their special gifts. Peter rebuked him, saying his heart was not right—Simon only wanted special powers to continue manipulating people. (Acts 7:9–24)

In 1985, 30 percent of Americans failed to pay off their credit card debts each month. In 1995, the figure had risen to 50 percent. Charge-card fever keeps going up. In 1996, *Money* magazine reported that installment debt in America, including auto loans and credit card balances, increased one-third of one percent during the previous two years.[5]

Does that sound familiar? We're just like the little kid in the toy store pitching a fit because we want it and we want it now and we'll maneuver our finances around until we get what we want . . . now!

As much as I would like to blame plastic for our financial crisis, I can't. We need to take a look inside, put away childish behavior, and start anew, following the Apostle Paul's example: *"When I was a child, I talked like a child, I thought like a child, I reasoned like a child. When I became a man, I put childish ways behind me"* (1 Corinthians 13:11). We can find true contentment in Christ if we honor God with our finances and material possessions.

Delilah: *means "dainty one"*

Samson: *twelfth judge of Israel; known for his strength*

Judas Iscariot: *disciple who betrayed Jesus*

Think About It

REMEMBER THIS

Words of a wise woman shopper:

- "Honey, what about this?" (Make joint decisions on purchases over $100.)

- "Where's your sales rack?" (Never pay full price.)

- "Gucci? Gucci who?" (Buy quality, but without the designer label attached.)

- "Put it down, walk away, and nobody gets hurt." (Never buy on impulse.)

- "May I read the fine print, please?" (Investigate. Never believe what advertisers say. "No money down" translated is "Pay big interest later!")

- "It'll be cash." (Cash only! You'll spend 38 percent more if you charge it.)

- "I would like a refund, please." (Take it back if the product is faulty.)

- "Where's the scissors?" (Use coupons. Shop around and find a grocer that discounts, then buy in bulk.)

- "On the thirteenth day of Christmas my true love said to me, 'Let's go shopping!'" (Buy during after-Christmas sales for your kids' next winter coat and other big cost items.)

KEY Outline:

Smart Money Management

examine the desires of your heart

be content with what you have

What Others are Saying:

insatiable: never satisfied; constantly wanting more

Mary Hunt: I believe that this longing for contentment within every person was placed there by God himself. Further, I also believe he made that desire so unique that only a personal relationship with him through his son Jesus can bring lasting satisfaction and the contentment our souls long for. Contentment has a way of quieting **insatiable** desires.[6]

When we search for contentment in the wrong place we remain unfulfilled even when we reach our goals. A wealthy businessman visited a psychiatrist because of deep depression. "I have everything I ever wanted," the businessman said. "If I manage to find something to buy that I don't have, I don't even have to go get it myself. I have so much money I can pay someone to buy it for me. I have no reason for living."

The Big Question

COFFEE BREAK
WITH GEORGIA

My dining room table looked as if a tornado had swept up a mail truck and dumped all it's contents on my table. Copies of the newspaper I write for were stacked up high in one corner, a tall pile of paid bills teetered in the middle, and a shorter stack of unpaid bills hunkered patiently beside them. There were outdated magazines, statements, documents, business materials waiting to be filed, and a lone calculator. The table was proof I was a member of the Messie's Club of America.

Summer had been a whirlwind of out-of-town trips. While away, I had neighbors feed Alice the cat, pick up our mail, and drop it off on the dining room table. I intended to go through the mail and relocate it to my office, but I didn't follow through, so the mail piled up.

As I looked at the award-winning Messies Unite table, several words popped into my head: Priorities. Reorganization. Time management. Those bills were a telltale sign of where my financial priorities lie. The unfiled bank statements and documents screamed "Organize us!" and the unread magazines and business materials sent a message that flashed like a yellow neon sign: Time Management! Time Management!

That still small voice whispered these questions to my heart: *What are your priorities? Where are you wasting time? What can you delegate? What can you say "no" to? Is this a good role model for your child? What changes can you make in reorganizing your time and life? Are you glorifying God in whatever you do?*

As those questions whirled around in my head I knew I had some major planning to do. I still don't have all the answers, but I have one big question that is a great starting point: What is my purpose for living?

Actually, I already know that answer. It just has to be reaffirmed daily with these words: *"whether, then, you eat or drink or whatever you do, do all to the glory of God"* (1 Corinthians 10:31).

Sorry, I've got to cut this a little short. I have to go reorganize and manage my time.

KEY POINT

Find a way to unite in your finances.

Money and Marriage

identify problems

understand your spouse

change negative behavior

Think About It

☞ **GO TO:**

Philippians 2:1–4 (advice)

What Others are Saying:

KEY POINT

Stop arguing and find a solution to your financial problems before it's too late.

> **Philippians 2:14–15** Do everything without complaining or arguing, so that you may become blameless and pure, children of God without fault in a crooked and depraved generation, in which you shine like stars in the universe.

For Richer, for Poorer

In Philippians, the Apostle Paul encourages the believers at Philippi (see illustration, page 143) to mend relationships (see GWBI, pages 263–267). He wants them to work it out not only for their own sakes, but as a testimony to those watching. For realistic solutions to the money time bomb, as women of the Word we need to heed Paul's advice and stop arguing, grumbling, and complaining. We need to get along with our better half when it comes to finances. Our lives are to be a beacon of Christ and his power in our community, not fodder for gossip in divorce court.

Money problems can, at times, cause explosive marriage problems. Whether rich or poor, too many happy couples end up in divorce court because they allowed their financial behaviors to destroy their marriage. Make an effort to resolve the money issue not only for your marriage, but for your witness.

When it comes to marriage and money we can learn from Paul's <u>advice</u> to the Philippians. No matter what your temperament and spending behavior, in marriage you must work together on a budget, come to an agreement, and commit to a financial plan you can both live with. (You may also have to add an extra dose of patience, forgiveness, and apologies along the way.)

O. S. Hawkins: What does money say about our commitment to Christ? I've often said if I were commissioned to write someone's biography and could have only one thing to use as a reference for that biography, I wouldn't want his family tree nor his prayer journal. I would want his checkbook. A checkbook will show us what things in our lives are more important to us. It's a testimonial. After we're gone from this earth, it's a testimonial to everybody of what we thought was really important in life.[7]

The book of Proverbs points out, *"All hard work brings a profit, but mere talk leads to poverty"* (Proverbs 14:23). We need to take action and quit just talking about getting finances in order. Actually sit down together, remember your love for one another, and unite in your purpose, vision, and spirit. Don't let money pull you apart. It's not worth it.

I recently heard a friend of ours preach a series on money. It was based on a 10-10-80 plan (see illustration, this page). He entitled the sermons "Give God Your Best, Put a Few in Your Nest, and Live Wisely on the Rest." His simple plan: tithe 10 percent of your income, save 10 percent, and on the 80 percent left, choose to live wisely.

In marriage it seems most of us get stuck on the "live wisely" part. Since opposites seem to attract, it's inevitable that you'll have differences of opinion on how to live on the 80 percent. As a wise counselor once told me, "If you have a budget when conflicts arise, then you can blame the budget instead of attacking and blaming each other. Then make adjustments, either in your budget or your behavior."

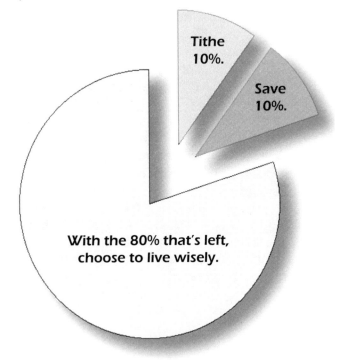

Tithe 10%.

Save 10%.

With the 80% that's left, choose to live wisely.

Everyday Life

Think About It

☞ **Check It Out:**

Genesis 19:1–26

KEY Outline:

Simple Financial Planning
give God your best
put a few eggs in your nest
live wisely on the rest

Pie Chart for Your Money

This chart gives you a picture of the 10-10-80 approach to financial planning. As you can see, after tithing and saving, you will still have plenty left over.

Dave Ramsey: Successfully married couples learn that the "you" in "unity" is a silent syllable. You win at marriage by losing your selfish need to get your way in every battle. I am not saying that you must be a doormat, but I am saying most of the turf that couples battle over isn't nearly as important as the damage the battle brings to a relationship. You get happy marriages by giving up selfish desires in order to win together—winning at creating your visions and goals that flow out of your shared values.[8]

SNAPSHOTS OF WOMEN IN THE BIBLE

Lot's Wife

Lot and his family <u>separated</u> from his Uncle Abraham. The land could not support the wealthy possession of livestock and herdsmen they both owned, so Lot chose the plain of Jordan, a beautiful oasis outside the cities of Sodom and Gomorrah. There Lot's clan pitched their tents and set up camp.

Was it Lot's wife who wasn't content? Maybe the plains were too boring and she longed for the festivities and excitement of the city housekeeping (see illustration, page 137). Or was she tired of living in a tent, and wanted a big stone house of luxury inside the city gates? For whatever reason, eventually Lot and his family moved from living near this wicked sinful city, to living in the middle of it. When next we see Lot, he is sitting daily at the city **gate**, the ancient equivalent of city hall.

The Lord <u>warned</u> Abraham of the forthcoming destruction of Sodom and Gomorrah (see GWWB, page 37). Abraham begged God to spare Lot, so the Lord sent angels to warn Lot and lead him to safety. Upon their arrival at the gate, Lot greeted the angels (unaware of their real identity) and quickly led them to his home, for fear the townsmen would harm them.

Lot's fears became reality as men, young and old, surrounded his house and demanded sex with the strangers. As these sinful townsmen shouted at Lot, he feared they would break in and wipe out not only the strangers, but also his family. In desperation, he stepped outside and offered the mob his daughters for their sexual gratification in place of the angels.

The angels pulled Lot inside the house and blinded the men who were trying to break down the door. Eventually the angels led Lot's family out of the city, warned them of the cataclysmic punishment about to descend from heaven, and told them to flee

☞ GO TO:

Genesis 13:1–18 (separated)

Genesis 18:16–33 (warned)

gate: the inside entrance of the city, where judges sat to witness legal transactions

ACT OF GOD

angels blind men, and God destroys Sodom and Gomorrah

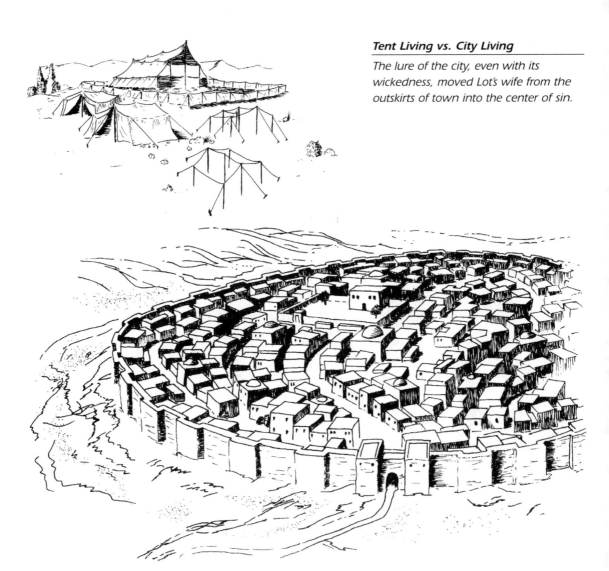

without looking back. But Lot's wife couldn't let go. As she fled, she cast one glance back at the lifestyle she loved, and God turned her into a pillar of salt.

In Lot's wife's reaction we see an example of how she and her husband were not like-minded. Lot followed God's instructions and ran for his life, while Lot's wife loved the things of the world more than God.

Your own personal relationship with God should be your top priority. He will direct you to put your family next in priority. Wealth and riches may or may not come, but we

Think About It

have to cherish and be content with God and let go of what holds us back from surrendering all to him. Are we pitching our tents ever closer to wickedness, putting our families a distant second, all in the name of money and career? My prayer is found in Proverbs 30:7–8: *"Two things I ask of you, O Lord, do not refuse me before I die: Keep falsehoods and lies far from me; give me neither poverty nor riches, but give me only my daily bread. Otherwise, I may have too much and dis-own you and say, 'Who is the Lord?' or I may become poor and steal, and so dishonor the name of my God."*

> **Proverbs 23:12** Apply your heart to instruction and your ears to words of knowledge.

Daddy Warbucks or Mommy Warbucks?

As Scripture encourages, *"apply your heart to instruction and your ear to words of knowledge"* (Proverbs 23:12), we can improve our financial portfolio if we understand and face our traits, and learn how to tame the negative side of our temperaments and build on the strengths.

 Everyday Life

Who's the "Big Spender" in your family? You or your husband? It is unusual to find a couple with the same temperament. If you do, you usually read about them in the paper, like Bonnie and Clyde.

We talked about different temperaments in Chapter 3 when dealing with getting along with family. When it comes to finances and spending behaviors, you've got to know the personality traits, temperaments, strengths, and weaknesses of you and your spouse. This will give you more insight on the "whys" of your spending behavior and will help make a positive change.

Our temperaments affect everything we do. Temperament can determine how big or small our house will be, how much we spend or save and even what type of car we cruise around in or limp along with.

KEY POINT

You and your husband are not financially challenged; you just have different person-ality challenges. You can change your behavior.

📖 EXAMPLES FROM THE BIBLE

Couples' temperaments and differences:

1. Isaac and Rebekah (Genesis 24)
   - Isaac: loner, peace loving, trusting
   - Rebekah: high spirited, helpful, scheming
   - Compatibility: probably good; they shared a heritage of faith and family

2. Jacob and Rachel (Genesis 29)
   - Jacob: resourceful and hardworking with a deeply spiritual and emotionally vulnerable side
   - Rachel: bright, determined, competitive
   - Compatibility: assumed to be good; Jacob adored Rachel

3. Boaz and Ruth (Book of Ruth)
   - Boaz: loyal, hardworking, sincere, brave
   - Ruth: loyal, fair, generous, honorable, optimistic
   - Compatibility: apparently excellent; both partners were honorable, kind, and loyal

4. Samson and Delilah (Judges 15)
   - Samson: charming, brave, rebellious, vengeful, a womanizer
   - Delilah: greedy, self-centered, manipulative
   - Compatibility: low; neither partner seemed to truly value the other

5. Elkanah and Hannah (1 Samuel 1–2)
   - Elkanah: patient, gentle, kind, devout
   - Hannah: passionate, intensely devout, true to her word
   - Compatibility: excellent; mutually devoted to God[9]

Vivian Baniak: While I have been teaching Money Mentors financial planning workshops and the personalities for many years, I continue to be amazed that when people begin to understand how they were uniquely designed to function, with their particular strengths and weaknesses, they are freed to apply that knowledge of themselves to the area of personal finances. A financial plan that is designed for a detail-oriented Perfect Melancholy [see page 107] will never work for a fun-loving, non-structured Popular Sanguine. Therefore, in order to gain financial success in budgeting, your basic personality must be taken into consideration.[10]

What Others are Saying:

> **Proverbs 21:5** The plans of the diligent lead to profit as surely as haste leads to poverty.

Balance More Than Your Budget

We all have weaknesses in our behaviors, but we can't use that for an excuse. God wants us to honor him with everything, including our finances. Are you a fun-loving sanguine who buys on impulse and somehow you've gotten yourself in way over your head with debt? Get control and plan ahead. Are you a controlling choleric who manages money pretty well, but you come across like a drill sergeant demanding to know down to the penny how much was spent? Lighten up, show a little love and tenderness, put family feelings over money. What about those budget-minded melancholies (that's me!) out there who are afraid to let go of the money, and if you do it takes you forever to plan the release? Don't be afraid, take a little risk. And last but not least, what about Mrs. Easy Going Phlegmatic, who never has a say and lets everyone do what they want, just to keep peace? Speak up, be heard, you are a valued member of your family.

EXAMPLES FROM THE BIBLE

How spending time with Jesus transformed:

- Simon Peter: impulsive, passionate, fearful—moved from fear to boldness. (Luke 22:31–34; Matthew 14:22–31; 16:13–19; Acts 2:14)
- James: ambitious, short-tempered, judgmental, self-righteous—became committed enough to die for the sake of Christ. (Matthew 4:18–21; Mark 3:17; 10:35–40; Luke 9:52–56; Acts 12:1–2)
- John: ambitious, self-righteous—moved from judgmental to loving. (Luke 9:52–56; John 19:26–27; 21:20–24)
- Andrew: eager to please—became someone who told others about Christ. (Matthew 4:18; John 6:8–9, 12:22)
- Bartholomew: doubtful, honest, straightforward—turned from doubt to belief. (John 1:45–51; 21:1–13)
- Thomas: doubtful—turned from doubt to belief and courage. (John 14:5–6; John 20:24–29; 21:1–13)[11]

Jerry and Ramona Tuma: God will allow us to operate according to our own wisdom if we so choose, but he holds out a promise to those who desire his higher ways. The promise is that we can gain his wisdom and not be forced to rely on our own flawed reasoning. As we learn how to receive God's wisdom, we must first distinguish between our wisdom and his. God's wisdom is unlike that of the world's. As it is written in 1 Corinthians, *"For the wisdom of this world is foolishness in God's sight."*[12]

> **Malachi 3:8–10** "Will a man rob God? Yet you rob me," says the Lord of Hosts. "But you ask, 'How do we rob you?' In tithes and offerings. You are under a curse—the whole nation of you—because you are robbing me. Bring the whole tithe into the storehouse, that there may be food in my house. Test me in this," says the Lord Almighty, "and see if I will not throw open the floodgates of heaven and pour out so much blessing that you will not have room enough for it."

Stop Thief!

We find in the book of Malachi that God had been faithful to his people, yet Israel kept turning away from him. One glaring wrongdoing was their refusal to follow the <u>Law</u> in giving **tithes** and offerings. God required the Israelites to give a standard amount (one-tenth of their income) back to God. The Israelites were required to give their tithes to the priests, Levites, aliens, widows, and orphans.

Because they refused to tithe, everyone suffered. The widows and orphans suffered because they went hungry. The priests suffered because they were supposed to benefit from the offerings of animals and food, but these were lacking. Those who refused to give their tithes suffered as God held back his blessing on the people. God suffered heartache and disappointment as he watched his people rob him of love and honor. Though they started out robbing God, they ended up robbing themselves.

☞ **GO TO:**

Leviticus 27:30–34;
Genesis 14:20 (Law)

tithes: contribution to God of one tenth of the produce of one's land or income

Everyday Life

I think by nature we are takers, not givers. From day one as cute little babies we enjoy receiving every need or want we might have. I think God set up the principle of giving because he knew that if we didn't have guidelines, it would be easy for us to slip back into that selfish-baby mode, just receive with a smile, and forget to pay honor to whom honor is due.

EXAMPLES FROM THE BIBLE

☞ **GO TO:**

Luke 21:3–4 (mites)

Jesus praised the widow who gave her offering of two <u>mites</u>, hardly enough to buy a loaf of bread.

When compared to the gifts of the wealthy, the cash value of her gift was hardly enough to notice. But the devotion behind it was another matter. That devotion, beginning there and spreading throughout the world, has built hospitals and helped the needy, fed the hungry, and encouraged the imprisoned. Today the world knows more about that poor widow than about the richest Jew of her day.[13]

What Others are Saying:

Bill Hybels: There are three positive results of tithing. First, a church can finance their ministries without having to resort to manipulative arm-twisting, cheap gimmicks, or secular fund-raising schemes. Second, those who tithe enjoy the benefits of divine intervention in their financial affairs. And third, the Money Monster (seduction of money) suffers a direct hit! Giving money away is like spitting in his face.[14]

KEY POINT

Failing to tithe is like robbing God and robbing ourselves.

> **2 Corinthians 9:6–8** Remember this: Whoever sows sparingly will also reap sparingly, and whoever sows generously will also reap generously. Each man should give what he has decided in his heart to give, not reluctantly or under compulsion, for God loves a cheerful giver.

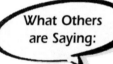
KEY Outline:

Tithing
ministries are financed
God intervenes in our finances
the love of money disappears

Give It Away

You don't have to be a farmer to understand what the Apostle Paul wrote to the Corinthian church (see illustration, page 143). A picture is worth a thousand words, and Paul is painting a masterpiece. He reminds us of what any smart farmer knows: in order to produce a bountiful harvest, he has to plan for it, plow it, plant it, and then pick a peck of produce. He also knows what to expect from what he sows. A few seeds will not produce a bumper crop.

Mary Hunt: There is something about the act of giving that cannot be explained in purely rational terms. I believe with all my heart that the act of giving invites God's supernatural intervention into our lives and our finances. I don't know about you, but the idea of opening my life to that kind of power is too awesome to miss.[15]

REMEMBER THIS

Some Christians respond to this teaching by saying, "I don't have to tithe! That system was the Old Testament law. I live in the New Testament era of grace!" While you are technically correct, the teaching of the New Testament regarding money calls for far more generosity than the Old Testament.

The Roman Empire

Within 30 years of Jesus' resurrection the Gospel had spread through the Roman Empire. There were Christian groups in most of its major cities. The well-known apostles Peter and Paul were influential in sharing the Gospel throughout the empire.

Laugh Out Loud

☞ **GO TO:**

Luke 6:38 (helping others)

Jesus said *"Give to the one who asks you, and do not turn away from the one who wants to borrow from you"* (Matthew 6:42). *"Give to everyone who asks of you, and if anyone takes what belongs to you, do not demand it back"* (Luke 6:30). Would you rather give a tithe, or give to every single charitable cause who makes a request of you? Hello? If you get as many fundraising solicitations as I do, ten percent is a bargain!

Jesus taught "when you give to the needy, do not let your left hand know what your right hand is doing" (Matthew 6:3). So genuine New Testament giving would be to close your eyes, plunge your hand into your wallet or purse, blindly clutch at a bunch of bills, and give away whatever you grabbed!

Okay, maybe that's not the most accurate explanation of Matthew 6:3. But don't miss my point. The New Testament indicates that our priority list should have money on the low end and <u>helping others</u> on the high end. We should not only tithe, but give from our hearts with additional expressions of love and honor as we watch God work through our gifts.

When I write out a check to my church in a tithe or a love gift to a ministry in need, it's like I'm sending a thank you note to God, honoring him for his many blessings on my life.

> **Deuteronomy 6:6–7** These commandments that I give you today are to be upon your hearts. Impress them on your children. Talk about them when you sit at home and when you walk along the road, when you lie down, and when you get up.

It's the Economy, Sweetie

As parents we have the responsibility to teach our children all the commandments, laws, and principles found in Scripture. As we go about living life we are to constantly impress these principles in our children's hearts and minds.

A catchy little sentence took the country by storm back in the '92 Clinton campaign. James Carville, Clinton's campaign manager, will go down in history for his slogan, "It's the economy, stupid."

I hate to admit it, but Carville did have a point. Economy and life go hand in hand. We must teach our children at an early age the basics of economy. We don't want them to grow up and be the poster children for the sequel to *Dumb and Dumber*. They must know how to manage their income. Who better to teach them than their parents?

KEY POINT

One of the greatest investments for your children's future is to teach them about money.

Remember the 10-10-80 rule? "Give God your best, put a few eggs in the nest, and live wisely on the rest." That's a great way to start with your children. When it comes to kids and what they learn, more is caught than taught. That means the best way to teach them is by example. Then follow up on your example with short instructive lessons. We can put a positive spin on that campaign slogan and say, "It's the economy, sweetie."

REMEMBER THIS

Dave Ramsey: The values and practices that operate in the family dynamic today are the ones that will be practiced tomorrow by the following generations, only magnified. If you make a firm decision to add discipline and knowledge to your financial life, and then to firmly instill those values in your children, you have the ability to not only begin changing your life today, but more importantly that of generations after you.[16]

What Others are Saying:

Money-Back Guarantee

I learned my first lesson on giving at an early age. When I was eight my parents became Christians and were baptized. They were trying to raise a young family with four kids, build a family business, put shoes on our little feet and set food on our table. They barely scraped by. But from studying the Scriptures my dad became convinced that he needed to begin tithing. He didn't know how the family would manage it, but he felt it had to be done.

COFFEE BREAK WITH GEORGIA

So, he began praying about his decision. Then his best friend came to him with a business opportunity. A national specialty advertising company was looking for a representative in that area. They had initially approached Dad's friend, but he had too many irons in the fire. He suggested Dad's name. So along with his family business, Dad added a moonlighting job and began selling immediately. Within several weeks the income from his moonlighting covered his initial tithe, plus the tithe from his advertising sales.

That was over thirty years ago. In retirement Dad still sells advertising part-time and continues to increase his earnings year after year. Needless to say, he is an advocate of tithing and giving above one's tithe. And he always practiced what he preached. Dad has used his sales techniques to encourage other Christians to tithe, offering a money-back guarantee. To this day, he's never had a dissatisfied customer.

KEY Outline:

Teach Your Children
to tithe
to save
to spend wisely
to give from the heart

So that's how I grew up in a tithing family. My parents taught me first to tithe from my allowance, then from cash gifts, and eventually, as I joined the workforce, from my paycheck. As a kid, I was merely practicing the letter of the Law. But as I grew and began my own personal relationship with Jesus, I discovered the fulfillment of the Law and the love of God. That's when I began giving above my tithe. I just followed my heart.

When you study Old Testament history, you will see that the people of Israel did not regard the laws of God as burdens, but as a joy. The Law was God's expression to Israel that they were his holy people. Their gratitude and obedience motivated God's continued generosity and set them free from slavery. They strayed from the Law, but whenever they repented, God always blessed them. (For one example, read about Josiah in 2 Kings 22:17–20.)

If we're really children of God, we won't consider giving a burden, but a joy. Let's willingly give our gifts to God, for his glory.

Think About It

KEY POINT

If we're really children of God, we won't consider giving a burden, but a joy.

STUDY QUESTIONS

1. What does the scripture say about being in debt?
2. The prophet's widow overcame financial ruin. What was the first step she took in solving her problem?
3. What is the key that unlocks the door to a plastic prison? According to 1 Timothy 6:6–10, where do you find that key?
4. Why is it so important to get along with your spouse when it comes to finances?
5. What kept Lot's wife from being like-minded with her husband?
6. Why did Jesus praise the widow who gave a small offering that was barely enough to buy a loaf of bread when others gave large amounts of offering?
7. According to the Apostle Paul in 2 Corinthians 9:6–8, how are we to give?

- The road to debt-free living requires taking a good look at the woman in the rear view mirror, then reading these road signs: STOP using credit cards. GO seek wise financial advice. YIELD to sound counsel. CAUTION, don't give in to the entrapments of materialism. If you can't afford it, don't buy it. Replace compulsion and consumption with contentment.

- If you allow it to, money problems can destroy your marriage. If you can't come to an agreement on your own, seek counsel in working together and devising a plan you can both live with.

- Our temperaments play a vital role in our financial behaviors, good or bad. Discover yours and your husband's temperaments. God made us unique, don't let those differences tear you apart. If we learn from one another, we can both benefit from those very things that drive us nuts.

- We honor God with our giving through our tithes and offerings of love. Everyone benefits from giving it away . . . especially the giver.

- The future of our world economy lies in the hands of our children. It is our responsibility to teach our children godly principles of finances, for what they do or don't know about money will either hurt or help them and generations to come.

KEY Outline:

Sound Financial Advice

Stop
- using credit cards

Go
- seek wise financial advice

Yield
- to sound counsel

Caution
- watch out for materialism

GEORGIA'S BOOKSHELF

Some of Georgia's favorite books on the subject of finances:

- *Financial Peace*, Dave Ramsey, Viking Press
- *More than Enough*, Dave Ramsey, Viking Press
- *The Financially Confident Woman*, Mary Hunt, Broadman & Holman
- *Making Life Work*, Bill and Lynn Hybels, InterVarsity Press
- *Breaking Out of Plastic Prison*, James D. Dean, Revell

6 TAKE THIS JOB AND LOVE IT

Finding Meaning and Fulfillment on the Job

Here We Go

Believe it or not, work is not a dirty "four-letter word." Our Creator experienced great fulfillment and pride in his creation of the universe. As a matter of fact, Scripture tells us that God saw his handiwork and said it was good. He liked his work!

He even had a job in mind for Adam: God placed him in the Garden of Eden to tend and care for it. Work was <u>good</u> . . . that is, until sin entered the Garden and man turned away from God's original plan. The privilege and pleasure of gardening turned to dread and drudgery as God **cursed** the land. Man would forevermore struggle to make a living.

Not only did Adam work, but God's Son worked, too. Jesus spent all but the last three years of his life as a <u>carpenter</u>, either helping his earthly father or working on his own.

The Bible is filled with stories of women who worked and worked and worked. As a matter of fact, those who were <u>idle</u> were told to get busy. (And you thought Arsenio Hall came up with "Let's get busy!")

If work for you seems like a "four-letter word," let's take a look at what the Bible has to say about women and their toil. With God's help, maybe you can recover your whistle while you work!

☞ **GO TO:**

Genesis 1:26 (good)

Genesis 3:16–19 (cursed)

Mark 6:3 (carpenter)

1 Timothy 5:13 (idle)

cursed: to say a thing is worthy of evil or trouble

> **Colossians 3:23** Whatever you do, work at it with all your heart, as working for the Lord, not for men, since you know that you will receive an inheritance from the Lord as a reward. It is the Lord Christ you are serving.

All I Do Is Work, Work, Work

Whether or not you have a boss you consider a slave driver, you can learn from the Apostle Paul addressing the slave/master relationship. Millions of slaves kept the Roman Empire functioning. As slaves such as <u>Onesimus</u> became believers in Christ, Paul admonished them to do their work as if they were doing it for the Lord. They were to work having the attitude of a sincere, obedient servant. But Paul knew slaves were not compensated according to the difficulty or quantity of their work, so he reminded them that ultimately our eternal inheritance and relationship with Christ is our reward.

His instructions parallel with our employee/employer relationships. As with the Roman slaves, in everything we do, the first step in making work . . . um, *work*, is: strive to please Christ. Put him first, and then everything else will fall into place.

☞ **GO TO:**

Philemon 1:8–25
(Onesimus)

Everyday Life

Women have always worked. The ancient Bible woman worked from dawn until dark. Her tasks included:

- providing food and clothing for her family (Genesis 27:9; 1 Samuel 2:19)

- educating the younger children (Proverbs 1:8)

- baking bread (1 Samuel 28:24)

- sewing each garment by hand (Exodus 35:25)

- gathering water every night at the local well for her family (Genesis 24:11)

She worked! She didn't have the conveniences of a local Seven-Eleven store or a department store. And we think we have it hard with only one microwave and limited grocery delivery!

KEY Outline:

Work
Slave/Master
Employee/Employer
- strive to please Christ
- all else will fall into place

In early America, the Native American woman worked just to survive. The black slave woman worked at backbreaking labor for no wage. The white woman worked on farms and raised food to help make a way for her family. Women have always worked. And worked, and worked. It wasn't until the late eighteenth century, when textile mills in New England needed women's sewing skills, that women began to "go to work" and punch in at the time clock.

The face of the work clock is forever changing. For sheer quantity, America now has the highest number of women in the workforce ever. We're seeing a nontraditional time clock tick toward a more flexible schedule as women attempt to structure work in new ways so they can spend more time with their families at home. It's always a struggle to juggle career fulfillment, finances, and a balanced family life.

Gwen Ellis: I once heard about a concert violinist who said, "If I don't practice for a day, I know it. If I don't practice for two days, my audience knows it, and if I don't practice for three days the whole world knows it." It isn't much different in our walk with Christ. We need daily contact with the source of our strength and life. Miss one day and you know something's amiss. Miss two days and your work companions know it. Miss a week or more, and the whole office will probably know it.[1]

SNAPSHOTS OF WOMEN IN THE BIBLE

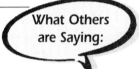

Lydia

Lydia's long purple tunic seemed to float in the breeze as she hurried through the streets to escape the city crowds. She looked forward to the peaceful countryside as a **reprieve** from the sounds of the prancing horses, the footsteps of the Roman legions, and the cries of the local merchants selling their goods.

Lydia was known all over the region as the <u>seller</u> of **purple**. Her customers were the Roman imperial family and Babylonian buyers who adorned their temples with her purple cloths. She was on a first-name basis with the rich and built her business as one of the best **dyers** in the region.

She hoped all the women she invited to the riverbank would be waiting for her, under the shade of the trees. This **Gentile** wor-

KEY Outline:

Fulfillment at Work
understand that work is good
work hard as you would for the Lord
find balance

What Others are Saying:

☞ **Check It Out:**

Acts 16:13–15

reprieve: rest; break

purple: royal purple was the most expensive and most coveted dye in the ancient world

dyers: people who colored clothing

Gentile: a non-Jew

☞ **GO TO:**

Acts 16:14 (seller)

synagogue: house of worship where Jews gathered

Sabbath: seventh day of the week; day of rest

snails: purple dye is produced from a liquid secreted in snails' hypobranchial gland

Messiah: expected and promised Savior, Jesus Christ

☞ **GO TO:**

John 4:25–42 (Messiah)

KEY Outline:

Lydia

was a godly
businesswoman
led a prayer group
was a seeker of wisdom
was converted and
baptized
housed a church

KEY POINT

Lydia's influence as a businesswoman helped her effectively witness to other businesspeople.

Think About It

shiped the God of the Jews, but there was no **synagogue** in Philippi, so she and others gathered at the riverbank on the **Sabbath** to pray and worship. She felt safe in the familiar surroundings, since they always met near the vats where her workers boiled the dye from the sea **snails** they harvested—a dye so beautiful, yet so foul in odor, that they had to process it away from the city (see illustration, page 153).

Lydia greeted the women, pleased at today's turnout. After exchanging pleasantries, each woman removed her sandals, pulled her prayer shawl over her head, and began to pray that God would guide her to better understanding. They wanted to know God.

The voices of men drawing near interrupted their prayers. Lydia greeted the strangers. They introduced themselves as Paul, Silas, Luke, and Timothy, followers of the **Messiah** (see GWRV, pages 269, 291, 318; GWBI, page 107).

Lydia invited the newcomers to join them, for she was anxious to hear more about the Savior they spoke of.

Paul (see GWBI, pages 220, 324–325), the apparent leader of the men, explained he had not planned to visit Philippi, but just days before his travels he dreamed of a man who pleaded with him to come to Macedonia (see illustration, page 143). Sensing the dream was from God, Paul changed his plans accordingly.

Having explained why he was in Philippi, Paul then began preaching about Jesus. Lydia's heart filled with an unspeakable joy. Her prayers had been answered. Her faithful God had sent these men to help them better understand. She asked Paul to tell her what she must do to become a follower of Christ. Lydia and her household were baptized in the name of Jesus that very day at the river.

Lydia opened her spacious home to Paul and his companions, a rare treat for first-century Christians used to meeting in catacombs and the equivalent of government project slums. In Lydia's house, the first church in Europe was established. The woman who knew kings and merchants now carried along with her expensive purple dye an even more valuable treasure: a personal relationship with Jesus. The purple she sold was made for earthly kings, but now everything she owned, every decision she made, was for the true King of Kings.

Lydia was open to the full knowledge of Jesus Christ because she had prepared her heart through worship and prayer. Because of her openness, Christianity spread to Europe. This businesswoman of God witnessed to friends and coworkers while she worked.

Sources of Dye

Lydia's business dealt mainly in purple dye, which came from snails. Purple, associated with royalty, was the most highly prized color. However, other colors of dye were produced from the plants in this illustration.

Everyday Life

There's an ongoing battle that has caused division among women in the Christian community. It's the "to work or not to work outside of the home" debate. We've already seen that work is a necessity and ordained by God. How and where God wants you to work is between you and him. *"The mind of man plans his ways, but the Lord directs his path"* (Proverbs 16:9).

What Others are Saying:

Ancient Irish Hymn ("Be Thou My Vision"): Riches I heed not, nor man's empty praise. Thou my inheritance, now and always. Thou and thou only, first in my heart. Thy King of heaven, my treasure thou art.[2]

> **Proverbs 31:27–29** She watches over the affairs of her household and does not eat the bread of idleness. Her children arise and call her blessed; her husband also and he praises her.

Mild-Mannered Reporter by Day, Supermom by Night

The ancient woman of Proverbs 31 appears to have a busy but balanced life. The writer describes her as a precious jewel—a rare woman we can all admire. The passage paints a beautiful, idealized portrait of a woman who has it all together. She works from dark to dark, she cooks, sews, quilts, buys and sells real estate, teaches her children and servants, takes care of the needs of her children and husband, has time for volunteer work, and she's prepared for the future. She basically "brings home the bacon and fries it up in a pan." (Oops, maybe not bacon. We need to think kosher here.)

Think About It

At the end of Proverbs 31, the writer gives the secret of this ideal woman's balanced life: *"A woman who fears the Lord is to be praised"* (Proverbs 31:30). When she sets priorities, she honors God first and foremost, and her life has a way of balancing all of its busyness.

Everyday Life

You look up from your desk and see the clock ticking away. How did that second hand get so fast? You realize you have another job to do and drop everything, run to the nearest phone booth, shut the door and *wham, bang, boom!*—you fly out in your Supermom cape, racing home at the speed of sound to resume the job you left earlier that morning.

Nearly a third of all employed women in the U.S. have children under age 13, and 38 percent have children under 18. One study reported of two thousand managers, 11 percent of the women reported that they currently work part-time in order to spend more time with family. Fifty-six percent say they have a "nontraditional" work situation, meaning any variation from 9 A.M. to 5 P.M., Monday through Friday. This is a good thing . . . finding balance between work and family.

GEORGIA'S TIPS . . .

Gwen Ellis offers these simple tips for a balanced life in her book, *Thriving as a Working Woman*:

1. Make your devotion or quiet time top priority. You must find that time to balance the rest. (You can read and pray while you relax in a hot bath with the door locked to ensure privacy.)

2. Keep everything simple. Complicated systems, tools, appliances, and clothing only take more time.

3. Divide big jobs into many smaller ones.

4. Stop trying to be perfect.

5. Get help from anyone who will help.

6. Buy duplicates of items that are in high demand—hair spray, toothpaste, toilet paper—to avoid emergency trips to the store.

7. Have a special place for your keys, your purse, and any other items that are repeatedly being lost.

8. Try to do two things at once: Talk on the phone and cook supper; watch television and mend.

9. When you have shopping and errands to accomplish, make a night of it. Plan your route from one shopping place to the next so that there is no backtracking.

10. Use delivery services as much as possible (if budget allows). In the Pacific Northwest, you can do all your grocery shopping online at www.homegrocer.com. Other regions have similar services under different names.[3]

KEY POINT

Make your devotion or quiet time top priority.

Riding on Cloud Nine

I breathed a sigh of relief as the wheels touched the runway. So far, so good. I'd caught an early morning flight to attend a speaker's conference in San Diego. The sessions would begin in about an hour, so I knew I would cut it close if there were any delays.

COFFEE BREAK
WITH GEORGIA

As directed by the shuttle operator, I made my way across the street and found Cloud Nine Shuttle Service. The driver had room for one more in the back seat, so we loaded up and I belted in for the ride of my life.

Cloud Nine Shuttle Service was proud because they ran their vehicles on propane fuel. That fact was painted beneath their logo. But you couldn't fool me; by the way this guy drove, I knew it was jet fuel. He took off like lightning. Dodged in and out of traffic. Passed vehicles like they were sitting still. He must have been the cum laude graduate at Mr. Toad's Wild Ride Driving School.

With white knuckles clutching my shoulder belt, I knew the real problem I faced: I wasn't in control. It was a strange city, and I had no directions to the resort; just an address. I was strapped into a vehicle with total strangers, traveling down the freeway at the speed of sound and there wasn't a thing I could do about it. (Of course I could have jumped out at the first stop, but the clock was ticking—I had a session in less than an hour.)

I was the last passenger to be dropped off. We made it with a few minutes to spare and I even had time to check into my room and grab a bite to eat.

Sometimes on life's road you feel as if you're on Mr. Toad's Wild Ride. Propelled by jet fuel and a busy schedule, you pass by people in your life as if they are sitting still. You can't slow down long enough to reach out and help someone in need. You dodge in and out of commitments, afraid to slow your pace. And then there are those slippery "relationships" roads where our pell-mell drive feels especially treacherous.

We have to look to the one who is truly in control and relinquish the driver's seat to him. We need to let God strap us safely into the back seat (or, given the maturity level of some of us, the child seat). The ride won't always be smooth. There will definitely be bumps along the way. But with him in control you'll feel like you're riding on Cloud Nine.

Laugh Out Loud

KEY Outline:

Let God
be in control
strap you safely in

> **1 Peter 3:8–9** Finally, all of you, live in harmony with one another; be sympathetic, love as brothers, be compassionate and humble. Do not repay evil with evil or insult with insult, but with blessing, because to this you were called so that you may inherit a blessing.

Catfight!

Peter wrote to the Jewish believers in the churches of Asia Minor during a time of major persecution (see GWBI, pages 304–306). Christians were being put to death by the Roman government, and Peter anticipated that the persecution would soon move into the lives of the believers he was writing to.

In a hostile world, what Peter wanted most was for his fellow believers to live in harmony. As never before they needed one another to accomplish their work of spreading God's word.

Though we don't usually experience life-or-death persecution at work (thank you Lord!), struggles and occasional conflicts seem unavoidable. We can be encouraged by Peter's words and overcome on-the-job friction by implementing his advice into our actions.

 Everyday Life

If there's something more chilling than being woken up in the middle of the night by the savage screams and hisses of a catfight, I don't want to know about it. Those wild screeches make you visualize paws and claws flying, fangs and teeth shining, backs arched and hair standing on end as the cats battle. With sunrise, you may see the reality of what you envisioned. Your cat may limp in sporting caked blood and swollen eyes, looking for a safe haven in which to curl up and sleep off the trauma.

Does that description remind you of anyone at your job? Most of us have seen women at work turn into Catwoman. We're so territorial, I'm surprised I haven't seen someone take SCAT animal repellent from her purse and spray it around her desk. Women are notorious for gossiping, backstabbing, undermining, and sabotaging each other. Meeow! We can be dangerous.

 ## EXAMPLES FROM THE BIBLE

Catfights were not unknown in Bible times:

- Peninnah was one of the two wives of Elkanah. She is known for taunting Elkanah's other wife, Hannah. It is not known why Elkanah had two wives, but some commentators presume that Hannah was his first wife and because she was unable to have children, Peninnah came into the picture. Peninnah may have felt that the only reason she was included was for her ability to have children. She may have feared that when her work was done, Elkanah would have no more use for her. This bitterness and jealousy led Peninnah to mistreat Hannah with taunting remarks. (1 Samuel 1:2–6; 11:2–4)

- Syntyche and Euodias were co-laborers with Paul as he built the early Church. But in Paul's letter to the Philippians he told these two women to get along and even asked others to intervene and help them patch up their differences. (Philippians 4:2–3; 14:2)

As women of faith, we can't join in the catfight. (To get declawed, some of us may need to think of Jesus not as the Great Physician, but as the Great Veterinarian!) We are not responsible for, nor can we control, Catwoman's behavior, but we are <u>responsible</u> for our own actions. Our actions should follow Apostle Peter's encouragement to live in harmony, be sympathetic, love, be compassionate, and be humble. These actions reflect the love of Christ.

☞ **GO TO:**

Romans 12:18 (responsible)

Think About It

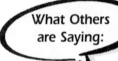

What Others are Saying:

Luci Swindoll: It's tempting to counterattack when your emotions are directing your actions. The reason is simple—it's because we're acting in the flesh. And when we operate in the flesh, it never brings glory to God. The flesh and the spirit are two entirely different things. When we're hurt, we want to lash back. Instead, we need to take what the other person is saying and look for the truth in it. There may be something in what we've been told that could help us grow.[4]

> **Matthew 5:13–15** You are the salt of the earth. But if the salt loses its saltiness, how can it be made salty again? It is no longer good for anything, except to be thrown out and trampled by men. You are the light of the world. A city on a hill cannot be hidden. Neither do people light a lamp and put it under a bowl. Instead they put it on its stand, and it gives light to everyone in the house. In the same way, let your light shine before men, that they may see your good deeds and praise your Father in heaven.

Lunch Is on Me

Jesus used salt and light as **metaphors** when he taught the famous <u>Sermon on the Mount</u> (see GWBI, page 179). We know that salt preserves, flavors, and creates thirst. Jesus' disciples were to become the "salt of the earth," and the "light of the world." As Christ's followers, we are as salt in the workplace. Our friendships can stop the decaying morals that surround us, flavor lives with the love of Christ, and create a <u>thirst</u> for God in our friends when they see something different about us and want to know more. As light we can illuminate the path, give direction, and introduce others to Jesus, our closest friend.

metaphors: words used as comparisons

 GO TO:

Matthew 5–7 (Sermon on the Mount)

Psalm 42:1–2 (thirst)

Friendships and women go hand in hand. I think it's the nurturing trait that makes us enjoy friendships so much. I have several levels of friendships:

Everyday Life

- school-mom friends
- church friends
- work friends
- best friends

Now, my small circle of best friends are my "forever friends," while the others seem to be "situational friends" that go in and out of the doorway of my life. Sometimes "situational" friends are people God places right smack on my doormat.

Work always has situational friendships. You can look at in two ways: either it was just the situation that brought you together, or God made your paths cross. You may have taken the job to fulfill your own purpose, but God has his own purpose in placing you there. Look for God's purpose. Develop friendships with women at work. Spring for lunch (or, depending on your budget, brown bag it) from time to time.

Think About It

GEORGIA'S TIPS . . .

Simple ways to express friendship to your fellow workers:

1. Sow seeds of encouragement when your coworkers are down, by giving a listening ear and directing their path to the Word. *"Perfume and incense bring joy to the heart, and the pleasantness of one's friend springs from his earnest counsel"* (Proverbs 27:9).

KEY POINT

While brown-bagging it with a friend at work, switch on the "light" by adding a pinch of "salt" to your conversation.

KEY Outline:

**Express Friendship at
Work**

encourage
celebrate
share sorrows
brighten lives

KEY POINT

Your heart controls
your life; fuel it with
God's Word.

2. Celebrate coworkers' accomplishments and express how God has blessed them with their special gift or talent. Give a small gift. (Women love gifts. But you already knew that.) Inspirational gifts are a great way to celebrate and deliver a message of God at the same time. *"Rejoice with those who rejoice"* (Romans 12:15).

3. Offer sympathy when your fellow workers grieve. Inspirational cards and books are a wonderful comfort when a seeker is trying to understand a loss. She can turn to the books in the privacy of her own grief and seek answers. *"Blessed are those who mourn, for they will be comforted"* (Matthew 5:4).

4. Shed light when days are dark. A smiling face and an encouraging word can brighten a coworker's soul. They look to you for strength as you reflect the light of Christ. *"Let your light shine before men, that they may see your good deeds and praise your Father in heaven"* (Matthew 5:4).

EXAMPLES FROM THE BIBLE

The Bible gives us examples of forever and situational friends.

- David and Jonathan were forever friends. Jonathan, the eldest son of King Saul, was David's closest friend. Their friendship began the day the two first met after David killed the giant Philistine, Goliath. David's friendship with Saul remained intact even though Saul's animosity towards David grew to the point of attempting to kill him. Jonathan was willing to surrender all claims to the throne rather than go against his beloved friend. (1 Samuel 18:1–4)

- A good example of situational friends were Joseph and his cell mate, the king's cupbearer. Their unusual situation brought them together along with the king's baker. The cupbearer and the baker each had a dream which made them worry. With God's help Joseph interpreted the dreams. He asked the appreciative cupbearer a favor. If the cupbearer were restored to his office, as Joseph predicted, he asked only that the cupbearer remember him. The cupbearer was restored to his position in the king's palace, but forgot about Joseph until another situation occurred where remembering their friendship would benefit the cupbearer. (Genesis 40:1–41:40)

Mary Whelchel: Before you march into work tomorrow, determined to be a friend to all, I offer a word of wisdom. We need to remember that we don't make friends in the workplace solely for the purpose of witnessing. We make friends because that is what Jesus would do and because we care. The love of Jesus in us says to others, "I care about you personally. Jesus died for you. I'd love to be able to share Jesus with you. I hope someday you'll come to the Lord, but that's not why I'm making friends with you."[5]

> **Proverbs 4:23** Above all else, guard your heart, for it is the wellspring of life.

Office Romance: the Good, the Bad, and the Ugly

Years ago I read a handbook for marriage. The author had some good thoughts but when he came to writing about the workplace, we parted company. He suggested that a woman should never be in the workplace, under any circumstances, because she was too weak. She would be tempted and would give in to an office affair. I couldn't believe my eyes. Now that's the solution—build a fortress around your house so temptation can't get through your door! Did he forget about the mailman, the UPS man, and the pool man? Just lock her up and throw away the key.

We live in a world filled with **temptations** but we are promised in 1 Corinthians 10:13, "*God is faithful; he will not let you be tempted beyond what you can bear. But when you are tempted, he will also provide a way out so that you can stand up under it.*"

As we encounter romance at the office, we must always be on guard and protect our hearts.

What does the Bible say about the heart?

1. From it springs personality, inner life, and character (mentioned 257 times in the Scripture): "*Yet Pharaoh's heart became hard and he would not listen to them, just as the Lord had said. Then the Lord said to Moses, 'Pharaoh's heart is unyielding; he refuses to let the people go'*" (Exodus 7:13–14). "*But the Lord said to Samuel, 'Do not consider his [Eliab's] appearance or his height, for I have rejected him. The Lord does not look at the things man looks at. Man looks at the outward appearance, but the Lord looks at the heart'*" (1 Samuel 16:7).

temptations: *things, thoughts, or people that try to make a person do sinful things*

Think About It

---

2. Emotional states (found 166 times in the Scripture):
   - Intoxication: Nabal was merry in his heart and drunk (1 Samuel 25:36)
   - Joy: the priest's heart was glad (Judges 18:20)
   - Sorrow: Hannah's heart was sad (1 Samuel 1:8)
   - Anxiety: Eli's heart trembled in fear because the ark of God was taken (1 Samuel 4:13)
   - Love: the king's heart longed for his son Absalom (2 Samuel 14:1)

3. Purpose of the heart: to follow God (found 195 times in the Scripture). The right attitude of the heart begins with the heart being broken or crushed. Brokenness is necessary because a hard stony heart does not submit to the will of God. But if you desire a clean heart, God will make your heart clean. *"I will give them an undivided heart and put a new spirit in them; I will remove from them their heart of stone and give them a heart of flesh. Then they will follow my decrees and be careful to keep my laws. They will be my people, and I will be their God"* (Ezekiel 11:19–20).

4. Prayer for a clean heart: *"Search me, O God, and know my heart; test me and know my anxious thoughts. See if there is any offensive way in me, and lead me in the way everlasting"* (Psalm 139:23). *"Create in me a pure heart, O God, and renew a steadfast spirit within me"* (Psalm 51:10).

5. Benefits of a pure heart: *"Blessed are the pure in heart for they will see God"* (Matthew 5:8). *"I pray that out of his glorious riches he may strengthen you with power through his Spirit in your inner being, so that Christ may dwell in your hearts through faith"* (Ephesians 3:17).[6]

KEY POINT

If you're looking, look for a single man at the office who "knows God." (Better: Do your shopping at church!)

☞ **Check It Out:**

Ruth 2

> **Ruth 2:4–5** Just then Boaz arrived from Bethlehem and greeted the harvesters, "The Lord be with you!" "The Lord bless you!" they called back. Boaz asked the foreman of his harvesters, "Whose young woman is that?"

The Good Office Romance

Ruth's and Boaz' (see GWWB, pages 197–204) relationship started on a field during harvest—the workplace. Old Testament Law allowed the poor to follow harvesters and gather the grain that fell to the ground during harvesting. This is what Ruth did on Boaz' field. Boaz took notice of her, asked his foreman about her, and offered her special protection and care. Following the appropriate customs, Ruth asked for Boaz to extend his protection to the point of matrimony. Boaz was deeply moved at her request because he was an older man and Ruth could have run after the younger fellas. Eventually they did get married and lived happily ever after. (For the whole story, see Chapter 4, "Home Front or Battlefront?".)

Everyday Life

Bill Gates met his wife Melinda at Microsoft. They seem to be living a fairy tale romance. Robin and Shaun are friends of mine who met at the office. You didn't read about their wedding on the cover of *Newsweek*, but they too are living happily ever after.

The office can be a great place for a single woman to observe her possible future mate from a safe distance. You can be a fly on the wall and learn all kinds of things about a man. Robin sized Shaun up the first day. She thought he was pretty cute but was a little too **aloof**. But after further observation, she found she had mistaken self-confidence for arrogance. She watched how others responded to him—everybody liked him! He always managed to calm a crisis, and if emergency help was needed, he was always there. No one had anything bad to say about Shaun, and he never said anything bad about anyone else. He even talked about his church unashamedly. Robin fell in love with a man of integrity, character, and faith.

aloof: distant; unaware

Does Mr. Romance at the office have the character traits Scripture lists for a husband's role in a marriage? He should be willing to:

Think About It

1. provide (Genesis 3:17–19)
2. protect (Ephesians 5:23)
3. serve and lead (Ephesians 5:23)
4. love sacrificially (Ephesians 5:25, 28–29)
5. nourish and cherish (Ephesians 5:28–29)
6. be understanding (1 Peter 3:7)
7. wash his wife with the water of the Word (Ephesians 5:26)
8. grant his wife honor as a coheir of the grace of God (1 Peter 3:7)

What Others are Saying:

malice: a wish to harm someone

Bill Hybels: The first and most important area in which spouses need to be compatible is in regard to their relationship with God. If knowing God *"leads to life"* (Proverbs 19:23), it would seem to follow that it is one of the keys to building a satisfying marriage and also something spouses should share in common.[7]

> **Ephesians 4:31–32** Get rid of all bitterness, rage and anger, brawling and slander, along with every form of **malice**. Be kind and compassionate to one another, forgiving each other, just as in Christ God forgave you.

The Bad Office Romance

In Apostle Paul's time, the Ephesians needed a little instruction on how to live the new life that they had in Christ. I think we can add Paul's guidelines to our Get Over the Bad Romance Survival Kit.

After a breakup, a hurting heart can turn to anger and bitterness. We are encouraged to tame our anger, work through our issues, be kind, and give up the right to get even. You may not want to patch things up with your ex. You may even need to distance yourself from all contact. But whatever you do, instead of anger, try kindness.

 Everyday Life

 **KEY Outline:**

Office Romance
  may be good for singles
  is bad if there are breakups
  will be ugly if there are affairs

Down through time, Dear John letters have seemed the easiest way to end a romance. You write the letter, bid farewell, and never have to see the person's sad little face again.

Too bad that's not reality in the office. If you choose to date coworkers, you risk the consequences of an office romance gone bad. You may zip him a Dear John e-mail, a Dear John alphanumeric pager message, and a Dear John video conference call, but chances are, he's not out of your life. Unless you transfer out of the office, you'll probably see him in the elevator, at management meetings, at office parties, in the parking lot, and so on. That's where it gets tough.

It's awfully hard to practice what we preach when our hearts are wounded. But remember—the whole office is watching and our actions speak louder than our words. Let your actions reflect kindness, compassion, and forgiveness, as we are a reflection of Christ.

The best advice to avoid this bad situation from the get-go: don't date coworkers.

Items to help you get over the bad romance:

1. Kindness—*"Be kind and compassionate to one another, forgiving each other, just as in Christ God forgave you"* (Ephesians 4:32).

2. Compassion—*"Therefore, as God's chosen people, holy and dearly loved, clothe yourselves with compassion, kindness, humility, gentleness and patience"* (Colossians 3:12).

3. Forgiveness—*"Forgive us our debts, as we also have forgiven our debtors"* (Matthew 6:12).

Think About It

Jan Silvious: Overcoming evil with good can be a daunting task if you are harboring bitterness in your heart. The most effective thing you can do to rid yourself of bitterness is to make the choice to forgive . . . You may find that it is still not possible to be at peace, but you will have provided the atmosphere for peace to reign on your side of the street.[8]

What Others are Saying:

Genesis 39:9–10: [Joseph said to Potiphar's wife] "My master has withheld nothing from me except you, because you are his wife. How then could I do such a wicked thing and sin against God?" And though she spoke to Joseph day after day, he refused to go to bed with her or even be with her.

☞ **Check It Out:**

Genesis 39

The Ugly Office Romance

Joseph was a handsome man and the boss's wife took notice. She made no bones about it—she wanted to sleep with Joseph. We can learn from Joseph's reaction, for he was the forerunner of the Just Say No campaign. He didn't look in the mirror and think he still had it, returning to her the next day so she could stroke his ego. He stayed as far away from her as he possibly could. He didn't say, "Let's do lunch," and keep it a secret from the boss. He didn't feel sorry for this lonely woman, and try to be her savior or counselor and say, "I'll call you later to help you out with your problem." He didn't fan the flame. Instead he hosed her down with the fire extinguisher called NO and then ran away.

Joseph was single. He didn't have a wife and family to betray, but he had a God he could not turn his back on. He knew that even unseen sins have consequences.

KEY POINT

Guard your heart. Say no to an office affair and run, girl, run.

Everyday Life

infidelity: lack of sexual or emotional faithfulness

REMEMBER  THIS

What Others are Saying:

☞ **GO TO:**

1 Corinthians 10:13 (escape)

Most soap operas and TV melodramas deal with "who's sleeping with whom" at work. Some offices could provide the script word for word, because every day in the land of "equal opportunity," what started out as an innocent friendship with a married man at the office turns into either an emotional or physical affair. Marital **infidelity** leaves a path of deadly destruction: destruction of self-worth, destruction of the spouse and marriage, destruction of the innocent bystanders called children, and in many cases, destruction of a career.

An affair is the ugliest of all office romances. Guard your heart and say NO. Honor yourself, your spouse, and God. There is no temptation so great that we cannot resist, for God will provide an escape. Look for the escape route and do like Mr. Gump: "Run, Forrest, run!"

Mary Whelchel: As difficult as you may think it is to cut off a relationship that feels good and meets some of your needs for companionship and acceptance, the pain you are going to deal with later if you allow this relationship to develop into an affair is greater than anything you can imagine. The earlier you turn around and head in the right direction, the easier it is to untangle yourself. [9]

> **Proverbs 16:3** Commit to the Lord whatever you do, and your plans will succeed.

Bringing Work Home

If you think working from home is for you, the first thing you must do is seek God's guidance. We have peace of mind when our thoughts and plans are established in, and our works are entrusted to, him.

Thousands of women want the flexibility and freedom to be at home with their kids. Each one wants to be her own boss and use her own unique creativity to turn her passion into profit.

Are you considering joining the ranks of women who work from their home? You're not alone. According to IDC/LINK, a market research firm that tracks the home-business industry, almost 30 million people work from home either part-time or full time. All projections suggest that the number of home-based workers will continue to increase significantly over the next 10 years.[10]

Think About It

• • •

I've seen women use unique abilities and turn fun into profit. Here's a list of a few businesses I know of personally that are run out of the home:

KEY POINT

Make your decision and build your business on prayer.

Services:
- home decorating
- floral designs
- wedding consultant
- wedding photographer
- clothing alterations
- day care center

Sales:
- kitchen accessories
- cosmetic sales
- children's books
- photo album memory maker sales
- long distance provider
- sales representative

Specialty Items: (Sold at specialty stores, but made at home.)
- lotions
- candles
- jewelry
- noodles (yes, noodles)
- candy

If there is a market and you have talent and determination, you have a great combination for a winning business.

Lindsay O'Conner: To be a truly great nation we must get back to strong families and strong faith. We must stop letting society dictate the family structure. Our country's wave of downshifting (evidence that people are voluntarily choosing simplicity) shows that both men and women are doing just that, by working from home.[11]

What Others are Saying:

Disheartened and worried by recent events, my friend Helen lay in bed next to her husband, Martin, and admitted things had to change. She had to get out of her work situation so she could spend more time with their eight-year-old daughter, Stephanie.

A few weeks before, Stephanie had broken her arm and dearly wanted her mom to be a temperature taker and sickbed sitter. Helen's job in sales drew her away from home 50 percent of the time, and her inflexible boss hadn't let Helen stay home with Stephanie. Martin was wonderful about picking up the slack, but she knew her priorities had shifted away from home to work. Her heart told her she needed to turn her priorities around and be home with Stephanie.

That night Helen and Martin talked about starting a sales company Helen could own. Helen says that was a turning point when she surrendered everything to God. They prayed, seeking wisdom and guidance. Helen finished her prayer with, "If you want this to happen, let it; if not, close the door."

That was four years ago, and God flung the door wide open. Helen quit her position, set up a home office and started Sales Pointe, a business which contracts with manufacturers and provides a service for retailers by demonstrating products to customers. (Sales Pointe people are the smiling faces you see in retail stores offering you samples of the latest product.)

Helen didn't have a paycheck for five months, but she trusted God to make a way, and he did. Somehow all the bills were paid. Each year the business has grown and is now a national company. Helen will tell you the income is great, but the freedom of spending more time with her daughter is the greatest blessing of all. Helen uses her success story as a testimony about the power of prayer. With a contagious smile she says, "This isn't my company. This is God's company, based on prayer."

Think About It

Helen and Martin took to heart Christ's teachings on prayer when he taught on the Sermon on the Mount. We are to

• ask,

• seek, and

• knock.

In other words, pray, pray, and pray.

Priscilla

Fear filled the air as news of persecution spread from house to house like wildfire. The emperor Claudius was expelling all Jews from Rome. There was no time to gather all of their possessions. Priscilla and Aquila collected only their tent-making tools (see illustration, page 170), wrapped them in the cloth used for their tents, tied them to their camel, and headed for Corinth. They left their home, friends, and family behind and clung to each other as they fled for their lives.

Priscilla knew God would provide for all their needs and was thankful that their tent-making craft seemed well suited for Corinth (see illustration, page 143). The metropolitan city was the world's seaport, with an international marketplace of merchants selling everything from Babylonian ivory to Phrygian slaves. But Priscilla also knew they would meet opposition as they entered a city that embraced the temple of **Aphrodite**, which had over one thousand **consecrated prostitutes**. Priscilla had the reputation for speaking out for her Lord. She knew she had to continue speaking out about Jesus and leave her life open to God's lead in business and life.

Priscilla and her husband Aquila had begun their business in Corinth by the time Paul, a missionary and an apostle of Christ, visited. God had prepared a place for Paul to renew his energies and spirit as Priscilla and Aquila opened not only their home to him, but also included him in their tent-making trade.

Weak, fearful, and trembling, Paul had arrived in Corinth from Athens. He had been driven out of Macedonia by angry Jews. The people of Athens barely put up with him, and now in Corinth he met the familiar hostility he had experienced from other Jews in his travels.

As Paul worked away his stress with his trade, Priscilla and Aquila had the opportunity to learn firsthand from this apostle. Day after day they produced goods that provided for their daily needs and also provided funds for the new church to continue to grow. They surrendered all to God, ministering to Paul and endangering their lives to speak out, but God protected them in their work. They touched the lives of others and as a result the Gospel continued to spread.

☞ **Check It Out:**

Acts 18:1–3

🔑 *KEY Outline:*

Priscilla
worked from home
was uprooted from Rome
started over
was hospitable
evangelized
was faithful

Aphrodite: *the goddess of love*

consecrated prostitutes: *religious prostitutes of pagan temples*

☞ **GO TO:**

Acts 18:26 (speaking)

1 Corinthians 2:1–5 (weak)

Acts 18:3 (trade)

Romans 16:3–5 (endangering)

Acts 18:18–28 (others)

Awl

Priscilla, Aquila, and Paul probably used an awl, along with needles and thread, to make their tents. Awls were usually about six inches long and made of bone or metal. They were also used by carpenters and leather workers for punching holes.

Think About It

Everything Priscilla and Aquila did and everything they owned was God's, no matter where they went. God blessed the work of a wife and husband who together made a living from self-employment, and together lived their lives for God.

> **Proverbs 1:5** Let the wise listen and add to their learning.

If I Learned Everything I Need to Know in Kindergarten, Why Am I Still in School at 40?

Sometimes we find ourselves forced into learning a new skill. Something changed, and like it or not, you have to respond. You may have never planned to work full time, but now you're a single mom and you need to go back to school to get a higher education to earn higher pay. Maybe your spouse is unable to work, or the pink slip just landed on his desk. Or maybe your children have flown from the nest and now you have the time to do and learn something you've always wanted to learn. One way or another, you find it necessary to retrain and to enter the workforce.

Whatever the circumstances may be, consider learning a pleasure. God will give you <u>strength</u> and stretch your brain as you <u>walk</u> this new path. Remember, just by wanting to learn you're a step ahead. The writer of Proverbs says, *"the wise listen and add to their learning"* (Proverbs 1:5).

☞ **GO TO:**

Psalm 28:7; Isaiah 40:29 (strength)

Isaiah 2:3–9 (walk)

EXAMPLES FROM THE BIBLE

Major changes required these men and women of the Bible to learn something new:

- Adam and Eve learned a new occupation in agriculture. Their status changed from overseers of the Garden of Eden, to tillers of the soil. (Genesis 3:17)

- Miriam was probably in her eighties when her brother Moses led the children of Israel out of Egypt. Her occupation changed from "slave" to "freedom fighter" as she helped Moses and Aaron in leadership. (Micah 6:4; Exodus 15:21)

- Esther (see GWWB, page 142) was an orphan Jewess who was chosen to be the new queen. She rose to the occasion and kept the Jews from being massacred by the wicked leader, Haman. (Book of Esther)

- Deborah (see GWWB, page 126) was a homemaker who counseled those who sought her advice. This led her to a position as one of the Judges of Israel. Her wisdom was needed in time of war and Deborah learned to lead an army to victory. (Judges 4:9; 5:2)

KEY POINT

Wise women learn.

Everyday Life

Recently the Discovery Channel showed a special on seniors active into their 90s. A study had proven that if we continue to learn, our brains stay in good shape into old age. I guess, in other words, we need to give the old gray matter a jump start from time to time to keep the juices flowing. (Granted, some need a bigger jump than others.) Commit to learning one new thing every year!

What Others are Saying:

Lynda Hunter: Don't let fear paralyze you. Sometimes we ignore or avoid change, but it doesn't go away. You make the choice. Take charge. Look for opportunities to make change work for you.[12]

Sister Heads Back to School

For all of you eavesdroppers out there, you get a special treat in this Coffee Break. This is a story my sister Connie e-mailed me on the subject of going back to school. After being out for twenty years she returned to the world of academics to fulfill requirements for advancement in her career. How often do you get to read an author's mail? Here's your chance:

"I left extremely early for my first class back in school. As you know, early is not my M.O. [modus operandi], but it was part of The Plan. The Plan was a simple one: attend and blend. Don't stand out in any way, try not to draw attention, just listen and learn.

"I wasn't sure I wanted to leave my current position, but I felt that the continuing classes certainly couldn't hurt. You know I love learning, and I honestly enjoy studying, especially history. I hurt inside every time we pass one of those historical markers on the highway and Bruce [Connie's husband] won't stop to read it. Something happened there, something important enough to erect a marker, and I wanted to know what it was! I couldn't believe I was adding all this extra work in my already-full schedule. I asked myself, Am I nuts?

"In formulating The Plan, I went to campus a week early to register, map out my route to the classrooms, and scout out a perfect parking place. The parking was stressful, mainly because there isn't any! But I was able to find a lot close to my building, so that first morning I felt confident as I left for classes. I was ready. I had my campus essential, the ten-pound backpack. I dressed to match the students I had checked out the week before, and I made myself leave early.

"Well you know what they say about the best-laid plans. My plans crumbled as I turned onto Campus Drive. All lots were blocked because of a special event. I managed to find metered parking, but I had no change. I ran to a nearby convenience store for a pocketful of quarters, fed the meter, and looked around to get my bearings. I had no earthly idea where I was and time was wasting. I found the YOU ARE HERE map and then rushed to class.

"I opened the door and stood gasping for breath. My backpack felt like it weighed a ton, and my shoes were untied. It was like I

Laugh Out Loud

had a neon sign flashing "I'm late!" over my head as I made my way into the classroom. After parading down a couple of aisles (nearly injuring several kids with the deadly, oversized backpack), I sat at the front of the class, close enough to read the instructor's notes. So much for blending in. This was not what I had planned. I only hoped it would get better.

"It didn't. The real blow came to this forty-something student during our lunch break when the young man behind the register in the food court asked for my Faculty ID, so he could give me the faculty discount. I must have looked dumbfounded because before I could get a word out, the girls in my class gave him my student status. He mumbled an apology and I mumbled, 'Thanks anyway.'

"I ate with the girls and they asked why I was taking these classes. I couldn't formulate a cool explanation, so I just told them I love to learn. They were totally confused. I already had a degree and a career. Why would anyone in their right mind put themselves through all this? (That was something I began to question myself at that point.) They said that once they got out of there, they didn't want to go back to school.

"I suddenly remembered how I felt when I was their age. The year Bruce and I graduated from college, I was married, Curtis [their son] was five months old, and I was more than ready to get out there in the world and make a place for myself. I was struck with a revelation as I thought about those girls. They were just beginning to learn. They had not lived their learning. There were experiences yet to come, lessons to be learned, and a life to be lived. It was all ahead of them. But I had already lived and learned. My experiences were broader, my understanding deeper, and my life richer because of it, but I never want to quit learning. There are things out there I still don't know, and places with markers erected that I have not yet seen. I did not learn in kindergarten all that I need to know.

"So I have a new plan. It's no longer 'attend and blend.' It's not even 'listen and learn.' Instead, my new plan is 'live to learn, and learn to live.' I like my new plan. What do you think?

"Love ya'. Connie."

KEY POINT

Live to learn, and learn to live.

STUDY QUESTIONS

1. According to Scripture, how does God feel about work?
2. The Apostle Paul gave us a simple plan for work. What did he encourage the Colossians to do?
3. Lydia spent time in prayer. How was her prayer answered? What was the result of her open heart, open home, and willingness to follow the message of Jesus?
4. How should we handle catfights at work?
5. How are we the "salt of the earth" at work?
6. What was the secret of the Proverbs 31 woman?
7. How did Joseph have the strength to withstand temptation?
8. Priscilla worked with her husband in their tent-making business. How did their trade help spread the Gospel?
9. What type of woman continues to learn?

CHAPTER WRAP-UP

- Work is not a "four-letter word." You can find significance, fulfillment, and make a difference in the lives of others at work. But you must place Christ first in your life and do everything as if you were working for him. When he is the center of our lives we can balance the rest.

- Some workers will try to drag you into catfights. Turn the other cheek. Don't stoop to their level; instead, reflect Christ's love.

- The fragrance of romance will permeate the office from time to time. Be aware of the good, the bad, and the ugly of romance. Guard your heart, for it will determine the condition of the rest of your life.

- Working from home is not only a trend—it can be a wonderful way to get back in touch with your family. If this is for you, build the foundation of your business on prayer and God's guidance.

- Welcome continued learning as a challenge and a gift. "Live to learn, and learn to live" in this new adventure of your life.

GEORGIA'S BOOKSHELF

Some of Georgia's favorite books on the subject of women and work:

- *Thriving as a Working Woman*, Gwen Ellis, Tyndale House
- *A Christian's Guide to Working from Home*, Lindsey O'Connor, Harvest House
- *The Workplace: Questions Women Ask*, Judith Briles, Luci Swindoll, Mary Whelchel, Multnomah Press
- *Only Angels Can Wing It,* Liz Curtis Higgs, Thomas Nelson
- *Seasons of a Woman's Heart*, Lynn D. Morrissey, Starburst

7 I HAVE A GLUE GUN AND I'M NOT AFRAID TO USE IT

Rediscovering the Lost Art and Joy of Homemaking

Here We Go

Moms trade in briefcases and BMWs for diaper bags and mini-vans in order to come home. Kids step off of big yellow buses to come home. Dads click off their computers, check out of the of-fice, and hit rush hour traffic to come home. Runaways face the reality of the real world and call to see if they can come home. Every day men, women, boys, and girls turn their hearts toward home looking for a rest stop, a bite to eat, and a safe haven.

> I truly believe that a woman is the heartbeat of the home. She is usually the one whose open arms call everyone else home.

> Proverbs 14:1 says, *"The wise woman builds her house, but with her own hands the foolish one tears hers down."* The writer is not referring to a woman as a carpenter who constructs the structure of the house, but as a woman who cares for her household, loves the inhabitants, and helps construct the souls living under her roof.

A wise woman creates a home that reflects Christ and her love for her family. A creative woman does it while making her home a fun and special place. We sometimes feel like Cinderella when it

Think About It

KEY Outline:

A Wise Homemaker
prays
has fun
is diligent
shows hospitality
is unique

KEY POINT

A wise woman
"builds" her house.

What Others
are Saying:

malign: *to speak bad of
or slander*

☞ **GO TO:**

1 Timothy 5:14
(homemaking)

Ephesians 5:33
(husband)

 Everyday Life

comes to daily housework, but there is a secret key to turning hated housework into willing housework. Scripture gives us tools of wisdom to rediscover this lost art of hospitality. Let's see what the Bible says about the joy of homemaking.

Carole Mayhall: Being a keeper of the home is a big task, but it won't be overwhelming if you keep trying to simplify your home as well as your life and strive to please God, not people. One saying I like is that while the husband is the hearth, the wife is the fire that warms the home.[1]

> **Titus 2:4–6** Train the younger women to love their husbands and children, to be self-controlled and pure, to be busy at home, to be kind, and to be subject to their husbands, so that no one will **malign** the Word of God.

Occupation: Homemaker

In writing to Titus and giving advice to the younger women of the early Church, Paul ranked homemaking right up there with loving your husband and children.

This new life in Christ meant liberation from the oppression of the day for women. In Jewish culture they were inferior and treated as property. But for Christian women, Paul said, *"There is neither Jew nor Greek, slave nor free, male nor female, for you are all one in Christ Jesus"* (Galatians 3:28). They were equal with men! Still, homemaking and the traditional role of motherhood were treasured as a calling for a young woman. Paul did not see this role as demeaning or contradicting the female believer's exalted worth in the Lord.

For the first few years after our son was born and I left my career to come home, I cringed when I filled out tax forms. Why? Well, for all the same reasons you do, plus one other: on the line where you must fill in your occupation, I had to write "homemaker." I had worked hard and had a successful career. Writing that one word made me feel like I had fallen from the top of the ladder to the bottom rung. But that was before I held up the white flag and surrendered all my titles to the Boss upstairs.

Now I almost laugh out loud when I write "homemaker" as my occupation. I write it in bold letters with pride, for I know that it's one of the greatest and most challenging careers of all time. I've added some commas after my homemaker title—wife, mother, author, and speaker—but homemaker still ranks at the top of my credentials.

Think About It

 EXAMPLES FROM THE BIBLE

In Bible times women performed homemaking chores for their families every day.

KEY POINT

Homemaking can be a calling designed by God.

- Even in days of suffering and starvation the widow of Zarepath gathered firewood to bake bread for her family's last meal. (1 Kings 17:12)

- Another daily homemaking chore: carrying heavy pots filled with fresh water for the family, just as Rebekah (Genesis 24:15–16) and the Samaritan woman did (John 4:1–7).

- Women worked in the fields and brought home grain as Ruth did for her family. (Ruth 2:2)

- Homemakers like Sarah prepared meals for their families and guests. (Genesis 18:1–15)

- During times of celebration like the wedding of Cana, women prepared the feast at the home of the bridegroom. (John 2:1–11)

Patsy Clairmont: My favorite refrigerator magnet reads, "Mom, I'll always love you, but I'll never forgive you for washing my face with spit on your hanky." That statement is funny and effective because most of us have experienced ye ol' spit shine. It's part of our family heritage.[2]

What Others are Saying:

SNAPSHOTS OF WOMEN IN THE BIBLE

Martha

☞ **Check It Out:**

John 12:1–2

Martha (see GWWB, pages 257–272) woke before sunrise, took the dimly burning lamp from the shelf, and hurried down the narrow stairway that led to the kitchen in the basement. The bright yellow in the **mosaic** pavement sparkled like gold as the room brightened. There was so much to do and so little time, but she could hardly contain her excitement.

mosaic: small pieces of colored tile inlaid to form a pattern

☞ **GO TO:**

John 11:32–45
(resurrected)

resurrected: brought back to life after dying

KEY Outline:

Martha
organized
detailed
served

☞ **GO TO:**

Luke 10:38–42
(outburst)

ACT OF GOD

brought Lazarus
back to life

In a few hours the quiet of the morning air would be broken by the jingling of the tambourine and joyful singing and dancing. Only days before, her home had been a house of mourning, filled with sadness and wailing. But tonight they would feast and celebrate, for her brother Lazarus who had died now lived! The guest of honor was their dear friend Jesus, who had **resurrected** Lazarus. The whole town wanted to join in the celebration and see this dead man that walked, but her house could hold only so many. She knew that every single person she had invited would attend.

It didn't bother her today that her sister Mary still slept. She could find plenty for Mary to do later, and extra help would arrive soon. *Besides*, Martha thought with a smile, *if Mary cooked, no one would want to eat!* She would put Mary in charge of the dancers and music.

As Martha bustled around the kitchen she nibbled on pieces of bread and cheese and popped an olive in her mouth from time to time. She had to keep up her strength; she had a busy day ahead.

Martha stood in the doorway of her small storage room and stopped for a moment to gather her thoughts. With so many guests coming, there was not enough time to bake as much bread as they would need. She would pick up her bread at the baker's shop early before they sold out. She smelled the fresh garlic that hung on the wall. It was still fresh enough. There were plenty of vegetables (see GWHN, pages 49–63) and onions for the stew, but she needed more wine and fresh figs. Oh, and she couldn't run out of oil; they needed so much for dipping the bread. Everything had to be perfect. Not only was a dead man dining at her table, but Jesus had spoken of leaving. She feared this could be their last meal together.

Martha felt ashamed of her <u>outburst</u> from the previous meal Jesus and his disciples had eaten there. She had been overworked, cleaning the house and slaving over a hot oven while others enjoyed his company. She had gotten so caught up in doing, she forgot to enjoy herself. Instead, she'd spent her time complaining.

But not this time. Martha looked at life a little differently since she heard Jesus call Lazarus out of the tomb, alive. When Jesus spoke, his voice pierced her soul. He not only brought her brother back to life; he resurrected her heart. She didn't resent or begrudge being the homemaker; she saw it now as a calling, a way she could serve her family and her Lord.

What she once thought was a duty was now a gift—a gift she would gladly give her Savior.

> **Mark 8:8** The people ate and they were satisfied.

Mama's in the Kitchen

You may have heard of Jesus feeding a crowd of five thousand men with five pieces of bread and two small fish. Fewer people remember that Mark records a second miracle of Jesus feeding thousands of men, women, and children. Jesus being Jesus, he once again had <u>compassion</u> for the people.

For three days the multitudes had followed and listened to Jesus' teaching. Even if they had packed some lunch for the first day, by the third day they had nothing to eat.

There was no Jonah's Fish Fry fast food restaurant around. Jesus and his followers were miles out of town, and he feared people would collapse if they journeyed on empty stomachs.

The disciples managed to gather up seven loaves of bread. Jesus blessed the bread, fed four thousand people, and still had seven baskets filled with leftovers.

Jesus not only cares for our spiritual needs, he cares about our physical needs as well. He and he alone can satisfy both a hungry stomach and a hungry soul.

☞ **Check It Out:**

Mark 8:1–10

☞ **GO TO:**

Matthew 9:36; 14:14 (compassion)

Everyday Life

They say the way to a man's heart is through his stomach. If that's the case, then the kitchen looms large in Mrs. Homemaker's tool kit. The kitchen is the gathering place of the home where family friendships brew, menus and parties are planned, dreams are shared, and where you can whip up a fun meal to spice up family life.

Flashback

Growing up with four kids in the house, I felt like Mom was always in the kitchen. She made sure no matter where we lived we always had a big kitchen, situated beside the family room. The most important kitchen item to me was our large, well-worn kitchen table. The family and friends that pulled up a chair for casual table talk, meals, and prayers made that table mean more to my Christian heritage than any other object in the house. The table doubled as my mom's private prayer chapel. I often found her there with her cup of coffee and open Bible, silently enjoying her morning devotions.

EXAMPLES FROM THE BIBLE

In Bible times the whole family ate the evening meal together. In most cases it was prepared by the mother, assisted by other family members or servants. Let's see what's cooking in the Bible:

- Fatted calf, curds, and milk (see GWHN, pages 81–96) were what Abraham and Sarah prepared for their guests. (Genesis 18:6–8)
- Lentil soup was what Esau traded his birthright for. (Genesis 25:29–34)
- Fish (see GWHN, pages 97–107), cucumbers, melons, leeks, onions, and garlic were eaten by the Israelites during their captivity in Egypt. (Numbers 11:5)
- Bread, wine, sheep, roasted grain, raisins, and fig cakes were what Abigail provided for David and his men. (1 Samuel 25:18)
- Grain (see GWHN, pages 19–33), wine, and olive oil were included in God's blessings. (Deuteronomy 7:13)
- Salt was the main seasoning (Job 6:6), along with dill and cummin. (Isaiah 28:25–27)
- Corn got Jesus and the disciples in trouble when they picked it fresh in the field. (Matthew 7:1)
- Fish for breakfast? Yes, Jesus prepared it for the disciples over an open fire. (John 21:13)

We can make the kitchen a fun and special place that is always open and ready to satisfy the ones we love. Take joy in the food you prepare, knowing it will nourish and strengthen your family.

REMEMBER THIS

Appetite for Life

Food and memory seem to go hand in hand. An ordinary food once took me by surprise and brought back some great memories.

If you're a hamburger fan and you've dined in southern California, I'm sure you've heard of the infamous In-N-Out Burger restaurants. They are known for their simple menu of hamburgers, cheeseburgers, fresh cut fries, and thick shakes—just like the old drive-ins. Since I'm not a real fan of red meat, I never understood the big sensation about In-N-Out burgers, until this trip.

COFFEE BREAK WITH GEORGIA

One spring when my son Philip and I were in California to visit my sister Connie, we made the obligatory trek to In-N-Out. My brother-in-law Bruce ordered chocolate shakes; Philip had a cheeseburger, fries, and shake; and I sat down to my water.

We had places to go and things to do, and as usual Philip was taking a loooong time to eat. So to help him finish, I tore off a piece of his burger and popped it into my mouth. That's when it happened. My eyes welled up with tears. I could hardly speak because I was so choked up with memories, but I managed to look at my sister and get these words out: "It's a Fair Burger!"

She looked at her husband and said, "See, I told you so!"

Now to you that means nothing, but to my sister and me that's a cherished memory.

Every September in our small county fair, the Lions Club sponsored a special building where the best hamburgers in the world were sold to everyone who attended the fair. It was the biggest fund-raiser for the Lions. You couldn't beat a Fair Burger. The master chef was none other than my father, affectionately known as "Boodle." He cooked with flair, adding touches such as grilled buns, grilled onions, and cheese melted right on the burger as it slowly grilled. Yum! For my sisters and me, one of the highlights of our year, every year, was assisting in the booth. I guess that was our first experience as short order cooks. What memories!

With one bite, that burger turned into comfort food. It's no wonder my sister Sherry devours them. Even me, Miss No Burger, had an urge to stop for just one more on the way to the airport.

Fish grilled over an open fire must've been an ordinary meal that Simon Peter ate hundreds of times. I wonder how different it tasted to him after the resurrected Jesus made it for breakfast on the shore of the Sea of Tiberias. Peter had apparently given up on being a fisher of men, and had returned to being a fisher of fish. John 21 gives the impression that Jesus surprised the disciples when he appeared on the shore. The Scripture says he fixed them breakfast, then afterwards asked Peter, "Do you love me?" In that poignant conversation, Jesus reinstated Peter as his forgiven follower and clarified Peter's calling. From then on, whenever Peter tasted grilled fish, I'm sure he reminisced about his risen Savior and that emotional meal on the beach. Did the words *"Follow me . . . feed my sheep"* burn in his heart every time he tasted fish? Did each bite give him a renewed heart, a sense of mission, a new appetite for life?

Memories of past foods. Girlfriend, now that's what I call comfort food!

Savor the moments!

KEY POINT

Savor the moments!

> **Colossians 3:17** And whatever you do either in word or deed, do it all in the name of the Lord Jesus, giving thanks to God the Father through him.

My Name Is Not Cinderella

The Apostle Paul wrote to the Colossians because they seemed to be losing their focus. <u>Teachers</u> in Colossae (see illustration, page 143) were adding to their newfound Christianity elements of religions and practices they had previously been involved in. Young believers were falling away from the central theme of the Gospel: all **sufficiency** in Christ. Paul reminded them to do everything, whether in word or deed, as if doing it for Jesus. Christ was supposed to be the central focus of their new lives.

We homemakers sometimes lose our focus, too. We get such close-up exposure to the Cinderella work, we can end up hating homemaking. Sometimes when I pull on the rubber gloves, rev up the vacuum cleaner, and look at the housework that is before me I hear those mean stepsisters barking orders to sweet little Cinderella: "Cinderella do the dishes, Cinderella scrub the floors, Cinderella wash the clothes. . . ." I grumble and complain just like Martha did when she whined to Jesus that she was overworked preparing food for all the guests. Like Martha, I start looking for a sister Mary to shove some of my workload on to (Luke 10:38–42).

I know my name is not Cinderella, but some days, I sure feel like her. When that happens, I need to step back, refocus the lens of my life, and examine myself to see if I've gotten away from my life's mission of *"being about my Father's business"* (Luke 2:49 KJV).

When Jesus said he was being about his Father's business, that business was a mission of saving the world: **redemption**. I can't save the whole world, but I can help save a little piece of it by doing what I'm supposed to be doing daily, influencing those in my home. My assignment changes on a daily basis. One day being the best mother I can be takes priority; another day, the top task is to be the supportive spouse; or another day, the willing worker. But whatever we do, we need to remember the big picture, remain focused, and do it willfully as unto the Lord.

Was the Savior of all humanity wasting time when he washed his disciple's <u>feet</u>? No, in that **mundane** task he was showing them a divine approach to life. Just as that footwashing

☞ **GO TO:**

Colossians 2:8 (teachers)

sufficiency: capability; skill

☞ **GO TO:**

Hebrews 9:12 (redemption)

John 13:5–17 (feet)

Remember This . . .

redemption: Jesus paid the ransom so we could be free from sin

mundane: ordinary

Think About It

still impacts lives all these centuries later, household chores done with Jesus' attitude can have untold results for God's kingdom. Don't think of yourself as Cinderella. Think of yourself as Head Overseer of the Mop Ministry.

Marion Duckworth: In those moments when we do live in him at the office or supermarket or aerobics class, we know why we're here. Not merely to type fine business letters or find the best grocery bargains or get rid of cellulite. I'm here to stay at home in the Spirit and finish Jesus' work. Every moment I do that, my life will count.[3]

> **Proverbs 21:5** The plans of the diligent lead to profit as surely as haste leads to poverty.

Where's Helpful Heloise When You Need Her?

Proverbs indicates planning is the secret to a wise woman's success. You've heard people say, "Haste makes waste." This verse is where that idea came from. If you discipline yourself and make strategic plans, your <u>hard work</u> will not go to waste—it will reward great dividends.

Pick up any women's magazine and you'll be sure to find a section on smart ideas to make life easier. We're always looking for help. I'm sure "Hints from Heloise" has rescued many a stained blouse from the rag drawer. Emily Barnes, an author and home-management expert, can put your life together—15 minutes at a time.

Isn't it wonderful how God balanced the world with Organized Olivias and Disorganized Dotties? It's great for the economy too, because Olivia can make a killing off of Dottie as she zooms into Dottie's house and like Mr. Clean whirls up a white tornado. *Zap, zoom, zing*—Dottie has an instant home makeover, and Olivia pockets a "consulting fee."

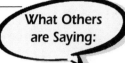

What Others are Saying:

KEY POINT

Wise women who build their house stay focused on *"being about [their] Father's business."*

☞ **GO TO:**

Proverbs 14:23 (hard work)

Everyday Life

EXAMPLES FROM THE BIBLE

Planning ahead helped many people in Bible times:

KEY POINT

A wise homemaker uses planning to build her house.

- God led Joseph to help Pharaoh implement plans that caused Egypt to prosper through seven years of famine. (Genesis 41:25–27)

- Jesus told the parable of ten virgins waiting for the bridegroom and the bridal party. Five were wise because they planned ahead and took extra oil for their lamps while they waited. The foolish virgins ran out of oil and went away to get more. While they were gone the bridegroom came and the foolish virgins missed the party. This was an analogy of Christ himself, the bridegroom of the church, and his second coming. (Matthew 25:1–3; John 3:29)

- Jesus commended planning through his parable of the servant who knew his master's will and was faithful and wise, prepared and waiting for his master's return. (Luke 12:35–47)

- We can also learn from Proverbs 22:3: "*A prudent man sees danger and takes refuge, but the simple keep going and suffer for it.*"

REMEMBER THIS

Say yes to planning, yes to organization, yes to uncluttered lives and schedules. Your hard work will bring you great dividends both financially and in the relationships with those you love.

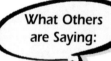

What Others are Saying:

Emilie Barnes: Simplify and unclutter your life by saying no to doing things and saving your yeses for the best things in life. Live a balanced life. Make time for yourself. Stop go-go-going. Be a person of "being" rather than a person of "doing."[4]

This Little Piggy Went to Market

There are some things you shouldn't put off. Grocery shopping just before a snowstorm hits is one of them. But honestly, I was oblivious to the snow report. Besides that, it's not supposed to snow before Thanksgiving. I just happened to have grocery shopping on my list for Monday night and moved it to the next day. I didn't know I would wake up to nine inches of snow and all my cupboards bare.

Sometimes I think I would rather go out and hunt my own food, or buy a farm and raise crops and livestock, than go grocery shopping. I personally don't know anyone who really enjoys this thankless task. It's time consuming, hectic, and definitely depressing when you see your weekly grocery bill cost more than your first car.

If you watch closely, you'll see different types of shoppers. There's Mother Hubbard who only goes to the store when there is nothing left in the house and the children are begging for bread. A friend of mine said one morning she was completely out of bread and had to resort to baking homemade biscuits. The funny thing was, her kids thought she was wonderful and wanted to know what they were celebrating.

Then there's Mrs. Busy, the one who goes shopping every day of the week, planning her evening meal in the car on the way home from work. The grocer loves her. He sees dollar signs as she bursts through the door, because research shows she'll spend a lot more money that way.

My favorite is Mrs. Commando, the shopper who declares war on shopping. Her strategy is laid out, the list completed, the menu decided weeks in advance, coupons clipped. Her weapon of choice, the pocket calculator, is grasped tightly in her hand. She marches into the store single-mindedly. She grabs a cart and begins dodging enemy fire (you know, those nice little ladies with the tempting sample carts of goodies). Mrs. Commando puts on her imaginary blinders and hustles through the store, aisle by aisle, depositing only items from her list into her cart. The yams are secured, sir! Rutabaga secured, sir! In order to avoid friendly fire, she never, ever takes her kids or husband with her, for they might try to sneak an unauthorized item into the cart.

I didn't always appreciate this shopper until she recruited me. Now I can say, I have declared war on shopping!

Laugh Out Loud

Since enlistment and boot camp I too am now Mrs. Commando, saving precious hours that I spend at home with my family counting the money my new tactics saved.

Life is too short to be standing in line at the so-called Express Lane with eight items or less. This little piggy went to market, but I'd rather raid it. The battle plan: get in, get out, nobody gets hurt. *"A wise woman is not afraid of the snow..."* (Proverbs 31:21).

> **Hebrews 13: 1–2** Keep on loving each other as brothers. Do not forget to entertain strangers, for by doing so some people have entertained <u>angels</u> without knowing it.

☞ **GO TO:**

Genesis 18:1–9 (angels)

☞ **GO TO:**

John 14:6 (truth)

Mark 6:10–11 (hospitality)

KEY POINT

Hospitality is "a good thing" for building your house.

Dial Martha Stewart 911

Hebrews was written to bring the Church to a deeper understanding of the <u>truth</u> of the Gospel. The writer of Hebrews wanted those truths put into action, and encouraged the believers to show love and hospitality to foreigners or strangers who needed food and shelter. Unlike today, in ancient times you couldn't find a Holiday Inn on every exit off the freeway. You couldn't even find a freeway. So it was a common practice to offer hospitality.

Jesus and his disciples depended solely on the <u>hospitality</u> of strangers as they went from village to village sharing their good news.

It's been said that Martha Stewart's first book, *Entertaining*, sparked the new transformation in how we welcome people in our homes. I've got to agree that Martha revived the long lost art of hospitality—and along the way built a giant "entertaining and hospitality" industry. She's everywhere: ten best-selling books, her own magazine, syndicated TV shows, newspaper columns. Now she's taking over K-mart with her own line of "entertaining accessories." Given Martha's track record, I think they'll eventually change the store name to K-Martha.

Think About It

You might think Martha's products sell because we're a bunch of self-indulgent entertainers who want to impress others. You may have a point there. But I believe Martha's products sell because somehow in our busy lives, we never learned how to be hospitable. We sense our lack and search for the lost art. Deep down, we want to know how to serve people and make them feel warm, welcomed, and loved. And if I may borrow one of Martha's favorite quotes, "It's a good thing."

We modern women need to be reminded and encouraged to share the spirit and love of Jesus by extending hospitality to strangers, friends, and family.

Dee Brestin: If you have a kitchen, purchase the ingredients for a meal which can be put together quickly to have on hand for unexpected company. Or, make a casserole and freeze it. Have a brownie mix in the cupboard. Then watch and see what needy (spiritually, emotionally, or physically) people God brings across your path.[5]

> **1 Timothy 3:4–5** He must manage his own family well and see that his children obey him with proper respect. (If anyone does not know how to manage his own family, how can he take care of God's church?)

Hospitality: the Warmth of the Home

Every organization needs leadership to survive. If it doesn't have someone at the helm, its members slowly lose <u>vision</u> and it will die a slow death. This is partly why the Apostle Paul wrote Timothy, a coworker, emphasizing the need for qualified <u>leadership</u> in the Church.

People who want to lead the church have to meet higher standards than "ordinary" believers. Leadership requires special skills and qualifications because new believers look to the leaders as examples and guides. Paul's **epistles** list fifteen "must have" qualifications, and the list includes hospitality (1 Timothy 3:2) and managing your household (Timothy 3:5). Leaders must enjoy having people in their homes and must be able to handle their own households.

You can learn a lot about someone by observing his or her family interactions. Does a leader's home reflect leadership? Do the children and spouse respect the leader? Do they love and respect God? Is God the head of their household? Paul makes a great point as he asks the rhetorical question, "How can a person lead a church, if he can't lead his home?"

 **KEY Outline:**

Hospitable Homemaker
creates a welcoming home
sees the need
hospitable toward
- family
- strangers

☞ **GO TO:**

Proverbs 29:18 (vision)

Acts 20:17; Titus 1:5 (leadership)

epistle: letters intended for public circulation

Paul's question applies to us, too. Put bluntly, he asks, Do you practice what you preach?

We can learn from the comparison of leadership in the home and church, for many of the same skills and qualifications are needed for both. As leaders in our home, we have higher standards to meet as our children look to us for vision and guidance. Before we offer hospitality to individuals beyond our home, are we showing hospitality to those inside our home?

Think About It

Homespun Wisdom: You don't have to be as great a cook as Julia Child and serve a delicious gourmet meal every night to be a successful homemaker. As Proverbs 15:17 says, *"Better a meal of vegetables where there is love, than a fattened calf with hatred."* The spirit of love and hospitality starts at home and is more important than the menu.

GEORGIA'S TIPS . . .

Here's a menu for a full course of hospitality:

1. Appetizer: Cut a big slice of gentleness.
2. Entree: Load a generous portion of patience on their plates.
3. Dessert: Roast marshmallows of mercy.

With fare like this, your husband and kids will quit skipping meals.

What Others are Saying:

Susan Alexander Yates: We need a vision. We must keep our vision of creating a family of friends clearly in mind. But remember, our vision is not ours alone. It is also that of our heavenly Father. In Him we have the unlimited resources of the universe: His wisdom, His power, and His forgiveness.[6]

Granny's Jam Cake

Fall brings back a multitude of rich memories. It has so many vivid sights, smells, and sounds: colorful harvest time, picking just the right pumpkin in the pumpkin patch, raking (and playing in) a pile of fallen leaves. It's usually my most homesick time of the year. But one year when I learned we would have out-of-state family around our Thanksgiving table, that homesickness gave way to preparation.

I thumbed through my recipe file and found the card for the most delectable food of the season—Jam Cake. Since we moved to Seattle, I found there are those who have never even heard of this fabulous cake. Evidently it's a dish from the South, but it's a family tradition and one of my most treasured comfort foods.

The recipe was written in my grandmother's hand. My eyes stung and my heart ached, but memories of Granny and her Jam Cake brought a smile to my face. I remembered her kitchen, filled with the spicy aroma of baking nutmeg mingled with the smell of brewing coffee. I could see her fluttering around the kitchen, busy as a bee, filled with excitement and anticipation because the holidays meant a house full of friends and family.

Sometimes I mirror my grandmother—especially in the kitchen. Just like her I start preparations weeks in advance, writing the menu in detail and compiling the grocery list. We have something else in common, too: like hers, when I'm in the process of cooking my kitchen looks as if the Pillsbury Doughboy® exploded. (At his funeral, they've *got* to sing "When the Roll is Called Up Yonder.") There's flour all over the countertops, utensils everywhere, and a sink full of dirty pots and pans, just like Granny's kitchen.

Laugh Out Loud

I hope I mirror my grandmother in other ways. No matter who gathered around her table any time of the year, she greeted them with love and hospitality. Her hospitality went beyond the Southern tradition; it was a love she mirrored from her Creator. Acceptance. Tolerance. A radiant love that gave you a sense of warmth and security. It's no wonder everyone cherished Granny and loved coming home for the holidays.

As the fall days grow colder, the smoke and smell of a crackling fire always chase away the chill of the air and stir up some late-autumn memories for me: heartwarming memories of Jam Cake, moments with Granny, and the treasure of her love.

> **Philemon 1:7** Your love has given me great joy and encouragement, because you, brother, have refreshed the hearts of the saints.

KEY POINT

Extending sincere hospitality lifts hearts and turns them toward God.

☞ **GO TO:**

Romans 12:13 (hospitality)

Philemon 1:2 (church)

Philemon: a wealthy Christian

Heartfelt Hospitality

The book of Philemon is a very short personal letter from the Apostle Paul to a coworker and friend, Philemon. Paul pens this letter from prison in Rome to his friend in Colossae. He addresses what our attitudes should be toward those who are different from us.

Paul opens by thanking God for Philemon's kindness. Philemon not only had been a blessing to Paul; he had *"refreshed the hearts"* of God's people. **Philemon** must have been known for his generous <u>hospitality</u> and kindness throughout the city. He even opened his home for the <u>church</u> to meet there. (I'll bet if he were from southern Colossae he would say, "Y'all come back now, hear?")

A simple, sincere gesture of hospitality can offer hope as you refresh the hearts of those in need. As believers, we extend hospitality not because we're just really nice people, but because those who are in need see a testimony of Christ.

REMEMBER THIS

What Others are Saying:

Linda Evans Shepherd: Trapped in life's pitfalls, you need a tug, a push, a gentle reminder to keep trying. You need the hand of a friend. That's the beauty of encouragement. It provides a way to go on despite life's hazards. Not only do we need to receive this gift, however, we also need to give it.[7]

☞ **Check It Out:**

2 Kings 4:8–37

prophet: person who receives messages from God

SNAPSHOTS OF WOMEN IN THE BIBLE
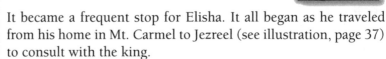

The Shunammite Woman

It became a frequent stop for Elisha. It all began as he traveled from his home in Mt. Carmel to Jezreel (see illustration, page 37) to consult with the king.

His reputation preceded him. But even if it hadn't, his hairy cloak gave away the fact that he was a **prophet**. Peasants and kings turned to him for help as he relayed messages to them from God.

A wealthy woman from Shunem (see illustration, page 37)

stopped him on his travels and persuaded Elisha and his servant, Gehazi, to eat with them. She didn't exactly need to twist Elisha's arm, since his stomach growled in hunger. He enjoyed the tasty stew, grains, and fresh fruit she provided. He left replenished, rested, and renewed for his travels.

The Shunammite woman recognized Elisha as a holy man and asked her husband to build a guest room for him. It was no king's palace, but it was better than many other lodgings Elisha had used during his travels.

Elisha was so grateful for her hospitality that he sent his servant, Gehazi, to see how they could repay her kindness. Elisha offered to use his political influence to have the king protect her. She declined the offer, for there was no need; she dwelt among her people where she felt safe and secure. She expected nothing in return from this prophet.

Gehazi told Elisha they had no children. In her old age and disbelief, she was shocked when Elisha promised her a son. But as he foretold, a miracle occurred: She conceived and bore a son.

Years passed. One day her little boy went to the harvesting fields with his father in the heat of the day and collapsed, apparently from heat stroke. The father quickly had a servant carry the son to his mother.

She cradled her son in her arms. She rocked him back and forth and dipped a cloth in springwater to cool his forehead. Then his body went limp in her arms. Her heart froze and she gasped.

Her only hope was to find the man of miracles. She carried her son to the guest room, laid him carefully on the bed, kissed his forehead, and shut the door. She dropped all formality as she and a servant rushed across country to fetch Elisha.

When at last she reached Elisha at Mt. Carmel, she ran and fell at his feet. Her mourning and anguish welled up as a tormented question: Why? Why did you give me this son, only to take him away?

Elisha responded as rapidly as possible. Elisha didn't answer her question. Instead, he brought the Shunammite woman's son back to life.

The room built for a stranger's refreshment became the room where a family was resurrected.

KEY Outline:

Shunammite Woman

discerning
hospitable
generous
had faith in God
was rewarded

KEY POINT

The Shunammite woman reaped blessing because of her hospitality.

ACT OF GOD

barren old woman conceives

ACT OF GOD

son brought back to life

Think About It

☞ **GO TO:**

1 Peter 4:9 (hospitality)

John 16:33 (courage)

John 9:2 (faith)

The Shunammite woman had an open, discerning heart. When she saw a man in need she was willing not only to feed him, but also to go the extra mile and provide lodging whenever he passed by. She expected nothing in return for her generosity, but was blessed through the miracle of birth and the miracle of resurrection.

In her time of crisis she knew who to turn to—a man of God. Because of her <u>hospitality</u>, <u>courage</u> and <u>faith</u> she received abundant gifts from God. She learned that it is truly *"more blessed to give than receive"* (Acts 20:35).

> **Exodus 31:1–3** Then the Lord said to Moses, "See, I have chosen Bezalel son of Uri, the son of Hur, of the tribe of Judah and I have filled him with the Spirit of God, with skill, ability and knowledge in all kinds of crafts.

Glue Guns and the Tabernacle

tabernacle: *place of worship*

Bezalel: *craftsman that helped build the tabernacle*

Aholiab: *craftsman, Bezalel's assistant*

☞ **GO TO:**

Exodus 31:6 (Aholiab)

2 Chronicles 2:4 (temple)

2 Chronicles 2:10 (compensated)

Since God designed the **tabernacle** (see GWBI, page 31) and gave Moses detailed instructions, it's not surprising that God also designed specific individuals with special creative abilities to fulfill his design.

God deserves and demands our best. The tabernacle was filled with gold, sliver, bronze, jewels, and carved wood. Each required a skilled workman which God provided when he had Moses send for **Bezalel** and <u>**Aholiab**</u>.

Generations later, as King Solomon went about his God-appointed task of building a magnificent <u>temple</u> (see GWBI, pages 70–71) of worship, he also needed the finest craftsmen to complete the project. Also believing God deserves only the best, Solomon negotiated with the Phoenician King Hiram of Tyre to send him skillful servants, who would be <u>compensated</u> for their work. King Hiram sent Huram-abi, his very own master craftsman.

EXAMPLES FROM THE BIBLE

Just as God designed specific abilities in the hearts of these craftsmen, likewise, I believe he gave women special abilities to accomplish their unique tasks.

• Sherah, a descendant of Ephraim, was mentioned as

Women Using a Spindle

After the flax fibers were clean and dry (right), they were drawn out by hand and wrapped around a spindle. The spindle was rotated to twist the fibers into thread (left).

building three villages that were ancient border towns between Benjamin and Ephraim. (1 Chronicles 7:24)

- Female perfumers used their talents to make scented waters from orange trees, violets, and roses. (1 Samuel 8:13)

- Dorcas was a seamstress and sewed garments for the needy widows at Joppa. (Acts 9:36–42)

KEY Outline:

Creative Homemaker
*unique God-given abilities
creative at home
shares creativity*

Everyday Life

I wasn't introduced to a glue gun until a couple of years ago. I don't know how I ever lived without one; it is such a marvelous invention.

Being creative is the craze. Even Rosie O'Donnell has a craft day on her talk show. Your own little craft corner can be more than a creative outlet for you as you design, weave, sew, glue, paint, or do what you do. It can also bless your family and those who admire your creations.

KEY POINT

Creations from the hands and heart are treasured possessions.

God created us all different. There's only one you, and you can decorate or create with your own God-given unique-ness. How would you like to display his beauty in your life? What's stopping you?

Think About It

Liz Curtis Higgs: Dear friends and others who have gifted me with their creations over the years could only guess at how their handwork has touched my life. Over a desk in our office is the cross-stitched phrase: "Working for the Lord doesn't pay much, but the retirement plan is out of this world!"[8]

KEY POINT

You can get heavenly results with your craft if you apprentice under the Master.

> **Exodus 35:25** Every skilled woman spun with her hands and brought what she had spun—blue, purple or scarlet yarn or fine linen.

Stitch by Stitch

tabernacle: Hebrew for "tent of meeting"

There was a magnificent amount of work required in order to complete the **tabernacle**. The whole community worked together as they responded with their gifts and talents. Spinning was considered women's work in Bible times (see illustration, page 195), so the women spun yarn and fine linens for the tabernacle—God's place of worship.

God opens doors for one who places her life, her heart, and her creations into his hands. You may never know how your craft touched someone. But you serve the Creator who can weave all of our gifts together into one beautiful masterpiece, the Body of Christ.

Everyday Life

☞ **GO TO:**

Psalm 51:12 (willingly)

2 Chronicles 2 (worship)

Melody's first attempt at crafting began when her church decided to hold a craft fair and they were short on vendors. She says even though she felt she was a little short on talent, she would <u>willingly</u> see what she could throw together to fill a booth.

The response was overwhelming. The booth swarmed with customers, and she walked away with the second highest sales of the day. Her simple floral arranging not only grew into a lucrative business, but a creative release and a Christian outreach as well. She also volunteers her creative talents to decorate her house of <u>worship</u>. Members and visitors alike comment on how beautiful her arrangements are. They feel as if they've walked into an elegant hotel lobby.

Melody says with gratitude and humility, "I never dreamed that this would be an area that God could use me in, but I am constantly thankful that I took the risk to see what God and I could whip up together."

Whether you are creating special memories for your children, decorating a church, or sitting around a quilting frame stitching a quilt for a woman in need, you are laboring in love. Share your creativity. *"She selects wool and flax and works with eager hands"* (Proverbs 31:13).

Think About It

STUDY QUESTIONS

1. What type of woman can build a house called home?
2. How was homemaking looked upon in the early Church? (Titus 2:4–6)
3. How does the Holy Spirit help us in building our homes?
4. Martha once grumbled about her everyday duties as a homemaker. What caused a change in her life?
5. When discouraged over the hassles of housework, what can we remember to keep us from grumbling and complaining?
6. In ancient Bible times, how did one offer hospitality? How can we do the same?
7. In return for her hospitality how was the Shunammite woman blessed?

CHAPTER WRAP-UP

- A home needs to be a safe haven for its family members. As the heartbeat of the home, a woman can rediscover the lost art and joy of homemaking if she realizes the profound impact the servant heart of Christ has on people. Welcome your family home with open arms.

- The occupation "homemaker" is one of the greatest and most challenging careers of all times. It is a God-designed, treasured calling for women.

- The kitchen is the gathering place of the home. Make it a fun and special place that is always open and ready to satisfy a hungry tummy or starving soul.

- There is eternal value to our everyday endeavors. If you stay focused on being about your Father's business, every seemingly mundane thing you do will count.

- Scripture reveals hospitality as a requirement in our walk of life. Extending heartfelt hospitality not only blesses those who receive but also is a great blessing for those who give. Hospitality starts at home. Then share Christ's spirit and love with those beyond your walls.

- Your own unique creations can serve as further expressions of God's love and glory. Being creative is part of being created in God's image, so don't hold back.

GEORGIA'S BOOKSHELF

Some of Georgia's favorite books on the subject of homemakers:

- *The Joy of Hospitality: A Bible Study for Women*, Dee Brestin, Chariot Victor
- *Creative Home Organizer*, Emily Barnes, Harvest House
- *A House Full of Friends*, Susan Alexander Yates, Focus on the Family
- *Disciples of a Beautiful Woman*, Ann Ortland, Word
- *Only Angels Can Wing It*, Liz Curtis Higgs, Thomas Nelson

Part Four

FELLOWSHIP AND COMMUNITY INVOLVEMENT

REVEREND FUN

"Don't get too excited fella, I'm the mediocre Samaritan . . .
I only give you a bandaid and then I'm off."

8 TOUCHING LIVES, SERVING OTHERS

Putting Your Gift to Work in the World

Here We Go

I wish someone would come up with a better recruiting mascot than Uncle Sam. As a child I got nightmares from that picture of a mean-spirited, tight-lipped, finger-pointing old coot. I could never imagine being a willing recruit for him.

In the spring of 1997 volunteerism got a jump start as Colin Powell chaired the president's Volunteerism Summit in Philadelphia. (Good choice for a recruiter. He's a lot better looking than Uncle Sam.) Celebrities, past United States presidents, and CEOs all jumped in, waving the volunteer flag and encouraging Americans to pull up their bootstraps, join hands, and volunteer. After all, it's our civic duty! As hoped, thousands of ordinary citizens volunteered their time and energy.

I believe it is our civic duty to volunteer. More importantly, however, it is our Christian duty to touch lives and serve others as we follow the example of Christ, our tender, loving, and caring Master. He commanded us to *"love one another as I have loved you"* (John 15:12). Now that's a great recruiting slogan!

Service is not reserved for a designated group of people to do. The act of serving is for everyone. Once we discover our own special abilities and spiritual gifts, we can put them to work and make a difference in the lives of others if we are willing to serve.

Serving may be as simple as responding to a next-door neighbor's crisis, being involved in a community canned food drive, or implementing your gifts at your local church. Your service may be a

KEY POINT

You (yes, you!) can make a difference in the lives of others.

KEY Outline:

Serving Others
touches hearts
nourishes the soul
fuels ministry

lifetime of committed involvement, or your situation may only permit you to commit to a short-term mission trip. Regardless of what shape it takes in each of our lives, we must reach out to others. When all is said and done, a whole lot more is said than done. We need to put more "show" in our Gospel "show and tell."

Let's see what the Bible says about touching lives by serving others.

> **1 Corinthians 12:4–5** There are different kinds of gifts, but the same Spirit. There are different kinds of service, but the same Lord. There are different kinds of working, but the same God works all of them in all men.

Unwrap Your Gift and Use It

☞ **GO TO:**

Galatians 4:6 (Holy Spirit)

Romans 12:3–8 (gifts)

Ephesians 4:7–11 (spiritual)

As Paul writes the church at Corinth (see illustration, page 143), he zooms in on problems relating to how the world views our actions. In this particular Bible passage he deals with how we discover and use our gifts to further the work of the Church.

When Jesus left to return to his Father, he gave us the gift of the <u>Holy Spirit</u> to dwell within us. The Spirit in turn gives us <u>gifts</u> that we can use in ministering to one another. These may come in the form of an added bonus to our traits, temperaments, and abilities, or they may be <u>spiritual</u> gifts. Whatever the gift, Paul encourages us to discover, unwrap, and put our gifts to work in the world.

 Everyday Life

 KEY Outline:

Believers Are Given
the Holy Spirit
ministering gifts
spiritual gifts

"We would be homeless and in a shelter without Rachel," says George Weathereby. For two decades, Rachel Sparkowich has been running Operation Blessing, a nondenominational Christian ministry that gives away clothing, furniture, housewares, and food in Portsmouth, New Hampshire. About two thousand families walk through the center's doors each year, referred by shelters, churches, and welfare organizations.

On a typical day at Operation Blessing, Rachel, a tall, thin, cheery woman spends most of her time in the office organizing the center's 70 volunteers, making arrangements for various pickups, and offering guidance and encouragement to people who ask for it.

Merriel Thomas, a volunteer, said, "Operation Blessing met my physical needs. Some people come in here wondering if God exists. When they leave, they know he does."[1]

I'm sure if you asked Rachel, she would readily admit that her work could not be completed without volunteers. Any director of a nonprofit organization would probably tell you the same. Some organizations are so short on help, they recruit almost frantically. The key to a successful volunteer is matching their unique God-given gifts with the appropriate ministry task.

GEORGIA'S  TIPS . . .

You have your very own special gift or gifts. There are ministry recruiters out there sitting on the edge of their seats waiting for the phone to ring as they pray for the perfect willing servant. Here are a few organizations that can use your gifts of service:

- Habitat for Humanity is always looking for serving hands that can handle a hammer and help build a home.
- Crisis pregnancy centers around the country are looking for women with tender hearts and listening ears that care not only about the unborn, but the unwed as well.
- Homeless shelters need cheerful smiling faces to offer food, shelter, and a ray of hope for lonely lives.
- The Salvation Army (and some church ministries) could use skilled mechanics to repair cars that have been donated for single mothers in need of reliable transportation.

Opportunities surround you in your community. What are you waiting for? Unwrap your spiritual gift and put it to use so the world can see Christianity in action.

EXAMPLES FROM THE BIBLE

As we see the acts of women in the Bible, we can examine their stories and see what spiritual gifts these women most likely possessed. Here are some examples of women who had serving gifts.

- Hospitality is the God-given ability to welcome and graciously care for and serve both strangers and guests through a receptive and warm attitude (1 Peter 4:9).[2] **Lydia** used her gift of hospitality by inviting the Apostle Paul into her home and provided practical provisions of fellowship, food, and shelter (Acts 16:13–15).

KEY POINT

You have your very own special gift or gifts.

Lydia: a businesswoman who was converted by Paul

Dorcas: a woman disciple who died and was miraculously brought back to life by Peter

Phoebe: a first-century deaconess

KEY POINT

Do you know what your God-given gifts are? Discover and use them.

Priscilla: a Christian woman who served with Paul in Corinth

What Others are Saying:

- Helps, or service, is the God-given ability to complete practical and necessary tasks, thereby allowing others to succeed in their own giftedness (Romans 12:7).[3] **Dorcas** used her gift of helps as she made garments for the needy widows (Acts 9:36). **Phoebe** used her gift of helps as she assisted Paul in delivering his letter to the church at Rome. She also was known for helping others in her own church home at Cenchrea (Romans 16:1–2).[4]

- Faith is the God-given ability to trust that, in response to prayer, God will do what he says he is going to do (1 Corinthians 12:9).[5] Mary, the mother of Jesus, used her gift of faith as she trusted God to fulfill his promise of a virgin birth through her (Luke 1:38, 45; 2:19).

- Teaching is a God-given ability to comprehend, clearly explain, and apply the word of God to the lives of those who listen (Romans 12:7).[6] **Priscilla** used her gift of teaching when she and her husband helped Paul teach the churches and as they instructed Apollos in the full message of Christ (Acts 18:18–19, 24–28).

Arthur F. Miller, Jr.: Following God's will and plan for your life means ordering your life around his gifts to you—your design and giftedness. It means finding and remaining in a call that God has given you—sharing through all your gifts, bearing good fruit in your day-to-day life, and producing good products worthy of praise.[7]

COFFEE BREAK WITH GEORGIA

She Wasn't in the Count

It was Thursday afternoon and at our house, that's Skate Deck afternoon. If Philip is caught up on his homework, we meet his friends for two hours of in-line skating fun as they chase each other around and around the rink.

Every now and then the moms abandon the snack tables, lace up the ol' skates and get some exercise. Of course we have to be very careful not to skate too close to our children, or even act like we know them. So we skate incognito, zooming by our own children without saying a word.

One day we invited some friends to join the crew. They have a four-year-old named Taylor who tried with all of her might but

---

204 WHAT'S IN THE BIBLE FOR . . . WOMEN

just couldn't keep up with the big kids. That didn't bother her. She scooted around the rink with a big smile on her face and enjoyed every minute. Her mom was busy with her big sister, so when Taylor had a big spill I slowed down, helped her up, and asked if she wanted some company. Hand in hand we skated around the rink, stopping occasionally to pick Taylor up from another tumble.

Like most preschoolers, Taylor is a little talker. She chitchatted away, her brown little locks of hair blowing in the wind when speedsters whizzed by. She's an adorable, sweet child you just want to squeeze every time you see her. As she looked up at me with her beautiful sparkling blue eyes, I silently thanked God for ministries like Special Delivery.

Special Delivery is a pregnancy help center in Kirkland, Washington. Like other pregnancy centers across the country that reach out to girls and women with unplanned pregnancies, they offer an alternative to abortion. After receiving help from this crisis pregnancy center, Taylor's biological mother chose life and placed her in an adoptive home. She joined a wonderful, loving Christian family, who, unable to have children of their own, had already adopted a big sister (who anxiously awaited Taylor's arrival from the hospital).

She's only four, so January 22 holds no special meaning to her. But January 22, 1998, just a couple of weeks from the day we skated, marked the grim twenty-fifth anniversary of *Roe v. Wade*, the Supreme Court decision that legalized abortion. Twenty-five years later, 35 million babies are dead.

I thank God for organizations like Special Delivery and for willing servants who share their lives and spiritual gifts with others. I support and pray for ministries on the front lines that make a loving effort to help women choose life. I thank God someone chose to make a difference so my little friend and her sister were not counted among the 35 million.

Without a shadow of a doubt, I know one day my skating partner will understand that life is a precious gift from God. When she hears her story she will be overwhelmed by the abundant love that was poured out by so many, to keep her out of the death count. I held her little hand that day because someone became a servant and chose to make a difference.

KEY POINT

Praise God for ministries like Special Delivery!

> **Philippians 2:3–5** Do nothing out of selfish ambition or vain conceit, but in humility consider others better than yourselves. Each of you should look not only to your own interests, but also to the interests of others. Your attitude should be the same as that of Jesus Christ.

Who Me, Join the Peace Corps? No Way!

If the Apostle Paul had a favorite church, I think it would be the church at Philippi, which he referred to as his "joy and crown." Like a favorite son who's never any trouble and brings joy to a parent, so was this church. They followed Christ and served others.

But like children we need to be reminded from time to time how to get along in life. Paul called the Christians in Philippi to **humble** themselves, to look inward, and to examine their motives. In other words (paraphrased by Georgia) he asks, "Why are you doing your good works? Is it to build yourselves up in the eyes of man or is it to <u>please</u> God and honor his kingdom? Is it for your own selfish desires or for the joy your service will bring to others?"

EXAMPLES FROM THE BIBLE

Humility is lowliness, meekness, and mildness; a freedom from pride.

- Jesus made humility a cornerstone of character. (Matthew 18:4; 23:12)
- Jesus by his humility drew men to himself. (Matthew 11:28–30; John 13:12–17)
- Paul emphasized the humility of Jesus. (Philippians 2:3–5; 2 Corinthians 8:9)
- Paul commended us to be humble toward one another. (Romans 12:10; 1 Corinthians 13:4–6)[8]

During the Volunteer Summit I mentioned earlier, **philanthropy** reigned. Many large corporations not only organized their army of employee volunteers, but also donated big bucks. As I read the news coverage each day, I thought it was going to turn into a "Look at me, I gave more money than you" contest.

☞ **GO TO:**

Philippians 4:1 (joy and crown)

1 Peter 5:5–6 (humble)

John 8:29 (please)

humble: *not proud; not self-assertive*

KEY Outline:

Humble Yourself
as Christ did
as a child
as a servant

KEY POINT

Service is outward expression of inward compassion.

philanthropy: *charity; generosity*

REMEMBER THIS

You may not have the time or the special calling on your heart to sign up for a hitch with the Peace Corps and serve abroad in an underdeveloped area. But whatever vehicle you choose for your service, let your attitude be the same as Jesus when you reach out to help others. Take a good look inward to understand your motives. As important as the gesture of service is the spirit of service.

In ancient Israel, every man above the age of 20 was called to be a <u>soldier</u>; they were on permanent reserve duty. Just as Abraham <u>called</u> his men and gathered a posse to rescue Lot, a tribal leader could call on men in his tribe for service at any time. Each man had to submit and humble himself for his time of service. Under God's leadership we must be willing to submit and humble ourselves for acts of service.

☞ **GO TO:**

Numbers 1:3; 2:2; 10:14 (soldier)

Genesis 14:1–24 (called)

What Others are Saying:

Bill Hybels: Self-indulgence is a dead-end road. Look around and you will see example after example of shattered lives resulting from a "me first" mindset. Jesus wants his follower to know that true fulfillment comes only through faithful service to God and humble service to others. This is the only sensible way to live.[9]

> **Luke 18:29** "I tell you the truth," Jesus said to them, "no one who has left home or wife or brothers or parents or children for the sake of the kingdom of God will fail to receive many times as much in this age and, in the age to come, eternal life."

Career Soldier

When Jesus said this, he had just looked deep inside the rich young ruler and seen money on the throne of his heart instead of God (see illustrations, page 208). This young man was single-minded toward his riches, but not his God. Jesus wasn't saying you couldn't have riches and still be a follower. Money itself wasn't the problem; it was a heart condition that kept the wealthy young man away from God's kingdom.

Those listening thought people got rich because God approved of their lives, and thus poured out his blessings in wealth. Jesus corrected them, and explained that those who leave all to follow him would be blessed abundantly, not only now but also in eternity.

KEY POINT

God promises blessing upon you when you serve.

Lepton

This coin, circulating at the time of the rich young ruler, was worth less than 1/64 of the Roman denarius.

Denarius

The denarius, the coin most mentioned in the New Testament, was a day's wage for the average working man.

Think About It

 REMEMBER THIS

☞ **GO TO:**

Romans 12:14 (body)

Colossians 3:4 (focus)

A career soldier is a soldier who has committed to a lifetime of service in the military. As soldiers for Christ, many believers become involved in a short-term service. Then, once they have a taste of the action, they enlist for a lifetime of service. They become career soldiers under the authority and leadership of Christ the King.

Jesus could have meant that his followers would receive a spiritual blessing, or he could have been describing riches in the physical realm. I've experienced both. Over the years we followed God's lead even when it meant leaving our extended families and moving out of our comfort zones. Blessings have always followed. *Sometimes* wealth, but *always* spiritual blessings.

The Church body has many parts, yet is still one <u>body</u> with one central <u>focus</u>. Whether we serve in part-time, short-term, or full-time ministry, we are all essential to the function of the body.

EXAMPLES FROM THE BIBLE

The Bible gives examples of men and women who became career soldiers for God as they spent a lifetime of service in ministry.

- The twelve disciples left families, occupations, and homes to follow Jesus and teach his Word. (Matthew 4:18–22; 10:1–4; 11:1)
- Eli, the high priest of Israel, lived at Shiloh in a dwelling adjoining the Tabernacle. He gave a lifetime of service to God. (1 Samuel 1–4; 14:3; 1 Kings 2:27)
- John the Baptist lived as a Nazirite in the desert. He dedicated his life to preaching repentance in preparation for the coming of the Messiah. (Matthew 11:12–14; Luke 1:15; 3:4–14)
- Anna lived and worked in the Temple as she dedicated herself to serving God. (Luke 2:36–38)

Mother Teresa: We must grow in love and to do this we must go on loving and loving and giving and giving until it hurts—the way Jesus did. Do ordinary things with extraordinary love: little things like caring for the sick and homeless, the lonely and the unwanted, washing and cleaning for them.[10]

> **What Others are Saying:**

I Sat Next to a Legend

COFFEE BREAK WITH GEORGIA

His Bible fit in his hand like an old worn glove. Creased and cracked leather showed years of extended use. Only a few flecks of gold leaf remained on the tattered edges. The pages had a distinct and unusual curve in the middle. He lifted it. His thumb fit perfectly in the curve. With one flick of the wrist, pages that years ago were once stiff and crisp, floated by like feathers.

This was a great moment for me, for I sat next to a legend.

While visiting my sister in Kentucky, I had the opportunity to attend church services in Grayson, Kentucky, home of my alma mater, Kentucky Christian College. I walked into the auditorium and saw one of my favorite professors, Dr. Donald Nash, who instructed my Greek and New Testament courses.

I invited myself to sit with Dr. Nash and his wife. Before church we chatted for a few minutes and caught up on what he had been doing over the few years since his retirement. Suddenly, organ music filled the air and halted our conversation. A silence fell over the audience and services began, but I was reminiscing about days gone by.

As a young college student, I didn't realize the credentials and status my professors held. Usually I was too busy gossiping about their quirks to appreciate the knowledge they possessed. But as time has passed and I've lived life, I hold individuals like Dr. Nash in high regard. Before my visit, while doing research for a writing assignment, I had just reread one of his books. I was in awe of his writing ability and the insights I gained from him.

Funny thing is, I read that particular book years earlier in college. It was required. I don't remember it having the same affect on me then. I'm sure as it sat on my library shelf, crushed between other college reference books collecting dust, the content didn't magically change. Thank goodness I did.

The minister presiding over the church service, also a former student of this great teacher, began reading a passage of Scripture. I watched as Dr. Nash held his Bible and followed along. Knowing Dr. Nash, the constant wear on his Bible was not only from teaching his students, but from his personal walk with Christ. I wondered if years from now my Bible would show the same signs of use.

Dr. Nash is a master of his trade. He believes passionately in the subjects he has taught and written about. As a young man Dr. Nash unwrapped his spiritual gift of teaching and as he committed himself to a lifetime of Christian service, gave it away. Thousands of men and women have learned about the Bible in his classroom. Then as these students went out into the world sharing the gospel and serving others, countless more individuals have been indirectly touched by this one man.

I thank God for granting me a spiritual heritage that includes men of Dr. Nash's stature. Our prayer should be that we will be a part of someone's spiritual heritage as God uses us to touch the lives of others.

Thank you, Dr. Nash.

> **Matthew 25:34–36** "Then the King will say to those on his right, 'Come, you who are blessed by my Father; take your inheritance, the kingdom prepared for you since the creation of the world. For I was hungry and you gave me something to eat, I was thirsty and you gave me something to drink, I was a stranger and you invited me in, I needed clothes and you clothed me, I was sick and you looked after me, I was in prison and you came to visit me. I tell you the truth, whatever you did for one of the least of these brothers of mine, you did for me.'"

KEY POINT

Every little bit helps. It's better to serve in small segments of time than no time at all.

Reserves Soldier

In Matthew, Jesus spoke about the importance of doing good deeds. Looking to the coming **judgment** and the end of time, Jesus identified himself with those in need and taught the importance of making a difference in the lives of others through social involvement.

However, Jesus also explained that good works alone will not ensure someone a place in heaven. We can't board a chartered "Works Plane" to get us to heaven; God's <u>grace</u> through the death of his <u>Son</u> is our only vehicle. However, our actions and <u>good deeds</u> are proof of our faith, love, and commitment to Christ.

A reserve soldier is part of the country's armed forces, subject to call in an emergency. Like a reserve soldier, this may be a time in your life when you can only serve if an emergency arises. You may only be able to carve out a couple of hours of your week to offer help, or set aside a week of your vacation for a short-term involvement. However small it may be, make a commitment to serve.

Isaiah Shoels, a victim of the tragic Littleton, Colorado high school shooting, was remembered for serving others. Before his death he gave of his time and energy to build a house in Mexico during a short-term missionary trip with his church. The lives he touched will be changed forever.

Through the CNN worldwide coverage of his funeral, the testimony of his life and his dedication to God were heard

 GO TO:

Romans 14:10;
 2 Corinthians 5:10
 (judgment)

Ephesians 2:8–9 (grace)

John 14:6 (Son)

Matthew 5:16 (good
 deeds)

Everyday Life

judgment: punishment for sin. A reference to the last day, when all people will stand before Christ to be judged by him.

Think About It

throughout the world. I'm sure the King of Kings said, "Hey, I know you; come on in, Isaiah," as he welcomed this young servant to heaven with arms open wide.

What Others are Saying:

Kay Cole James: Do you want to know how to transform America? Look in the mirror. Look to God. Fall to your knees. Ask him to change you. Get up. Live life. As long as we can keep the problems at arm's length, we can keep the solutions there as well. It is easy to demand change in our government, change in our economic system, and change in our social institution—but to transform America, we must be a changed people.[11]

☞ **Check It Out:**

2 Kings 22;
    2 Chronicles 34:22

SNAPSHOTS OF WOMEN IN THE BIBLE

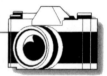

Huldah

It didn't surprise Shallum when five of the King's messengers showed up at his doorstep. As the keeper of the King's wardrobe, he was used to receiving members of the King's court. But never had the King sent a chief priest and a scribe for wardrobe business.

It wasn't wardrobe business. The King's representatives wished to speak to Huldah, Shallum's wife! They had a request from the King.

KEY Outline:

Huldah
  served for a lifetime
  loved Scripture
  taught
  was wise
  was discerning

When King Josiah's workmen were busy repairing the Temple that Solomon had built over three hundred years before, they discovered a treasure. It was customary to place important documents in the foundations of buildings. The workmen came across the Book of the Law (see illustration, page 213), the scrolls containing the laws of Moses. They were convinced that Solomon must have placed the scrolls in the cornerstone of the Temple.

During the reign of King Josiah's father, Manasseh, copies of the scrolls had been destroyed when Manasseh turned away from God and began worshipping false gods. Now the succeeding generation was not very familiar with the Law. But the King's men knew Huldah had studied the scrolls and the laws of Moses.

Huldah had made friends with Josiah's mother, Jedidah. Over the years Josiah had watched Huldah and found her to be wise and dedicated to God. He respected the women in his life and now wanted Huldah to tell him if his discovery was authentic.

KEY POINT

God uses us where we are and with whatever gifts we possess.

Shallum watched as his wife studied the Book of the Law. Huldah's years of preparation proved valuable. She found the scrolls totally authentic, and used her gift of prophecy to give the King a message.

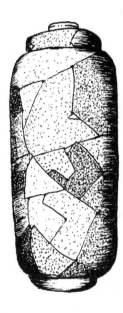

Dead Sea Scrolls

The Book of the Law was believed to be the scroll of the "law of Moses," the core of the book of Deuteronomy. It was a great discovery and would have looked just like the Dead Sea Scrolls discovered in 1947 that were fragments of every book of the Hebrew Bible except Esther. The scrolls were found in caves near Qumran, on the northwestern shore of the Dead Sea.

Huldah boldly foretold that the Lord would bring evil upon Judah because the country had turned to idols. But she assured King Josiah that because of his tender heart he would be spared; that he would be gathered unto his <u>fathers</u> before this doom would occur. He would not suffer.

Assured that these scrolls really held God's Law, King Josiah proclaimed them publicly and immediately put them into action.

Huldah had access to the palace through her husband's work for many years. How long did the king know of her? Did he know and respect her as he grew from a boy to a man? God uses us where we are and with what gifts we possess.

☞ **GO TO:**

2 Kings 21:16, 21 (fathers)

Think About It

Huldah, as a woman, could have been intimidated by suddenly being thrust into the highest level of Judah's politics. But she followed her calling, and through her service national revival ensued. Huldah let God use her in a mighty way.

> **Luke 10:27** He answered: "'Love the Lord your God with all your heart and with all your soul and with all your strength and with all your mind'; and, 'Love your neighbor as yourself.'"

KEY POINT

A neighbor is anyone in need.

Won't You Be My Neighbor?

Once when Jesus taught, a student of the laws of Moses stood up and asked what he must do to inherit eternal life. Jesus' response was like a first-century version of *Jeopardy*, since Jesus answered a question with a question. (Obviously, this is where Merv Griffin, *Jeopardy*'s creator, got the idea.) He answered by asking the young man, *"What is written in the Law and how do you read it?"* (Luke 10:26).

☞ **GO TO:**

Deuteronomy 6:5 (loving)

Leviticus 19:18 (neighbor)

Luke 10:25–37 (parable)

The law student knew that Jesus knew the correct answer, and may have believed that Jesus was looking for a way to trip him up. To play it safe, the law student quoted the Old Testament law concerning <u>loving</u> God and loving your <u>neighbor</u>. Ding! Jesus said they were the right answers. The student gained a thousand points and control of the board.

But that wasn't enough to win, and you know how lawyers hate to lose. So he asked a Double Jeopardy question: "Who is my neighbor?"

This time instead of playing a game of questions, Jesus answered with a story. It was the <u>parable</u> of the Good Samaritan, a traveler who helped a stranger he found beaten, naked, and left for dead beside the road. Religious leaders passed the victim by, but the Samaritan provided food, shelter, and medical care, expecting nothing in return.

So who is my neighbor? The correct *Jeopardy* response is, "Who is anyone in need?"

Jesus' answers always had a way of getting to the root of the problem. We often don't want to take time to help people, even those we know. Jesus' parable shows how important it is to stop to help everyone, even those we don't know or like.

For many reasons we have an aversion to getting to know our neighbors. Sometimes we even joke about it. We laughed as Tim, the "Tool Time" handyman on the sitcom *Home Improvement*, never saw his neighbor's face for seven years. We saw the neighbor's fishing hat and his eyes from time to time. He was great at giving "through the fence" advice, but he never actually reached over the fence.

If we are to love our neighbor, we're going to have to reach over the fence to touch a life. Yes, that means our neighbor might see us as we really are. But can't you put up with a slight drop in privacy in order to inherit eternal life?

There were how-to instructions built into the commandment Jesus gave the young man: Love your neighbor as yourself. We don't need to ask how to treat ourselves. Most of us never have a problem loving ourselves. One little nudge will provide me an excuse to pamper myself, and I'm off to Bath and Body Works for a refill of Tropical Stress Relief Bubble Bath so I can soak my worries away. We treat ourselves to a night on the town. If we're sick, we demand the best health care available. Yes, we love ourselves . . . and I need to love others as much as I love "little ol' me." If we all loved our neighbors as Jesus commanded, they would roll out the red carpet whenever they saw us coming.

Linda Evans Shepherd: We don't do to get. If our motive for kindness is some sort of payback, we are operating from the wrong spirit.[12]

> **Luke 23:55** The women who had come with Jesus from Galilee followed Joseph and saw the tomb and how [Jesus'] body was laid in it. Then they went home and prepared spices and perfumes.

Is There Anything I Can Do?

Jesus spoke his last words. He breathed his last breath. He hung on the cross dead. Joseph of Arimathea, a wealthy member of the **Sanhedrin** and a secret follower of Christ, mustered up the courage to go to Pilate and ask for the body.

Everyday Life

KEY POINT

Simple acts of kindness make a difference in the lives of others.

Think About It

What Others are Saying:

Sanhedrin: the official group of ruling priests and Levites among the Jews during New Testament times

☞ **GO TO:**

John 3:1–21; 19:39
(Nicodemus)

Deuteronomy 21:23;
Ecclesiastes 38:16
(delay)

Acts 9:37 (washed)

Everyday Life

☞ **GO TO:**

Matthew 2:11; Mark
15:23; John 19:39
(myrrh)

John 19:39 (pounds)

Think About It

*myrrh: an expensive,
pleasant-smelling plant
used to make perfume*

Joseph and <u>Nicodemus</u>, another secret follower, took away his body, and, in the Jewish tradition, without <u>delay</u> <u>washed</u> it, wrapped it in linens with spices of **myrrh** and aloe, and laid Jesus' body in Joseph's tomb, a cave carved out of a rocky hillside.

Mary Magdalene and Mary the mother of Jesus followed them to the tomb to see where Jesus was buried, with plans to return and anoint him with spices. Did they not know Nicodemus had already used 75 <u>pounds</u> of spices, an amount only a king would receive? Or were they simply trying to find something they could do to help the family in this time of sorrow?

Too many times when a crisis hits the home of a friend or neighbor we don't know what to do, so we do nothing. We may even ask how we can help, but in the midst of the storm they can't come up with a specific task. But "nothing" can be the worst thing to do. We need to offer simple acts of kindness to show we care—to show that God cares.

Simple acts of kindness usually do not take a significant amount of time but make a significant impact upon the lives of those in crisis. Do any simple thing that you can do (without barging in and taking over). Listen to what your friend or neighbor in crisis is saying, ask God for wisdom, and respond as you feel led. Your acts of kindness will not go unnoticed or unappreciated as you touch another's life.

GEORGIA'S  **TIPS . . .**

Georgia's list of simple acts of kindness:

1. Send a card with encouraging words.
2. Prepare a tray of food for quick bites.
3. Offer to watch the children.
4. Pick up some groceries.
5. Make phone calls.
6. Smile and wave.
7. Let a car go in front of you in a traffic tie-up.
8. Hold the door open for someone.

What Others are Saying:

Larry Burkett: I believe God's people are the warmest and most compassionate people in the world. Shortly after I announced [my] diagnosis of cancer on the radio, I began to receive cards and letters of encouragement from all over the world. I was deeply touched by the sentiments expressed by the writers and found great encouragement through their generosity.[13]

Neighbor to Neighbor

COFFEE BREAK
WITH GEORGIA

The bold headlines faded, but would return when the judge sentenced the youth in a couple of weeks. One troubled youth, David Dodge, had viciously taken the life of 12-year-old baby-sitter Ashley Jones, whom her father referred to as "a flower." A community was in shock, a family agonized over the murder of their daughter, and I'm sure the parents of the killer were devastated that their own flesh and blood could commit such a horrendous crime.

I read all the coverage from day to day and produced a radio show for my husband's talk show, *America Today with Phil Ling*, on the subject "Unprecedented Surge in Youth Crime." The research was disturbing. The October 1997 murder in Stanwood, Washington is repeated in similar acts of crime across America daily. Callers to the radio show were outraged and tried to offer solutions to juvenile crime.

On the show the goal is not to merely talk about the problems, but to interview individuals who are making a difference and offer biblically based solutions to issues and challenges America faces. Following the calls, our guest was Lisa Barnes Lampman, president of an organization called Neighbors Who Care, the first national Christian victim assistance program and a subsidiary of Prison Fellowship. Lisa is also author of a book on the same subject, *Helping Neighbors in Crisis*. Neighbors Who Care springs from the story of the Good Samaritan, who cared for a crime victim. Jesus finished the parable with the admonition to *"go and do likewise."* The organization recruits and trains volunteers to provide assistance to victims: crime-scene cleanup, property repair, transportation, filling out claim forms, referral to local church support groups, follow-up calls, home visits, and more. That's what I call a neighbor who cares.

In the newspaper coverage of the tragic death of Ashley Jones, I was impressed with the community's outpouring of love and support for the Jones family—their neighbors in crisis. But from the interview with Lisa Lampman we found out that the positive reaction from the Stanwood community was rare. Most individuals do not understand, or they are unsure how to respond to pain and grief, and they ignore or avoid the needs of those who are hurting.

I had to agree with Lisa when she said, "God calls us to minister one-on-one with each other. That's what makes an impact and a difference. We can't leave it up to the government anymore. We must, as a church, love our neighbor as ourselves."

> **1 Corinthians 15: 58** Therefore my dear brothers, stand firm. Let nothing move you. Always give yourselves fully to the work of the Lord, because you know that your labor in the Lord is not in vain.

Did She Just Call Me Church Lady?

As believers in the early Church faced persecution, the Apostle Paul reminded them of the hope we have in Christ's return and our resurrection. The fear of persecution and death should no longer have a grip on our lives for there is more that awaits us beyond this life—rooms in the heavenly <u>mansion</u> Jesus has prepared for us.

Paul encouraged the Corinthian Christians to have no fear and to remember that what really mattered was their service for the cause of Christ.

There is no better place of service than with your local church body. Look what happened when Christ recruited twelve willing workers—they turned the world upside down! With your acts of service the Church can have an eternal impact. We can change our families, our communities, and the world as we minister to one another and spread the news and love of Christ. "*And whatever you do, whether in word or deed, do it all in the name of the Lord Jesus, giving thanks to God the Father through him*" (Colossians 3:17).

☞ **GO TO:**

John 14:1–6 (mansion)

Think About It

My watching of *Saturday Night Live* ended twenty years ago when I graduated from college, entered the real world, and couldn't stay up so late. But I have seen clips of comedian Dana Carvey's character, the Church Lady. She looks outdated, as if she stepped out of the early episodes of *The Andy Griffith Show*, with puckered lips, an old-fashioned housedress, and a black Bible she carries on her crusade against Satan. I have to admit, Dana Carvey made me laugh. (I've even known a few Church Ladies in my time.)

You don't have to look or act like the *Saturday Night Live* Church Lady to be part of a church. (Thank goodness!) But being plugged into a church community is a vital part of growing in our walk with God. He intended the <u>Church</u> to come together to learn, pray, and worship as one body.

☞ **GO TO:**

Acts 2:42–47 (Church)

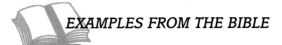

EXAMPLES FROM THE BIBLE

There are some women mentioned in the Bible who probably earned the title "Church Lady" in the early church:

- Euodias and Syntyche worked by Paul's side in spreading the gospel. (Philippians 4:2)

- Tryphena and Tryphosa were called *"those women who work hard in the Lord."* (Romans 16:12)

- Philip's four unmarried daughters prophesied and assisted their father. (Acts 21:9)

- Apphia was a *"sister"* in Christ at Colossae and wife of Philemon, who worked with Paul. (Philemon 1:2)

- Mary of Rome was mentioned by Paul as a laborer in the church *"who worked very hard."* (Romans 16:6)

- Persis *"worked very hard in the Lord."* (Romans 16:12)

- Rufus' mother was the spiritual mother of Paul and a worker in the church. (Romans 16:13–15)

Everyday Life

KEY POINT

Get plugged into a local church—they need your special abilities to help fulfill their mission.

GEORGIA'S TIPS . . .

Get plugged into the local church body. Does your spiritual gift match up with any of the following ministries?

1. "Encouragement gifts" strengthen and encourage those who are weary and build up the faithful.
   - Recovery Ministry
   - Prison Ministry
   - Counselors
   - Premarriage/Marriage Mentors
   - Mom's Support Groups

2. "Teaching gifts" teach and apply the scripture in order that the student will fully understand the message.
   - Children's Ministry
   - Youth Ministry
   - Bible Study Leaders

3. "Leadership gifts" are areas of ministry that motivate and lead a group in a focused direction.
   - Chairperson
   - Organize/Develop Programs
   - Finances/Accounting
   - Missions

4. "Hospitality gifts" are areas of service that welcome newcomers and serve the existing body of the church through practical provisions.
   - Greeters/Information Booth
   - Parking Crew
   - Communion Preparation
   - Creative Decorating
   - Meal Preparations for Shut-ins

These are just a few of the vital ministries in the local church you can become involved in. What are you waiting for? Get plugged in and consider it a compliment if someone calls you "Church Lady."

KEY Outline:

Gifts
encouragement
teaching
leadership
hospitality

KEY POINT

Get plugged in and consider it a compliment if someone calls you "Church Lady."

Bill Hybels: A way we can expand the horizons of our servanthood is by sharing our skills and abilities with others. The Bible clearly communicates that in the family of believers we should not only share our gifts with one another, but we should also be enthusiastically and eagerly sharing our talents, learned skills, and abilities.[14]

> **Mark 16:15** Jesus said to them, "Go into all the world and preach the good news to all creation."

KEY POINT

Inquiring seekers turn to believers in their times of crisis. Prepare to share.

Inquiring Minds Want to Know

The Gospel of Mark ends with Christ giving his followers their marching order to go into the entire world with his message. After Jesus' resurrection he ministered for 40 more days on earth before his **ascension** into heaven.

The final **commission** to go into all the world seems to have been uttered to the eleven at this ascension. It may, however, have been a summary of final instructions that Jesus repeated over and over during his 40-day postresurrection ministry. In substance it is recorded four times: 1) here in connection with his first appearance to the disciples; 2) at his Galilean appearance (Matthew 28:18–20); 3) at his final appearance in Jerusalem (Luke 24:47); and 4) at his ascension (Acts 1:8).[15]

When unbelievers face a crisis or turning points in their lives, they search for answers from authentic believers who may have shared the same struggles. In most cases, they silently observe day by day with inquiring minds, listening to your conversations and keeping a watchful eye on how you handle life's struggles and disappointments. People are looking for an authentic relationship with God. They look to see if your personal relationship with God makes an authentic difference.

☞ **GO TO:**

Mark 16:19 (ascension)

ascension: *Jesus' rising into heaven*

commission: *charge, command*

In one week of news I read the following stories:

- A youth worker molested an eight-year-old boy. Naturally, the family was devastated, angry, and confused.
- A physician was fired unjustly from his position at a local clinic. His wife was depressed and uncertain of what the future held.

Everyday Life

- A teen was arrested on drug charges. The parents were brokenhearted and needed wisdom and advice for their situation.

- A father driving across a mountain pass with his 32-year-old son witnessed his son's sudden death from a heart attack. With no civilization around for miles, he continued his journey to the next town with his son's lifeless body. Grief stricken and shattered, he sought help and comfort in his time of crisis.

These were all local headline news stories, but I knew of them because they were real hurting people who made their way to our church. They each had something else in common. Each situation involved non-Christians who, in crisis, turned to a Christian neighbor, a Christian teacher, or a Christian coworker.

Think About It

Are non-Christians searching for what we have? Absolutely! It is our mission to go into all the world and preach the good news to all creation. When tragedy hits our neighborhood, we can offer our neighbors the <u>peace</u> that passes all understanding—the only good news that can make an eternal difference in their lives.

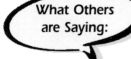

What Others are Saying:

Warren Wiersbe: Can people really know that we love them? Yes, most of them can. To begin with, if we really love people, we accept them as they are and identify with their deepest needs.[16]

☞ **GO TO:**

John 14:27; Philippians 4:7; Ephesians 2:14 (peace)

SNAPSHOTS OF WOMEN IN THE BIBLE

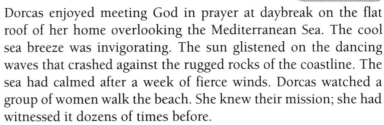

Dorcas

☞ **Check It Out:**

Acts 9:36–42

Dorcas enjoyed meeting God in prayer at daybreak on the flat roof of her home overlooking the Mediterranean Sea. The cool sea breeze was invigorating. The sun glistened on the dancing waves that crashed against the rugged rocks of the coastline. The sea had calmed after a week of fierce winds. Dorcas watched a group of women walk the beach. She knew their mission; she had witnessed it dozens of times before.

The group gathered around a dark object on the shore. They were there to identify the body of a fisherman lost at sea. The waves that took his life also returned his body home to the sandy beaches of Joppa.

Widows accompanied other women who searched for missing husbands. The widows had walked those same steps, felt their loss, known their pain. They were there to lean on. Dorcas could pick out individual widows who returned month after month with newly worried women. Dorcas noticed that as the widows struggled to survive, their clothes slowly turned to rags. She prayed for a way to help, and God answered her prayers. She knew what she must do. There was only one talent she had, but she did it well. She could sew. She could use her needle and thread to sew clothes for the widows. After all, God <u>commands</u> us to take care of the orphans and widows. Dorcas knew her <u>service</u> would please God and lift the lonely widows' spirits.

Dorcas began to sew and sew and sew. The widows in the community grew to know her well. They loved her generous gifts, loving heart, and listening ear. She became their friend as she shared their burden of sorrow and offered simple gifts of love to help mend their broken lives.

It was a normal day as she worked on a beautiful tunic for a woman who had recently been widowed. Dorcas couldn't wait to see the smile on the woman's face when presented with these new clothes. Then a shooting pain took her by surprise. Suddenly she felt faint. There was no strength in her arm. She dropped her needle and thread, clutched her chest, and everything went dark.

The women arrived in the afternoon at the time Dorcas had specified, but when they knocked no one answered the door. Fearing foul play, they eventually forced their way into her home. They found Dorcas slumped over, laying on the floor amidst the fabric and unfinished clothes. She looked as though she slept, but they knew she had died. They gently picked her up, washed her body for burial, laid her on the bed, and began to mourn the loss of their dear friend.

Some didn't lose hope. They knew of the miracles her fellow believers were performing. They sent two men for the disciple Peter and asked him to come at once. Peter rushed to her home and found the house filled with widows weeping the loss of their closest friend. They showed him the garments Dorcas had blessed them with.

Peter instructed them to leave the room. He knelt by her bed and prayed.

Out of the darkness, Dorcas heard someone call her name. She opened her eyes and saw Peter stretch out his hand. She felt his strong, rough fisherman grip as he helped her up. She had no pain. She wondered what had happened. As she walked out of the

☞ **GO TO:**

Exodus 22:22–24;
  Deuteronomy
  10:17–18
  (commands)

Romans 12:4–8
  (service)

KEY Outline:

Dorcas
  saw a need
  used her talent
  sewed garments
  filled the need
  became a friend to
    widows
  was resurrected

☞ **GO TO:**

Matthew 10:8 (power)

bedroom and heard the gasps and delighted squeals of her friends, it didn't take her long to discover she was a miracle—Peter had raised her from the dead, just as Jesus had given him the <u>power</u> to do.

The news spread quickly in Joppa about this woman who was always doing good and helping the poor; how she served the Lord, and the Lord rewarded her; and many believed in the Lord.

Think About It

The Bible records seven people raised from the dead, but Dorcas was the only adult woman:

1. the widow of Zarepath's son (1 Kings 17:21–23)
2. the Shunammite woman's son (2 Kings 4:36)
3. the daughter of Jairus (Luke 8:55–56)
4. the son of the widow of Nain (Luke 7:11–19)
5. Lazarus (John 11:40–44)
6. Jesus (Luke 24:1–12; John 20:1–9; Matthew 28:1–15; Mark 16:1–11)
7. Dorcas (Acts 9:40–43)

Dorcas' resurrection was a sign of God's power. The town knew this woman from her acts of kindness. Many gave glory to God because of how he worked in Dorcas' life. You never know what glorious things might happen when you use your abilities and willingly serve others.

REMEMBER  THIS

People are watching to see how God works in and through us.

STUDY QUESTIONS

1. Why is it our duty as believers to volunteer and serve?
2. What motive should we have in serving?
3. How do we prove our Christian commitment to the world?
4. King Josiah had Huldah check the Book of Laws for authenticity. What credentials did Huldah possess to complete such a task?
5. Do believers have special gifts? How are we to discover them?
6. The Jewish lawyer asked how he could inherit the kingdom of God. What was Jesus' response?
7. Why is your work in the Lord not in vain, even if it seems to go unnoticed?
8. What instrument did Dorcas use in her service to God?

- The gift of serving touches hearts, nourishes souls, and fuels ministries that share the love of Christ.

- Serving is for everyone. We each have special abilities and God-given gifts we can share with others. We need to look beyond ourselves, unwrap our gifts, and commit to the act of serving. But do it for God, not for personal glory.

- Yes, you can make a difference in the lives of others. No act of kindness, no matter how great or small, will go unnoticed by God. Whether you can only carve out a small piece of time or you decide to commit to a lifetime of service, whatever you do will enrich not only your life, but those you touch.

- Our neighbor is anyone who is in need. It could be our next-door neighbor, a community member or someone across the continent. Make a special effort to reach out to a neighbor in their time of crisis through your simple acts of kindness. Let them know that you and God truly care.

- The Church needs you! You need the Church! Believers are the fuel for ministries. Twelve willing workers changed the world, but they did it together. If you've been staying on the fringes of the Body of Christ, find a church and get involved.

GEORGIA'S  BOOKSHELF

Some of Georgia's favorite books on volunteering in your church and community:

- *Encouraging Hands, Encouraging Hearts*, Linda Evans Shepherd, Vine Books

- *Serving Lessons* (Putting God and Others First Study Series), Bill Hybels, Zondervan, Willow Creek Resources

- *A Simple Path*, Mother Teresa, Ballantine Books

- *Christian Community* (Bible Study Series), Rob Suggs, InterVarsity Press

- *Helping Neighbors in Crisis*, Lisa Barnes Lampman (Prison Ministry Fellowship, 1-800-692-7770)

9 MADAME PRESIDENT?

Using Your Voice to Improve Your Community

WHAT'S IN THIS CHAPTER

- Women in Leadership
- Speak the Truth
- Protect Your Family's Future
- Be Persuasive

Susan B. Anthony: Early activist in American **temperance** *and anti-slavery movements*

temperance: *antialcohol*

segregation: *the practice of separating racial groups from each other*

civil rights: *rights guaranteed to individuals by the Constitution of the United States and other acts of Congress*

Here We Go

It's no secret that over the centuries women have played a major role in politics and leadership. American history books are filled with women who made a difference through involvement in politics. **Susan B. Anthony** helped win the fight for the American woman's right to vote in the nineteenth century. Rosa Parks, an African American passenger on a bus, decided in December 1955 that she was tired of the injustice of **segregation** and refused to move to the back of the bus. Rosa Parks became a hero in the **civil rights** movement.

Women who voice their biblical beliefs can change lives, shape communities, and transform a nation. We have to be willing to stand up, speak out in love and do our part to protect our families. It's guaranteed we will face opposition, but with God's strength and <u>guidance</u> we can make a difference.

Let's see what the Bible has to say about women and our involvement in politics.

EXAMPLES FROM THE BIBLE

Bible women were very involved in their communities and their governments.

- **Miriam**, the first Hebrew **prophetess**, accompanied her brothers Moses and Aaron as they led the children of Israel out of Egyptian <u>captivity</u>.

☞ **GO TO:**

Psalm 25:9; 32:8; Isaiah 58:11; John 16:13 (guidance)

Zechariah 10:12; Philippians 4:13; 1 Peter 5:10; Exodus 13–15 (captivity)

Miriam: *Hebrew prophetess*

prophetess: *a woman who is inspired to speak the will of God*

Deborah: *a prophetess, counselor, judge of Israel*

Esther: *queen of Persia and Media*

- **Deborah** was a woman of great power as she served the children of Israel in the role of counselor, judge, and deliverer in time of war. When no man had the courage to take action, Deborah rallied troops, inspired them, and led them to victory, which was Israel's first united action in 175 years (Judges 4).

- **Esther**, a courageous orphan Jewess who became queen of Persia, was faced with a choice to speak out and possibly die, or remain silent and deny her faith. When she learned of the plot to kill all the Jews in the kingdom, she risked her life in revealing that she was a Jew. By speaking out she was able to save her people from massacre (Esther 2–10).

> **Romans 13:1–2** Everyone must submit himself to the governing authorities, for there is no authority except that which God has established.

From the PTA to the Oval Office

Throughout the book of Romans, the Apostle Paul gives us guidance in our everyday lives and shows the purpose of God's laws and God's grace. Paul gives us the answer as to why we, God's children, should obey man's government. Paul explains that the government was established by God, and we are subjects under God.

Scripture records that God set up three institutions:

1. God established the home and family (Genesis 1:28) to increase humanity's numbers and to subdue the earth. (Genesis 2:22–24)

2. God established the church to increase the number of disciples and spread the good news of Christ and salvation. (Acts 2:42–44, 47)

3. God established the government to be accountable unto God and to keep his commandments and laws. (Genesis 9:5–8)

EXAMPLES FROM THE BIBLE

Leaders in government in Bible times loved God and his Laws, and made a positive impact on society:

- Joseph: became ruler of Egypt under Pharaoh and saved his family and a nation from a famine. (Genesis 37:1–50:26)
- David: the second king of Israel followed God's direction during his reign. His descendant, Jesus, was the Messiah. (1 Samuel 16:13, 19–23)
- Josiah: a young king *"did that which was right in the eyes of the Lord and walked in all the ways of his father David, not turning aside to the right or to the left"* (2 Kings 22:2). Josiah led his kingdom back to the Law of God and renewed the nation's covenant with God.

Some leaders in government disobeyed God's laws and had a negative impact on society.

- Athaliah: ruled for six years over Judah. She was extremely wicked and worshiped Baal (see illustration, page 36). She nearly destroyed all of the royal House of Judah, her own blood relations, but missed one boy. (2 Chronicles 22:3–23)
- Jezebel: wife of King Ahab who persecuted prophets of God. She tried to force her worship of Baal on God's people. (1 Kings 16–2 Kings 9)
- Saul: the first king of Israel disobeyed God. God, in turn, rejected Saul. *"The Lord was grieved that he had made Saul king over Israel"* (1 Samuel 15:35).
- Herod Antipas: king of the regions of Galilee and Perea during the time of Christ. He had John the Baptist beheaded and took part in Jesus' trial. (Luke 3:1; Mark 6:17–29)

Whether joining the **PTA** or running for the Oval Office, if believers incorporate God's laws and grace into their home, church, and government they will have a life-changing and eternal impact on our world. The question should not be "Why should we be involved in government?" The question is "Why not be involved in a God-ordained government?"

KEY POINT

God established the home, the church, and the government.

PTA: Parent Teacher Association

Think About It

William J. Bennett: Reclaiming our institutions is less a political opportunity than a civic obligation. It involves hard work. But it is work of immense importance. At the end of the day, somebody's values will prevail. In America, "we the people" have a duty to insist that our institutions and our government be true to their time-honored tasks.[1]

> **Isaiah 6:8** "Then I heard the voice of the Lord saying, "Whom shall I send? And who will go for us?" And I said, "Here am I. Send me!"

Send Me?

Isaiah preached in Jerusalem, the capital of **Judah**, during a time when King Uzziah had brought the nation to great prosperity. But the nation must've suffered from spiritual heart disease, for they turned away from God.

Isaiah saw a **vision** of God seated on his throne with angels praising him by saying, *"Holy, holy, holy is the Lord Almighty"* (Isaiah 6:3). When Isaiah saw the glory and **righteousness** of God and his own unrighteousness he repented of his unclean lips. Isaiah clearly saw the poor spiritual condition of his own heart and the heart of his people, and he grieved for his nation.

God asked whom he could send to deliver his message. Isaiah willingly said, "Here am I. Send me!"

Over the years this passage of Scripture is used in reference to missionary work, but we can be used in mission work in our own backyard if we, like Isaiah, willingly become a voice for God to our community.

Since God established the government, the most active citizens should be Christian citizens. We should have input in leadership, in the laws of our land, and in the enforcement of those laws.

EXAMPLES FROM THE BIBLE

Women of the Bible who willingly followed God's lead:

- Sarah left her home and country and faithfully followed her husband to a land of the unknown. God blessed her as the *"Mother of Nations."* (Genesis 21:1–13)
- Rahab hid the spies of Israel, which led to the capture of the city of Jericho. God spared the life of Rahab and her family. (Joshua 2:1–24; 6:1–25)

☞ **GO TO:**

Isaiah 6:3 (vision)

Isaiah: *"the salvation of Jehovah"*

Judah: *the twelve clans, or tribes, of Israel were divided into two nations. The two tribes in the south were called Judah; the 10 tribes of the north organized as Israel.*

vision: *a prophecy or revelation in which a person sees something that God wants him or her to see*

righteousness: *harmony with God, his will, and with others*

KEY Outline:

Isaiah
  grieved for a nation
  saw a vision
  repented of his own
    unrighteousness
  was God's messenger

- Mary, the mother of Jesus was willing to face possible death by being unwed and pregnant as she became God's handmaiden and bore the son of God. (Luke 1:25–38)
- Jesus was Jewish, and Samaritans regarded Jews as their political enemies. The Samaritan woman said yes to Jesus and opened the door of Samaria to Jesus and his message. (John 4:4–26)

Our society is screaming out for answers and boundaries. I think that's why Dr. Laura Schlessinger, the radio talk show host who has 18 million listeners, is so popular. She's not afraid to offer biblically based advice that works. As <u>witnesses</u> of Christ we can implement spiritual values in our governing body and impact our communities with the spiritual truths of the Scriptures.

Elizabeth Dole: My grandmother taught me that what we do on our own matters little—what counts is what God chooses to do through us. She stressed the importance of ministering to others and Jesus' instruction to his followers to "Feed my sheep." Public service is a part of that.[2]

KEY POINT

Christians should be active citizens.

Think About It

☞ **GO TO:**

Acts 1:8 (witnesses)

What Others are Saying:

We Are Out Here

Remember how 1998 started? Maybe this sounds familiar: "In breaking news from the White House . . .", "Stay tuned for the latest developments in the sex scandal," and, "It's all a vast right wing conspiracy." Whew! You heard it from all sides, from CNN to *Entertainment Tonight* to radio talk shows.

COFFEE BREAK WITH GEORGIA

I raise the subject not because of the scandal itself, but the allegations made against other Americans during the scandal. I heard one local talk show host say, "Every American male has committed adultery. If that [not committing adultery] was a prerequisite for being elected President of the U.S., no one would qualify." Now, that's ridiculous! Contrary to that commentator's absurd opinion, there are moral individuals out here living lives of character.

Kathleen Parker's editorial in *USA Today* (2/1/98) examined the women involved in the White House scandal. Ms. Parker was really depressed that there were no more "classy women" or "great broads" left in this country. She said, "What ever happened to privacy and discretion, sophistication and class?" She continued, "I'm talking about the kind of woman who, if she's had an affair, doesn't feel compelled to share the experience with CNN." She wasn't concerned about the moral fiber of this nation. Her concern was merely whether women who kiss, tell!

Speaking on behalf of all the women of character, sisters in Christ who dare to live their lives and raise their children on biblical truths, who preserve their marriage living by the book, and make a difference by sharing their truths and principles with others—we are out here! We are saying to God, "Here I am, send me!" We're praying for our families, our church, and our country knowing that when the media frenzy is over, lives will be broken, our country wounded, and conservative thinking bruised.

But unlike the doomsayers, I have hope. I have a heritage of faith—faith in the same God our Founding Fathers placed their trust in when they developed America. A heritage of faith that's been tested through time and still stands. This faith has always played a role in the history of our nation. Faith in God is our only hope and the future of this nation.

> **Acts 13:50** But the Jews incited the God-fearing women of high standing and the leading men of the city. They stirred up persecution against Paul and Barnabas, and expelled them from their region.

Overcoming Hurdles

On Paul's missionary journeys he worked in the cities establishing churches and training new believers.

As Paul preached about Christ, many received his message with open hearts and spread the exciting news throughout the city. However, the Jewish leaders opposed Paul because he included the **Gentiles** in his invitation to hear about Christ. Out of envy, the Jewish leaders stirred up many leading men and women of the community to persecute Paul. They cast him and his missionary companion **Barnabas** out of the city. As they left, Paul and Barnabas shook the dust off their sandals, just as Jesus had instructed his disciples to do when their message was rejected.

When Paul faced persecution for carrying the message of Christ, the Lord protected him. Can we be as brave as Paul? When we take a stand for biblical principles in our governing bodies, we

☞ **GO TO:**

Romans 15:19, 23 (establishing)

1 Thessalonians 1:1–12 (training)

Matthew 10:14 (instructed)

2 Timothy 3:11; Acts 14:19–20 (persecution)

Gentiles: non-Jews

Barnabas: "son of encouragement"

will face resistance and will have to overcome the hurdles. But remember, *"the foolishness of God is wiser than man's wisdom, and the weakness of God is stronger than man's strength"* (1 Corinthians 1:25).

Some think that gaining a voice in the political arena is the biggest hurdle women have to overcome. Yet, we're better off than we were three decades ago. In the United States, three of fifty governors are women, nine of one hundred senators are women and fifty-six of four hundred thirty-five House members are women. In state legislatures, city councils, and country commissions, women represent twenty to twenty-five percent of elected officials. And who knows? The United States may end up with a female President in the next election.[3]

In the News

Women are making an impact throughout our country as we come together for one cause—to influence our society for Christ. Concerned Women for America was founded in 1979, after Beverly LaHaye watched a television interview with Betty Friedan, founder of the National Organization for Women. Offended by Miss Friedan's claim to speak for all American women, Mrs. LaHaye founded CWA to protect the interest of American families and provide a voice for women who believe in Judeo-Christian values. Concerned Women for America members are active in all levels of the American public policy arena, from the halls of Congress to state capitols, city councils, and local school boards. They are working to advance the values they believe in and to make a difference in their communities and nation.[4]

If you have stood up and said, "Send me," don't let opposition and fear stop you. God is not a God of <u>fear</u>. He has given us the power of love. As God-fearing women we can accomplish <u>anything</u> he calls us to do.

Think About It

KEY Outline:

Paul

preached Jesus
established churches
trained believers
faced persecution

KEY POINT

Expect opposition when standing up for what is right, but remember God empowers us to stand for him.

REMEMBER THIS

☞ **GO TO:**

2 Timothy 1:7 (fear)

Philippians 4:13 (anything)

Tony Campolo: In addition to being a voter or a campaigner, you may want to consider becoming a candidate for office yourself. Contrary to what many believe, holding political office is truly a noble Christian calling. Edmund Burke, in a famous quote, once said, "All that is necessary for evil to triumph, is for good men to do nothing." You may choose to run for public office for no other reason than to keep evil in its place.[5]

SNAPSHOTS OF WOMEN IN THE BIBLE

Esther

Esther's family was taken into captivity under King Nebuchadnezzar's reign. She once lived a life of nobility, but now she was a Jewish orphan raised by her cousin **Mordecai**.

The provincial king, Xerxes, was looking for a replacement for his queen. Queen Vashti had refused one of Xerxes' requests, so he banished her and ordered that a new queen be found. So the search began throughout 127 provinces for a new queen.

Mordecai served in the royal court. As soon as he heard news of the search, he sent for Esther. Out of all the **virgins** presented to the king, Xerxes chose Esther and placed the royal crown on her head. Esther became loved and respected throughout the palace and the kingdom as she enjoyed the status of her new title.

But all was not well in the palace for Mordecai was hated by the king's chancellor, Haman. The king respected Haman and ordered everyone to bow down to him. But Mordecai only <u>bowed</u> down to God and refused to bow to Haman.

Because of Haman's wounded pride, he decided to kill Mordecai and all other Jews in the empire. Until this time, for her own protection, Queen Esther had kept her Jewish heritage a secret. When she found out that the king plotted to eliminate the Jews, she was faced with an awful dilemma.

Mordecai asked Queen Esther if she would go to the king to save their people. Esther's former guardian told her that this may be the very reason she sat on the royal throne. Maybe this was her purpose in life. Maybe God placed her there *"for such a time as this"* (Esther 4:14), for there was no one else close to the king who could stop the slaughter.

No one could go to the king uninvited, not even the queen. Esther feared she was placing her own life in danger, but knew she had to speak up. She said, *"If I perish, I perish"* (Esther 4:16).

☞ **Check It Out:**

Esther 1–10

Esther: orphan girl, chosen to be queen

Mordecai: Esther's cousin

virgin: a person who has never had sex

☞ **GO TO:**

Exodus 4:5; 32:8–9 (bowed)

KEY Outline:

Esther
*was an orphan Jew
was crowned queen
discovered injustice
prayed and fasted
spoke up
saved Jews from
      massacre*

Knowing she could not do this alone she called for all the Jews to <u>fast</u> and pray for three days as she prepared to meet the king.

Esther went before the king unannounced. The penalty should be death, but instead he welcomed her into his court and asked what her request would be. She first made a small request that the king and Haman would join her for a banquet.

At the banquet the king once again asked what request she had. Esther did not feel the timing was right and asked the king to return the next day.

That evening the king was restless and could not sleep. He asked a courier to read from the book that recorded memorable deeds of his people. Mordecai's name was recorded as one who had revealed that two **eunuchs** plotted to kill the king. His speaking up had saved the king's life. It was also recorded that Mordecai had never been rewarded. The king resolved to reward Mordecai for his acts.

The next morning as Haman came to ask for permission to kill Mordecai and the Jews, he was surprised by the king's order to honor Mordecai.

Later at the banquet, Xerxes met with Esther and asked what he could do for her. She fell at his feet in tears and begged for the lives of her people. When Haman's plot was revealed, the king ordered that Haman be hanged from the very gallows that Haman had built for Mordecai.

The king instructed Esther to write a contradictory order that would stop the annihilation of the Jews. He signed it and sealed it with the royal seal.

Esther was a woman who would not tolerate the injustice for her people. She would not stand by and do nothing. Esther stood up for God and her people and spoke up to her ruler. Esther's actions saved her people from extermination. One woman made a difference for an entire race.

☞ **GO TO:**

Ezra 8:23; Daniel 9:3; Zechariah 7:3 (fast)

eunuchs: men who have been castrated

KEY POINT

Esther was only one woman but through her God saved a nation.

> **Ephesians 6:10** Finally, be strong in the Lord and in his mighty power. Put on the full armor of God so that you can take your stand against the devil's schemes.

Protecting Your Family's Future

The Apostle Paul reminded the believers in Ephesus to remember who we are at war with—**Satan.**

From earliest times, mankind wore devices for protecting the body in battle. These devices varied and were made of different

☞ **GO TO:**

Isaiah 4:9; 2 Corinthians 11:3; Revelation 9:11 (Satan)

Satan: "adversary" or enemy

Just as this Roman soldier is protected by his armor, Paul told the Ephesian Christians to put on the full armor of God as described in Ephesians 6:11–16.

KEY POINT

In order to protect your family, you must first be fitted with the "armor" of God, ready for battle.

REMEMBER  THIS

material, from heavy leather to hardened steel. Usually armor consisted of a shield carried on one arm, a coat or breastplate, leather or iron casings for the legs and feet, and a helmet for the head.[6]

Paul compares a soldier armed and ready for battle to our spiritual walk, encouraging us to put on our *"full armor of God"* (see illustration, this page) and prepare for battle.

In our society we are at war over man's values versus God's values. Our children are caught in the middle of that war as we try to protect them. In order to protect our families we must be ready for battle. Armor, anyone?

The Full Armor of God

Sword of the Spirit	Hebrews 4:12
Belt of Truth	John 14:6
Breastplate of Righteousness	Colossians 2:6
Feet Fitted with Readiness and Peace	1 Corinthians 7:15
Shield of Faith	Mark 11:22
Pray in the Spirit	Colossians 4:2

SNAPSHOTS OF WOMEN IN THE BIBLE

Shiphrah and Puah

Shiphrah and Puah loved the sound of a newborn baby's cry. As midwives they had delivered dozens of babies, but tears welled up in their eyes with each new birth.

The Pharaoh, however, did not share the midwives' joy over each new life. He feared the Hebrews he held in captivity would soon outnumber the Egyptians. He devised a plan to have all the Hebrew newborn males killed during childbirth, and called for the midwives to be brought before him.

Shiphrah and Puah wondered why they would be ordered before the Pharaoh. Had they done something wrong? They went to his court with great uncertainty. Their hearts were troubled as they heard his orders. He commanded them to kill all the baby boys at birth, but to let the girls live.

Shiphrah and Puah knew that children were a gift from God, loved by him. They refused to murder children.

Moses, the great prophet, would have been a victim of the command if Shiphrah and Puah had obeyed Pharaoh's laws instead of obeying God's laws. In this snapshot, two women took a stand against murder and stood for their beliefs. They feared God more than man, and God rewarded and blessed them.

Today across America women involved in crisis pregnancy centers take a stand for God as they try to protect children from **abortion**. Lives are saved and hearts are mended as they share Christ's message of life and love.

> **1 Peter 3:15–16** But in your hearts set apart Christ as Lord. Always be prepared to give an answer to everyone who asks you to give the reason for the hope that you have. But do this with gentleness and respect, keeping a clear conscience, so that those who speak maliciously against your good behavior in Christ may be ashamed of their slander.

Speak the Truth in Love

The Apostle Peter deals with Christians and their relationship with the world. First, God must be the center of a believer's life. He must be first in your heart. You must know the Word and be ready

☞ **Check It Out:**

Exodus 1:15–21

KEY POINT

Puah and Shiphrah obeyed God's laws when man's commands contradicted God's.

☞ **GO TO:**

Luke 17:2 (loved)

1 John 2:4–5 (obeying)

Exodus 1:17 (feared)

Exodus 1:21 (blessed)

abortion: ending a pregnancy by removing an unborn child from the mother's uterus

☞ **GO TO:**

Romans 6:4 (newness)

and prepared to not only defend your position, but also tell why you have hope in your message. We must present ourselves with gentleness and respect, not hatred or violence. Peter encourages us to live correctly, walk in the <u>newness</u> of life with clear consciences before God so our lives witness of Christ's love to the world.

What Others are Saying:

Think About It

homosexual: *person with sexual desires for those of the same sex*

☞ **GO TO:**

Hosea 4:6 (lack)

Romans 12:21 (overcome)

KEY POINT

We must speak the truth in love.

Janet Parshall: Politics and culture are inseparable. Our cultural progress is built on the idea that people will be working, in face-to-face community, to improve our country through compassionate efforts that lie outside the government's expertise.[7]

As you become an active Christian citizen you must remember your commission to *"be about [your] Father's business"*—it's not our business, it's God's business. We are only his representatives. Not only should we know the truth of the Word, we must know the truth behind referendums, bills, special education programs, and issues that are being placed in our communities. We can be destroyed within from the <u>lack</u> of knowledge. If the issue is dealing with a hot topic such as abortion or **homosexual** marriage, we must know the ills that they place on society, the consequences, and the reason for our beliefs. All must be done in a Christ-like manner, in order that evil can be <u>overcome</u> with good.

Scripture Concerning Abortion

Exodus 20:13—*"You shall not kill."*

Psalm 139:13–14—*"For you created my inmost being; you knit me together in my mother's womb. I praise you because I am fearfully and wonderfully made; your works are wonderful, I know that full well."*

Proverbs 24:11–12—*"Rescue those being led away to death; hold back those staggering toward slaughter. If you say, 'But we knew nothing about this,' does not he who weighs the heart perceive it?"*

Jeremiah 1:5—*"Before I formed you in the womb I knew you, before you were born I set you apart; I appointed you as a prophet to the nations."*

Scripture Referring to Homosexuality

Romans 1:24–27—*"Therefore God gave them over into the sinful desires of their hearts to sexual impurity for the degrading of their bodies with one another. They exchanged the truth of God for a lie, and worshiped and served created things rather than the Creator—who is forever praised. Amen. Because of this, God gave them over to shameful lusts. Even their women exchanged natural relations for unnatural ones. In the same way the men also abandoned natural relations with women and were inflamed with lust for one another. Men committed indecent acts with other men, and received in themselves the due penalty for their perversion."*

1 Corinthians 6:9–10—*"Do you not know that the wicked will not inherit the kingdom of God? Do not be deceived: Neither the sexually immoral nor idolaters nor adulterers nor male prostitutes nor homosexual offenders nor the greedy nor drunkards nor slanderers nor swindlers will inherit the kingdom of God."*

Leviticus 18:22—*"Do not lie with a man as one lies with a woman; that is detestable."*

In *Roe v. Wade*, Norma McCorvey fought for and won the right to secure an abortion. She became the poster child for the abortion movement. On August 8, 1995, twenty-three years later, headlines shocked the world with her conversion to Christ, complete with a photo of her baptism. In her book *Won by Love*, Norma tells how a little girl's affection, a mother's trust, and a gregarious man's friendship surprised her and led her to Christ.

She wrote, "After years of working in a cauldron of hatred, factional infighting, bitterness, and resentment, I was won by a people of love. Their love included telling me that I was a sinner, that abortion was an offense to God, and that I would someday pay for this activity if I did not repent. But it was a love that also showed me there was a way out, an opportunity to experience forgiveness, grace and mercy. I was won by love."[8]

KEY Outline:

Christians in the World Should

be God centered

know the Word

defend the Word

be gentle

live correctly

Flashback

COFFEE BREAK
WITH GEORGIA

What a Week!

The week of May 5, 1997, the country had a triple header in the news. Two of the stories had great coverage, with newspapers and magazines filling their pages with commentary on challenges and issues surrounding the stories. Then there was one great story that only had a little coverage, but involved millions of individuals across the country.

Up to bat first was the president's Summit for America's Future—also known as the Volunteer Summit. Volunteering is not strange to the Christian community. According to the Gallup organization, over 60 percent of the volunteer effort in this country comes through churches and religious organizations. Yet, I have to admit, these volunteers have an ulterior motive: to share the love of Christ, change hearts, make a difference in our world. Other than that, they ask nothing in return.

Next in the lineup was the "coming out" of Ellen DeGeneres. Ellen was the lead character in a TV sitcom, *Ellen,* who revealed that she was a lesbian, not only in the show, but offscreen as well. The *USA Today* headline read, "Liberating 'Ellen'—Sitcom elevated to honest heights." For days in the news all you heard about was Ellen and "Coming Out Parties" planned all over the nation. There was an awful lot of coverage, considering that homosexuals comprise less than three percent of the population.

Our cleanup batter for the week was the forty-sixth annual National Day of Prayer. It only received minimal news coverage, but millions of Americans across the nation gathered for prayer on courthouse lawns, sidewalks, or silently in their homes, and prayed for the leaders of their nation and their generation.

My prayer is that we have a (pardon the phrase) "coming out" party for believers to stand up for what we believe is the right choice for ourselves, our children, and our communities; to share our belief in God and Scripture. If our society would open Scripture, it would find answers to all the questions of society's woes. We need to reclaim the culture for good.

"Let us not lose heart in doing good, for in due time we shall reap if we do not grow weary. So then, while we have opportunity, let us do good to all men, and especially to those who are of the household of faith" (Galatians 6:9).

KEY POINT

We need to reclaim the culture for good.

> **2 Corinthians 5:11** Since then we know what it is to fear the Lord, we try to persuade men. What we are is plain to God, and I hope it is also plain to your conscience."

You Can Be Persuasive

The Apostle Paul, writing the Christians in Corinth, was looking toward life after death and the judgment each of us will receive *"according to what he has done, whether good or bad"* (2 Corinthians 5:10). Death frequently knocked at Paul's door as he faced persecution, bodily harm, and imprisonment. At times he realized it would have been easier to <u>die</u>, knowing in death he would see Christ face to face and dwell in His presence. Humans fear judgment on this earth, but we are responsible to the judgment of God for all that we do and say as we persuade others of his message of forgiveness, love, and eternal life.

☞ **GO TO:**

Philippians 1:21, 23 (die)

As believers we have a huge load on our shoulders. We carry the weight of persuasion. Like Paul, at times we just wish it would all be over and God would just take us home. We look around and see the mess our world is in, and we are tempted to think that what we do in society doesn't matter, what happens in the world doesn't affect us, and when we all face judgment God will take care of everything.

Don't give up. It does matter. We must remember our first goal is to fill our bus and take as many people to heaven as we possibly can. And secondly, God will hold us responsible for our actions or the absence of our actions.

You can be persuasive and make a difference in our world.

GEORGIA'S TIPS . . .

One person can influence the opinions of many people:

1. Use the power of the press: The editorial section of the newspaper is a great place to present your thoughts, facts, and convictions on an issue. You don't have to be an expert to get in print. The letters column is open to everyone. You can persuade thousands of people who read your words.

2. Call in to your local radio talk show: Radio is not just all talk. Thousands upon thousands of listeners tune in to hear what's on the mind of John and Jane Doe. Live radio

is a little more nerve-wracking than writing to a newspaper, so I suggest you write your thoughts on paper before calling in and be prepared to defend your statements. Try to have fun!

3. Write your legislators: Did you know that your representatives view each letter received as representing at least one hundred other constituents? Write only about one issue at a time. Be sure to include the bill number and title. Bring it to a personal level and tell why this bill would affect you, your family, and your community.

4. Call your legislator's hotline: Call the hotline with the same information you would include in your letter. If you don't talk directly with your representative your message will be recorded and given to him or her.

EXAMPLES FROM THE BIBLE

The Bible gives us many examples of faithful people who made a difference for God through their persuasive words. Listed are just a few who spoke up for him:

- Daniel (see GWDN, pages 16–17) the prophet lived 70 years under Babylonian rule, yet did not compromise his convictions. He resisted political pressure. When called upon by the king, he spoke the truth of God's Laws and was placed in leadership in the glorious city of Babylon (see illustration, page 243; Daniel 5:18–21).

- Jeremiah was a prophet who stood up for God's laws as he preached to a wicked nation of disobedient Jews. He wrote God's warnings and impending disasters out on a scroll. Even though imprisoned, persecuted, and hated by those he dared to confront, Jeremiah remained faithful and foretold a new law that would be written on men's hearts. (Jeremiah 24:7; 31:31–34; Hebrews 8:1–9:28)

- Stephen's preaching caused many to accept the Word of God. Scripture records, "*Now Stephen, a man full of God's grace and power, did great wonders and miraculous signs among the people*" (Acts 6:8). Though Stephen was falsely accused before the **Sanhedrin**, he defended his belief in Jesus. "*All who were sitting in the Sanhedrin looked intently at Stephen, and they saw that his face was like the face of an*

Sanhedrin: powerful Jewish ruling council, comparable to Congress and the papacy combined

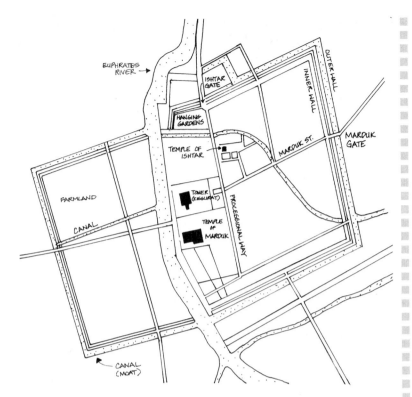

Ancient City of Babylon

One of the greatest cities of all times. The palace alone took up over 6 square miles, and the Hanging Gardens were one of the Seven Wonders of the World.

angel" (Acts 6:15). Even after Stephen's **stoning**, the Church grew as persecution scattered the believers throughout the Roman empire, where they preached the Word.

stoning: *method of capital punishment where the accusers hurled rocks at the condemned*

STUDY QUESTIONS

1. Why should we obey man's government?
2. What three institutions did God establish?
3. What did Isaiah do that allowed God to use him?
4. Are Christians immune to opposition?
5. What did Esther do that made such an impact on her nation?
6. What gave Esther the strength to go to the king, and possibly face death?
7. How can we protect our families as we battle societal values that contradict God's values?
8. Why did Shiphrah and Puah disobey a direct command from the Pharaoh?
9. In what attitude are we to speak out against the injustices of society?
10. To whom are we ultimately responsible for our actions?

- Women have made an impact in leadership across the centuries. The Scripture records how God used women and men to accomplish his goal of turning hearts back to God. It's our duty as believers to be involved in government as we try to have a life-changing and eternal impact on our world.

- Our actions are a witness of Christ to the world. As we go about the great commission of teaching about Jesus, we must always speak *"the truth in love"* (Ephesians 4:15).

- In order to protect our families we must be ready for battle as we put on the full armor of God. We must constantly be in the Word, walk with Christ, place our faith in God, and devote ourselves to prayer.

- You can make a difference right where you are as you go about sharing God's Word with others. As Esther, Deborah, Shiphrah, and Puah did in ancient days, today we women of faith can make a difference if we stand up, speak up, and reclaim the soul of America for God. Get active.

GEORGIA'S  BOOKSHELF

Some of Georgia's favorite books influencing culture:

- *Transforming America from the Inside Out*, Kay Cole James, Zondervan

- *Following Jesus without Embarrassing God*, Tony Campolo, Word

- *Reclaiming the Culture*, Alan Crippen II, editor, Focus on the Family

- *Burden of Truth*, Charles Colson, Tyndale House

- *The De-Valuing of America*, William J. Bennett, Focus on the Family

APPENDIX A—THE ANSWERS

CHAPTER ONE

1. God's Word is perfect and true. It makes us wise and brings us joy in life if we follow its guidelines. It leads us to do right and satisfies the appetite of our souls. (Psalm 19:7–11)
2. Sarah put her faith and trust in God by following his instructions. She left her homeland and followed her husband Abraham. (Hebrews 11:11)
3. Mary surrendered her time (Luke 10:39), her sorrow (John 11:32), and her precious possessions (John 12:1–11) to Jesus.
4. We should worship God, obey God, and praise God daily. (Psalm 86:11–12)
5. Elizabeth walked with God in service, in prayer, in praise, in obedience, and by faith. (Luke 1:8–25, 39–45)
6. Our souls are satisfied by God's words recorded in the Scripture. (Matthew 4:4)
7. The Samaritan woman found Jesus, who gave her the Living Water of the Holy Spirit. (John 4:4–26; 7:37–39)
8. Prayer nurtures your relationship with God as you communicate with him continually. (Romans 12:12)

CHAPTER TWO

1. Jeremiah told the children of Israel to keep living, be patient, and wait on God's plans for *"hope and a future."* (Jeremiah 29:1–32)
2. Jesus knows our suffering souls. When we turn to Christ in the midst of our suffering, we no longer live for ourselves but for God. (Matthew 27:1–66; John 10:14)
3. The widow of Zarepath followed Elijah the prophet's instructions and shared what she thought was her last meal with him. (1 Kings 17:1–24)
4. The Apostle Paul advised the Ephesians to restrain and control their anger. We can express our feelings of frustration and anger, but we are not to let anger turn to hatred and bitterness. (Ephesians 4:26)
5. They all listened and followed God. Noah's wife found relief and happiness when the floodwaters receded and the survivors built an altar to praise God (Genesis 8). Hagar was comforted by an angel and found strength to continue (Genesis 6). Naomi stayed true to God, and he blessed her with the companionship of Ruth (Ruth 1).
6. The psalmist was honest with himself and his state of mind and cried out to God for help in prayer. (Psalm 69:1–2)
7. Laughter gives you a break from your pain. Your heart may still ache, but laughter gives relief. (Proverbs 14:13, 17:22)
8. When we suffer, we can gain relief by allowing others to help us. (1 Corinthians 12:25–26)
9. Rahab harbored two spies from Israel's army and saved her family. She left behind her immoral life and believed in God as she joined the Israelites. (Joshua 2:1–21; Hebrews 11:31)

CHAPTER THREE

1. We are to impress upon our children that they should love the Lord with all their hearts, with all their souls, and with all their strength. (Deuteronomy 6:5–7)
2. The older women were to teach the younger women to love their husbands and to love their children. (Titus 2:3–4)
3. Hannah continually prayed for Samuel and turned his life over to God's hands. (1 Samuel 1:1–3:21)

4. The key advice parents should give children is to love the Lord and *"walk in his ways."* (1 Kings 2:2–4)
5. Samson's mother was obedient to the faith as she loved, prayed, confronted, and instructed Samson in the way of the Lord. (Judges 13:6; 9:23; 14:3)
6. Do not worry, live one day at a time, and live in Christ. (Matthew 6:25–27)
7. God gives us the gift of the Holy Spirit which dwells in our hearts when we accept Jesus as the Lord of our lives. (1 Corinthians 13:8, 13)
8. Eunice remained faithful to God and passed her faith along to Timothy as she instructed him in God's commands and principles. (2 Timothy 1:1–6)
9. In our daily walk we are to continue to encourage one another and offer each other support. (1 Thessalonians 5:11)

CHAPTER FOUR

1. God is the foundation we must build our families and marriages upon. (Psalm 127:1)
2. Rebekah showed two exemplary qualities: She was willing to leave the familiar behind, and she made a lifelong commitment to her marriage. God rewarded Rebekah with a husband who loved her and with twin boys. (Genesis 24:1–67)
3. Recommit your covenant to God and to one another. Let God be the foundation of your marriage. (Matthew 7:24)
4. The Bible permits divorce in the case of sexual unfaithfulness by a spouse (Matthew 5:31). The intended goal of separation is reconciliation (Colossians 1:19–20; Matthew 5:21).
5. The Apostle Peter was probably a "Powerful Choleric." (Luke 22:33, 50)
6. Jethro reminded Moses that he should be doing what he was called to do. (Exodus 18:20)
7. Ruth left her own country to take care of her mother-in-law. She gleaned the fields for food in order to feed herself and her mother-in-law. (Ruth 1:16–17; 2:1–2)

CHAPTER FIVE

1. The borrower is a servant to the lender. (Proverbs 22:7)
2. The prophet's widow went to the wise prophet Elisha seeking advice. (2 Kings 4:1–7)
3. Godliness with contentment unlocks the door to plastic prison (1 Timothy 6:6–10). Contentment is found in Christ.
4. The world is watching and our lives are a beacon of Christ and his power in our community. (Philippians 2:1–15)
5. More was not enough for Lot's wife. (Genesis 19:1–26)
6. The widow gave all that she had. The devotion behind her gift was what mattered to Jesus. (Luke 21:3–4)
7. We are to give cheerfully and willingly, not reluctantly. (2 Corinthians 9:6–8)

CHAPTER SIX

1. Work is designed by God and work is good. God's Son even worked while on earth. (Genesis 1:26; Mark 6:3)

2. Paul encouraged the Colossians to put Christ first and work as if they worked for the Lord. (Colossians 3:23)
3. God sent Paul to teach them about Jesus and a fuller understanding of the Scripture. Because of Lydia's willingness to follow the message of Jesus, Christianity spread throughout Europe. (Acts 16:13–15)
4. Our actions should reflect the love of Christ. We should get along, live in harmony, and not pay back evil for evil. (1 Peter 3:8–9)
5. As salt in the workplace we can stop the decaying morals that surround us, flavor lives with the love of Christ, and create a thirst for God. (Matthew 5:13–15)
6. She first and foremost feared and honored God. (Proverbs 31:31)
7. He knew God's laws and chose not to sin against God. (Genesis 39:9)
8. Their business provided funds for themselves and Paul as he stayed with them and assisted tentmaking. Part-time, they helped Paul in various teaching ministries and as a result the gospel continued to spread. (Acts 18:18–28)
9. A wise woman listens and adds to her learning. (Proverbs 1:5)

CHAPTER SEVEN

1. A wise woman builds a house called home. (Proverbs 14:1)
2. Homemaking was a treasured calling for a young woman. (Titus 2:4–6)
3. The Holy Spirit is the comforter and helper of those who love Jesus. (John 14:23)
4. Jesus rebuked her and encouraged her to take more time to commune with God. (Luke 10:41–42)
5. We are to be about our heavenly father's business and do everything as unto the Lord. (Luke 2:24)
6. Hospitality meant providing lodging and food. (Hebrews 13:1–2; Genesis 18:1–2)
7. The Shunammite woman was blessed with a son, and the added miracle of her son being brought back to life. (2 Kings 4:8–37)

CHAPTER EIGHT

1. Christ commanded us to "love one another as I have loved you" (John 15:12).

2. To please God and honor his kingdom. (Philippians 2:3–5)
3. Our actions and good deeds are proof of our faith. (Matthew 25:35)
4. Huldah was a prophetess whom God used as a messenger. She studied the laws and taught others. (2 Kings 22)
5. Every believer has at least one gift. To discover it, consider Scripture, seek God's wisdom as you look inward, and notice what you enjoy and are good at when you serve the church. (1 Corinthians 12:4–6; Romans 12:3–8; Ephesians 4:7–11)
6. Love God and your neighbor as you love yourself. (Luke 10:27; Deuteronomy 6:5; Leviticus 19:18)
7. What really matters is pleasing God. As a bonus, eternal reward awaits when you are obedient to God and his Word. (1 Corinthians 15:58)
8. Dorcas sewed garments, so her instruments were needle and thread. (Acts 9:36–42)

CHAPTER NINE

1. God established the government. (Romans 13:1–2)
2. God established the home (Genesis 2), the church (Acts 2), and the government. (Genesis 8:20–9:7)
3. Isaiah repented of his own unrighteousness and volunteered willingly by saying, "Here am I, send me." (Isaiah 6:8)
4. No. The early church faced persecution as we do today around the world. (Acts 13:50)
5. Esther remained true to her faith and her heritage as she spoke up to the king and revealed a plot to massacre all of the Jews in the kingdom. (Esther 1–10)
6. Esther called the Jews to pray and fast for three days as she sought strength from God. (Esther 4:15–17)
7. We receive spiritual protection when we put on the full armor of God. (Ephesians 6:10)
8. They chose to obey God's laws over man's commands. (Exodus 1:17)
9. We are to speak out in gentleness, respect, and love. (1 Peter 3:15–16)
10. We each will be judged by God. (2 Corinthians 5:11)

APPENDIX B—EXPERTS

Vivian Baniak and her husband, Andy, present financial workshops around the country.

Emilie Barnes is a nationally known home management expert and popular speaker. Her 15 books have sold over one million copies, including *More Hours in My Day, The 15-Minute Organizer,* and *If Teacups Could Talk.*

William J. Bennett is a best-selling author who served as director of the Office of National Drug Control Policy under President Bush and as Secretary of Education and Chairman of the National Endowment for the Humanities under President Reagan.

Sue Buchanan is an author, speaker, and the vice president of Dynamic Media, Inc. With her friends, Gloria Gaither, Joy Mackenzie, and Peggy Benson, she coauthored *Friends through Thick and Thin.*

Dee Brestin speaks at large retreats on the topic of women's friendships. She is the author of *The Friendships of Women, We Are Sisters,* and a best-selling line of Bible study guides.

Judith Briles is a speaker, author, and management consultant. She is the author of ten books including *When God Says No, The Confidence Factor,* and *Women in the Workplace.*

Jill Briscoe is known throughout the world for her Bible study and speaking ministry. Jill is director of Telling the Truth media ministries and has authored a number of books.

Stuart Briscoe is the pastor of a large church and ministers through weekly television and radio broadcasts. He is the author of over twenty-five books and a popular speaker.

Larry Burkett is a renowned financial adviser and host of a nationally syndicated radio talk show. He has authored several books.

Richard Carlson, Ph.D., is a frequent lecturer and a stress consultant in private practice. He is the author of *Don't Sweat the Small Stuff.*

Tony Campolo, Ph.D., is a pastor, author, and professor of sociology. He is founder of the Evangelical Association for Promotion of Education and creator of a school for inner-city children with learning disabilities.

Gary Chapman, Ph.D., directs marriage seminars throughout the country and is host of the nationally syndicated radio broadcast, *A Growing Marriage.* He is author of the best-selling books *The Five Languages of Love* and *The Five Love Languages of Children.*

Patsy Clairmont is the author of many books including *It's about Home.* She is a popular speaker.

Judith Couchman is the author of numerous books, including *Designing a Woman's Life; Lord, Please Help Me to Change;* and *Lord, Have You Forgotten Me?* She has published articles in such publications as *Discipleship Journal, Today's Christian Woman,* and *Moody Magazine,* and speaks at conferences around the country.

Alan R. Crippen, II, is the director of Institute for Family Studies at Focus on the Family in Colorado.

Verdell Davis is the author of *Let Me Grieve But Not Forever.* She is a popular speaker, the mother of three, and grandmother of three more. She recently retired from her career in education and lives in Dallas, Texas.

James D. Dean, CPA, is director of associate development for Cornerstone Management Associates, and he is the CEO and cofounder of the Institute for Debt Free Living.

James Dobson, Ph.D., is a psychologist, best-selling author, and president of Focus on the Family ministries.

Elizabeth Dole is an outspoken Christian woman and wife of Bob Dole, past Senate Majority Leader. She served as the president of the Red Cross, the world's largest humanitarian relief agency.

Gwen Ellis is managing editor of Focus on the Family book publishing and a time management expert. She has authored several books.

Kathie Lee Gifford is one of America's best-known television personalities and author of the national bestseller *I Can't Believe I Said That!*

Archibald D. Hart, Ph.D., is dean of the Graduate School of Psychology and professor of psychology at Fuller Theological Seminary in Pasadena, California. He has authored several books including *Stress and Your Child, Overcoming Anxiety,* and *The Hidden Link between Adrenaline and Stress.*

O. S. Hawkins is the author of numerous books and the pastor of the 25,000-member First Baptist Church in Dallas, Texas.

Liz Curtis Higgs is an author, speaker, and nationally known humorist. She has a monthly column in *Today's Christian Woman* magazine.

Mary Hunt is an author and founder and publisher of *Cheapskate Monthly,* a newsletter to encourage financial confidence and responsible spending.

Brenda Hunter, Ph.D., is a psychologist, internationally published author, and passionate defender of the mother-child bond. She has defended hands-on mothering on *The Today*

Show, CBS This Morning, and *Larry King Live.* She authored *A Mother's Love* and *Home by Choice.*

Lynda Hunter is an author, and founding editor of Focus on the Family's *Single Parent Family* magazine. She is a popular speaker and writer of a syndicated newspaper column for single parents.

Bill Hybels is pastor of Willow Creek Community Church, known worldwide for its "seeker sensitive" approach. He is the author of a number of books and Bible study series, including *Too Busy Not to Pray* and *Making Life Work.*

Kay Cole James is dean of the School of Government at Regent University. Kay has served as Virginia's Secretary of Health and Human Services, associate director for the White House Office of National Drug Policy under President George Bush, and vice president of Family Research Council.

Gregory L. Jantz, Ph.D., is a best-selling author, consultant, and keynote speaker. He is founder and executive director of The Center for Counseling and Health Resources, Inc., a mental health and chemical dependency treatment agency.

Deloris Jordan is cofounder and president of the Michael Jordan Foundation, a volunteer organization that raises funds to help disadvantaged children.

Florence Littauer is an international speaker and popular author. She and her husband, Fred, conduct marriage and personality seminars and are the founders of CLASS.

Marita Littauer is president of CLASS (Christian Leaders, Authors, Speakers Services) and author of many books. She is an international speaker.

John C. Maxwell is an internationally known speaker on the topic of personal and corporate leadership development. He is the author of several books and the founder of Injoy Ministries.

Carole Mayhall, a popular author and conference speaker, has traveled throughout the world teaching about marriage, family relationships, and how women can help each other.

Kathy Collard Miller is the best-selling author of *God's Abundance* and the *God's Vitamin "C" for the Spirit* series. She writes and speaks about issues facing women including how to heal and grow a marriage.

Connie Neal is a popular speaker and the author of more than 20 books, including *Dancing in the Arms of God.* She is a featured speaker with the Women of Faith conferences and Renewing Your Heart conferences.

Lindsay O'Conner is an author, wife, mother, and speaker.

Dean Ornish, M.D., is the author of several best-sellers, including *Love and Survival.* He is a speaker and professor of medicine as well as one of President Clinton's official physicians.

Janet Parshall is the host of the nationally syndicated talk show *Janet Parshall's America* and is presently the spokesperson for the Family Research Council, a political awareness organization based in Washington, D.C., under the ministry of Focus on the Family.

Donna Partow is the author of devotional and practical advice books, including *No More Lone Ranger Moms.*

Dave Ramsey is the best-selling author of *Financial Peace* and *More than Enough.* He is founder of the Lamp Group, Inc., and popular host of the nationally syndicated radio talk show, *The Money Game.*

Bob Russell is the pastor of the 10,000-member Southeast Christian Church in Louisville, Kentucky and has authored a number of books.

Linda Evans Shepherd is a popular speaker and the author of nine books.

Jan Silvious is the cohost (with Kay Arthur) of Precepts Ministry's national radio program, *Precepts with Kay and Jan.* She is an author, a counselor, and a popular speaker.

Gerald L. Sittser, Ph.D., is a professor of religion and philosophy. A former pastor, he is the author of four books and many book reviews and articles for popular and scholarly journals.

Charles R. Swindoll serves as president of Dallas Theological Seminary. He is also president of Insight for Living, a radio broadcast ministry aired daily worldwide. He was senior pastor of the First Evangelical Free Church in Fullerton, California, for almost twenty-three years and has authored numerous books on Christian Living.

Luci Swindoll is vice president of public relations at Insight for Living. She is a popular speaker and the author of six books.

Joni Eareckson Tada is author of over 20 books. She serves as president of JAF Ministries, a Christian organization that advances Christ's kingdom among the world's 550 million people with disabilities.

Mother Teresa started her own order, the Missionaries of Charity in 1950. She won the Nobel Peace Prize and was acclaimed internationally for her work among the destitute and the dying.

Cynthia Tobias is founder and president of Learning Styles Unlimited, Inc. She is a popular speaker and best-selling author of *The Way They Learn* and *Every Child Can Succeed.*

Jerry Tuma, a Certified Financial Planner, is president and founder of Cornerstone Financial Services Inc. He and his wife, Ramona, are both authors and popular speakers.

Sheila Walsh is the past host of *The 700 Club.* She is a popular speaker, vocalist, and author of several books, including *Honestly.*

Mary Whelchel is founder of the national radio program *The Christian Working Woman.* She is an author and popular speaker.

Warren Wiersbe, Ph.D., is best known as an author, pastor, and radio Bible teacher. He has written over eighty books and is the former director of *Back to the Bible.*

Susan Alexander Yates is a columnist and regular guest on the radio program *On Your Mark,* broadcast in Boston and Washington. She is a popular speaker and author.

NOTE: To the best of our knowledge, all of the above information is accurate and up to date. In some cases we were unable to obtain biographical information.

—THE STARBURST EDITORS

ENDNOTES

Introduction
1. Luci Swindoll, *Strengthening Your Faith* – Women of Faith Bible Study (Grand Rapids, Michigan: Zondervan, 1988), 9.
2. Kathy Collard Miller, *God's Word For The Biblically-Inept Series, Women of the Bible* (Lancaster, Pennsylvania, Starburst, 1999), introduction IX.

Chapter One
1. Dean Ornish, *Newsweek* Magazine (August 1994), 36.
2. Jill Briscoe, *Women in the Life of Jesus* (Wheaton, Illinois: Victor Books, 1986), 69.
3. Carole Mayhall, *Come Walk With Me* (Colorado Springs, Colorado: WaterBrook Press, 1998), 38.
4. Gien Karssen, *Her Name Is Woman* (Colorado Springs, Colorado: NavPress, 1975), 146.
5. Bill Hybels, *The God You're Looking For* (Nashville, Tennessee: Thomas Nelson, 1997), 147, 152.
6. Roger Frederickson, *The Communicators Commentary – John* (Waco, Texas: Word), 98.
7. Robert Sullivan, "Discovery: Sleepless In America," *Life* Magazine (February 1998), 56.
8. Charles R. Swindoll, *Flying Closer To The Flame* (Dallas, Texas: Word, 1993), 141.
9. Mother Teresa, *A Simple Path* (New York, New York: Ballantine Books, 1995), 8.

Chapter Two
1. Elizabeth Kübler-Ross, *On Death and Dying* (New York, Macmillan, 1969), quoted in Joyce Landorf, *Mourning Song* (Old Tappan, New Jersey: Fleming H. Revell, 1974), 16.
2. Joni Eareckson Tada and Steven Estes, *When God Weeps* (Grand Rapids, Michigan: Zondervan, 1997), 50.
3. Gerald L. Sittser, *A Grace Disguised* (Grand Rapids, Michigan: Zondervan, 1996), 47.
4. Jill Briscoe, *It Had To Be A Monday* (Wheaton, Illinois, Tyndale, 1995), 32.
5. Gary Chapman, *Loving Solutions* (Chicago: Moody Press, 1998), 123.
6. Joni Eareckson Tada, *When God Weeps*, 152.
7. Stuart Briscoe, *What Works When Life Doesn't* (Wheaton, Illinois: Harold Shaw, 1998), 142.
8. SmithKline Beecham Pharmaceuticals, A Health Education Material reviewed favorably by the American Academy of Family Physicians Foundations, "Symptoms of Depression," 3–4.
9. Gregory L. Jantz, *Becoming Strong Again* (Grand Rapids, Michigan: Fleming H. Revell, 1998), 18.
10. Verdell Davis, *Let Me Grieve But Not Forever* (Dallas, Texas: Word, 1994), 59.

11. Sue Buchanan, *I'm Alive and the Doctor's Dead* (Grand Rapids, Michigan: Zondervan, 1994), 128.
12. Verdell Davis, *Let Me Grieve But Not Forever*, 12.
13. Sheila Walsh, *Gifts for Your Soul* (Grand Rapids, Michigan: Zondervan, 1998), 48.
14. Gregory L. Jantz, *Becoming Strong Again*, 32.
15. Mary Alice Kellog, "A Frank Talk With Kathie Lee," *McCall's* Magazine (June 1999), 32.
16. Gerald L. Sittser, *A Grace Disguised*, 63.

Chapter Three
1. Brenda Hunter, Ph.D., *The Power of Mother Love* (Colorado Springs, Colorado: WaterBrook Press, 1997), 1.
2. Deloris Jordan, *Family First* (San Francisco: Harper San Francisco, 1996), 38.
3. Dr. James Dobson, *The Strong-Willed Child* (Wheaton, Illinois: Tyndale House, 1978), introduction X.
4. Cynthia Ulrich Tobias, *Every Child Can Succeed* (Colorado Springs, Colorado: Focus on the Family), preface.
5. Lynda Hunter, *Parenting On Your Own* (Grand Rapids, Michigan: Zondervan, 1997), 22.
6. Dr. Archibald D. Hart, *Stress and Your Child* (Dallas, Texas: Word, 1992), 68.
7. Ibid., 31.
8. Donna Partow, *No More Lone Ranger Moms* (Minneapolis, Minnesota: Bethany, 1995), 31.

Chapter Four
1. John Maxwell, *The Success Journey* (Nashville, Tennessee: Thomas Nelson, 1997), 178.
2. Gary Chapman, *Loving Solutions*, 51.
3. Bob Russell, *Marriage By The Book* (Cincinnati, Ohio: Standard, 1992), 20.
4. Washington Citizen Newsletter, "Five Things You Can Do To Strengthen Your Marriage" (Washington Family Council, Bellevue, WA, March 1999), 3.
5. Connie Neal, *Holding On To Heaven While Your Husband Goes Through Hell* (Nashville, Tennessee: Word, 1998), 31.
6. Gary Chapman, *Loving Solutions*, 135, 142.
7. Ibid., 30.
8. Jan Silvious, *Foolproofing Your Life* (Colorado Springs: WaterBrook Press, 1998), 178.
9. Florence Littauer, *Personality Plus* (Grand Rapids, Michigan: Revell, 1992), excerpts 24–81.
10. Lowell D. Streiker, *An Encyclopedia of Humor* (Peabody, Massachusetts: Hendrickson, 1998), 130.
11. Marita Littauer and Florence Littauer, *Personality Puzzle* (Grand Rapids, Michigan: Revell, 1992), 114.

12. Susan Alexander Yates, *A House Full of Friends* (Colorado Springs, Colorado: Focus on the Family, 1995), 140.

13. Charles Swindoll, *Growing Strong In The Seasons of Life* (Portland, Oregon: Multnomah Press, 1983), 349.

14. Joni Eareckson Tada, *The Life and Death Dilemma* (Grand Rapids, Michigan: Zondervan, 1995), 22.

Chapter Five

1. Jerry and Ramona Tuma with Tim LaHaye, *Smart Money* (Sisters, Oregon: Multnomah Books, Questar Publishing, 1994), 140.

2. Dave Ramsey, *Financial Peace* (New York: Viking, 1997), 90.

3. Ibid., 92.

4. Richard Carlson, Ph.D., *Don't Sweat the Small Stuff* (New York: Hyperion, 1997), 161.

5. James D. Dean, *Breaking Out Of Plastic Prison* (Grand Rapids, Michigan: Fleming H. Revell, 1997), 52.

6. Mary Hunt, *The Financially Confident Woman* (Nashville, Tennessee: Broadman & Holman, 1996), 54.

7. O. S. Hawkins, *Moral Earthquakes and Secret Faults* (Nashville, Tennessee: Broadman & Holman, 1997), 171.

8. Dave Ramsey, *More Than Enough* (New York: Viking, 1999), 69.

9. Ibid.

10. Vivian Baniak, contributing author, *Getting Along With Almost Anybody* by Florence and Marita Littauer (Grand Rapids, Michigan: Fleming H. Revell, 1998), 228.

11. Judith Couchman, *Women of Faith Bible Study Series – Celebrating Friendship* (Grand Rapids, Michigan: Zondervan, 1998), 29, 77.

12. Jerry and Ramona Tuma, *Smart Money*, 148.

13. Edith Deen, *All The Women of the Bible* (New York: Harper & Row, 1955), 353.

14. Bill Hybels, *Honest To God* (Grand Rapids, Michigan: Zondervan, 1990), 162.

15. Mary Hunt, *The Financially Confident Woman*, 72.

16. Dave Ramsey, *Financial Peace*, 121.

Chapter Six

1. Gwen Ellis, *Thriving As A Working Woman* (Wheaton, Illinois: Tyndale, 1995), 198.

2. Ancient Irish Hymn, "Be Thou My Vision."

3. Gwen Ellis, *Thriving As A Working Woman*, 36–37.

4. Luci Swindoll, Judith Briles, Mary Whelchel, *The Workplace, Questions Women Ask* (Portland, Oregon: Multnomah, 1992), 136.

5. Ibid., 38.

6. The New Bible Dictionary, J. D. Douglas, Editor (Eerdmans Publishing), 510–511.

7. Bill Hybels, *Making Life Work* (Downers Grove, Illinois: InterVarsity Press, 1998), 124.

8. Jan Silvious, *Foolproofing Your Life*, 171.

9. Mary Whelchel, *The Workplace, Questions Women Ask*, 28.

10. Lindsey O'Connor, *A Christian's Guide to Working from Home* (Eugene, Oregon: Harvest House, 1997), 10.

11. Ibid.

12. Lynda Hunter, *Parenting On Your Own*, 260.

Chapter Seven

1. Carole Mayhall, *Come Walk With Me* (Colorado Springs, Colorado: WaterBrook Press, 1998), 143.

2. Patsy Clairmont, *Sportin' a Tude* (Wheaton, Illinois: Tyndale, 1997), 169.

3. Marion Duckworth, *Renewed on the Run* (Victor Books, 1991), 17.

4. Emilie Barnes, *Creative Home Organizer* (Eugene, Oregon: Harvest House, 1995), 14.

5. Dee Brestin, *The Joy of Hospitality* (Colorado Springs, Colorado: Chariot Victor, 1996), 31.

6. Susan Alexander Yates, *A House Full of Friends*, 31.

7. Linda Evans Shepherd, Encouraging Hands, Encouraging Hearts (Ann Arbor, Michigan: Vine Books, 1999), 10.

8. Liz Curtis Higgs, *Only Angels Can Wing It* (Nashville, Tennessee: Thomas Nelson, 1995), 175.

Chapter Eight

1. Meadow Rue Merrill, "Operation Blessing" (*Family Circle* Magazine, February 16, 1999), 15.

2. Phyllis Bennet, *Women of Faith Bible Study Series – Discovering Your Spiritual Gifts* (Grand Rapids, Michigan: Zondervan, 1998), 39.

3. Ibid., 40.

4. Ibid., 43.

5. Ibid., 28.

6. Ibid., 28.

7. Arthur F. Miller, Jr., *Why You Can't Be Anything You Want* (Grand Rapids, Michigan: Zondervan, 1999), 108.

8. The New Compact Bible Dictionary (Zondervan, 1981), 236.

9. Bill Hybels, *Putting God and Others First, Serving Lessons*, Small Group Series (Zondervan, 1998), 21.

10. Mother Teresa, *A Simple Path*, 99.

11. Kay Cole James, *Transforming America From The Inside Out* (Grand Rapids, Michigan: Zondervan, 1995), 53.

12. Linda Evans Shepherd, *Encouraging Hands, Encouraging Hearts*, 117.

13. Larry Burkett, *Damaged But Not Broken* (Chicago: Moody Press, 1996), 223.

14. Bill Hybels, *Putting God and Others First*, 47.

15. Halley's Bible Commentary (Zondervan, 1965), 483.

16. Warren Wiersbe, *10 Powerful Principles for Christian Service* (Grand Rapids, Michigan: Baker Books, 1997), 47.

Chapter Nine

1. William J. Bennett, *The De-Valuing of America* (Colorado Springs, Colorado: Focus on the Family, 1994), 267.

2. Jennifer Ferranti, "Elizabeth Dole" (*Christian Reader*, May/June 1999), 23.

3. Richard Wolf, "Women's Political Gain in Past Three Decades" (*USA TODAY*, February 17, 1999), 7A.

4. Concerned Women for America Web Page: http:www.cwfa.org, February 3, 1999.

5. Tony Compolo, *Following Jesus Without Embarrassing God* (Dallas: Word, 1997), 162.

6. The Layman's Bible Encyclopedia (Nashville, Tennessee: The Southwestern Company, 1964), 63.

7. Janet Parshall, Washington Watch (a publication by Family Research Council, May 1999, Volume 10, Number 7), 8.

8. Norma McCorvey, *Won By Love* (Nashville, Tennessee: Thomas Nelson, 1997), 167.

The following excerpts are used by permission with all rights reserved:

Gary Chapman, *Loving Solutions* (Chicago: Moody Press)

Gwen Ellis, *Thriving as a Working Woman* (Wheaton, IL: Tyndale House Publishers)

Dr. Archibald Hart, *Stress and Your Child* (Nashville: Word Publishing)

Florence Littauer, *Personality Plus, Personality Puzzle*, and *Getting Along with Almost Anybody* (Grand Rapids: Fleming H. Revell, a division of Baker Book House)

Joni Eareckson Tada and Steve Estes, *When God Weeps, The Life and Death Dilemma*, (Grand Rapids: Zondervan Publishing House)

INDEX

Boldface numbers indicate defined (What?) terms in the sidebar.

human need for, 117–118
for neighbors, 214
qualities of, 66
teaching children about, 73
unconditional, for the prodigal son, 70
Luke, 152
Lydia, 83, 151–153, **203**
as businesswoman, 152
prayer of, 22

M
Macedonia, 169
Magnitude, **34**
Maidservants, **54**
Malachi, 141
Malice, **164**
Malign, **178**
Manasseh, 212
Manna, **13**, **38**
Manoah and Manoah's wife (parents of Samson), 76–77
Marriage:
abuse in, 99–100, 102
the Bible on, 95
Christ–centered love in, 121
Christian, 93
commitment to, 97
Community Marriage Agreement, 93
counseling, 95–97, 99
as covenant, 92–93
differences within, 90; examples in the Bible of, 139
difficulties in, 94–104
forgiveness in, 95, 97
God in, 93–94, 98
mending, 96
money and, 134, 138, 147
of Rachel and Jacob, 111
of Rebekah and Isaac, 92–93
Rebekah's qualities in, 93
of Ruth and Boaz, 120
reconciliation, tips for, 97
sexual practices forbidden in, 100–101
strengthening, tips for, 94
women's biggest complaint in, 21
Martha, 108, 179–180
(*See also* Mary of Bethany)
Mary (mother of Jesus), **64**
and the crucifixion, 83, 85–86
and Elizabeth, 16, 83
faith of, 5
prayer of, 22
at the tomb, 216
and the Upper Room, 85–86
Mary (mother of John Mark), **83**
Mary of Bethany, 7–9
Mary Magdalene, 216
Mary of Rome, 219
Maxwell, John C.:
on family, 90

Mayhall, Carole:
on God's word, 9
on housekeeping, 178
McCorvey, Norma, 239
Memories, 85
Mentor, **68**
Meribah, 102
Messiah, **17**, **152**
Metaphor, **55**, **159**
Michal, 28, 103
Midian, 111
Midwifery, 237
Miller, Arthur F., Jr., 204
Miller, Kathy Collard, xiv
Ministries:
getting involved in, 220
examples in the Bible of, 209
Miracles, **19**
Miriam, 46, 171, **227–228**
Miscarriage, author's experience of, 34–35
Missionary, **82**
Moabites, **119**
Money, 125–147
advice on, 147
budgeting, 135
coins used in Bible times, 208
greed and, 130
hard work resulting in, 135
management, tips on, 127, 132
marriage and, 134
Paul, on the love of, 130
personality types and, 138–140
the rich young ruler and, 207
Monogamy, **54**
MOPS (Mothers of Preschoolers), 84
Mordecai, **234**
Mosaic, **179**
Moses, 23, 39, 111–112
faith of, 23
father–in–law's advice to, 111, 112
Law of, 72, 212
mother saving life of, 29
old age of, 115
parents of, 23, 29
Pharaoh and, 23, 102
raised staff of, 49
the Red Sea, parting of, 23
Zipporah as wife of, 103
Motherhood, 63–87
instructions in Bible regarding, 63
children, time with, 66–69
and Christian community, 83–84
Mary, and adolescent Jesus, 65–66
"mother's heart," 70
Mothers of Preschoolers (MOPS), 84
single, 81–82
support needed in, 83–86
unconditional love in, 63–67
work and, 154
Mothers–in–law (*see* In–laws)
(*See also* Children; Parenthood)
Mother Teresa:

on love, 209
on prayer, 21
on service, 209
Mulgrew, Kate:
on parenthood, 66
Mundane, **184**
Myrrh, **216**

N
Nabal, 109–110, 162
Naomi, 41
(*See also* Ruth)
Nash, Donald, 209–210
National Day of Prayer, 240
Nazareth, **64**
Nazirite, **71**, 76, 209
Neal, Connie, 97
Nebuchadnezzar, **28**
Neighbor(s), 225
Jesus defines, 214
Neighbors Who Care, 217
Nero, 32
New Testament:
on giving, 143–144
Nicodemus, 216
Ninevah, **39**
Noah, 14, 23, **41**, 101
wife of, 41
Nomad, **53**

O
Obed, 120
Obey, **8**
O'Connor, Lindsay, 167
Office romance, 161–166
Oil, miracle of, 128–129
Old age: 114–115, 117–118
older women as example, 69
Old Testament, 146
on tithing, 143
scripture, as referring to, xvi
Olive oil press, **129**
Onesimus, 150
Operation Blessing, 202
Optimistic, **107**
Ordained, **74**
Ordinances, **3**
Ornish, Dean, 4

P
Paganism, 36
Paltiel, 103
Parable, **15**
Parents, honoring, 110, 113
Parenthood:
Biblical role models for, 69–70
difficulties and rewards of, 71
James Dobson on, 71
Kate Mulgrew on, 66
main responsibility of, 74
teaching inherent in, 72–73
(*See also* Children, Motherhood)

Widow, the prophet's, 128–129
Widows, Dorcas as friend to, 222–224
Widow with two mites, 142
Widow of Zarepath, 30, 36–38, 179
Wiersbe, Warren, 222
Winfrey, Oprah, 16
Wisdom, **10**, **15**, 99
    of Abigail, 109–110
    Solomon on, 104
    Proverbs as book of, 45
Witness, **57**
    Christian, 231
Woman; women:
    Christian, 232
    as helpmate, 90
    as heart of family, 89, 177
    as leaders, 244
    Paul on equality of, 178
    Proverbs on, 154
working, 149
work of, 154
Word of God (*see* Bible)
Work:
    Bible women and, 150
    family and, 81, 154
    God and, 154

from home, 166–168
friendship at, 159–60
mothers and, 66–68
romance at, 161–166
women and, 149–174
Working women, tips for, 155
Worry, **20**, 78
Worship, **8**
    (*See also* Prayer)

X
Xerxes, 234–235
X–Files, The, 16

Y
Yates, Susan Alexander:
    on having vision, 190
    on family relationships, 113
Youth, Jesus as, 65–66

Z
Zarepath, **30**
    widow of, 30, 36–38, 179
Zechariah, 11–13
Zipporah, 103, 111–112

Books by Starburst Publishers®

(Partial listing—full list available on request)

What's in the Bible for . . .™ Women
Georgia Curtis Ling

What does the Bible have to say to women? Women of all ages will find biblical insight on topics that are meaningful to them in four sections: Wisdom for the Journey; Family Ties; Bread, Breadwinners, and Bread Makers; and Fellowship and Community Involvement. This book uses illustrations, bullet points, chapter summaries, and icons to make understanding God's Word easier than ever!
(trade paper)   ISBN 1-892016-11-7 $16.95

What's in the Bible for . . .™ Mothers
Judy Bodmer
AVAILABLE SPRING 2000

Is home schooling a good idea? Is it okay to work? At what age should I start treating my children like responsible adults? What is the most important thing I can teach my children? If you are asking these questions and need help answering them, *What's in the Bible for . . . Mothers* is especially for you! Simple and user-friendly, this motherhood manual offers hope and instruction for today's mothers by jumping into the lives of mothers in the Bible (e.g., Naomi, Elizabeth, and Mary) and by exploring biblical principles that are essential to being a nurturing mother.
(trade paper)   ISBN 1-892016-26-5 $16.95

What's in the Bible for . . .™ Teens
Mark and Jeanette Littleton
AVAILABLE FALL 2000

This is a book that teens will love! *What's in the Bible for . . . Teens* contains topical Bible themes that parallel the challenges and pressures of today's adolescents. Learn about Bible Prophecy, God's plan for relationships, and Peer Pressure in a conversational and fun tone. Helpful and eye-catching "WWJD?" icons, illustrations, and sidebars included.
(trade paper)   ISBN 1-892016-05-2 $16.95

God's Word for the Biblically-Inept ™ Series:

- ☞ **The Bible** by Larry Richards
- ☞ **Daniel** by Daymond R. Duck
- ☞ **Genesis** by Joyce L. Gibson
- ☞ **Health & Nutrition**
  by Kathleen O'Bannon Baldinger
- ☞ **Men of the Bible** by D. Larry Miller
- ☞ **Revelation** by Daymond R. Duck
- ☞ **Women of the Bible** by Kathy Collard Miller

(see pages iii to vi for ordering information)

The Weekly Feeder: A Revolutionary Shopping, Cooking, and Meal-Planning System
Cori Kirkpatrick

A revolutionary meal-planning system, here is a way to make preparing home-cooked dinners more convenient than ever. At the beginning of each week, simply choose one of the eight preplanned menus, tear out the corresponding grocery list, do your shopping, and whip up each fantastic meal in less than 45 minutes! The author's household management tips, equipment checklists, and nutrition information make this system a must for any busy family. Included with every recipe is a personal anecdote from the author emphasizing the importance of good food, a healthy family, and a well-balanced life.
(trade paper)   ISBN 1892016095 $16.95

God Stories: They're So Amazing, Only God Could Make Them Happen
Donna I. Douglas

Famous individuals share their personal, true-life experiences with God in this beautiful new book! Find out how God has touched the lives of top recording artists, professional athletes, and other newsmakers like Jessi Colter, Deana Carter, Ben Vereen, Stephanie Zimbalist, Cindy Morgan, Sheila E., Joe Jacoby, Cheryl Landon, Brett Butler, Clifton Taulbert, Babbie Mason, Michael Medved, Sandi Patty, Charlie Daniels, and more! Their stories are intimate, poignant, and sure to inspire and motivate you as you listen for God's message in your own life!
(cloth)   ISBN 1892016117 $18.95

More of Him, Less of Me: A Daybook of My Personal Insights, Inspirations & Meditations on the Weigh Down™ Diet
Jan Christensen

The insight shared in this year-long daybook of inspiration will encourage you on your weight-loss journey, bring you to a deeper relationship with God, and help you improve any facet of your life. Each page includes an essay, scripture, and daily tip that will encourage and uplift you as you trust God to help you achieve your proper weight. Perfect companion guide for anyone on the Weigh Down™ diet!
(cloth)   ISBN 1892016001 $17.95

Desert Morsels: A Journal with Encouraging Tidbits from My Journey on the Weigh Down™ Diet
Jan Christiansen

When Jan Christiansen set out to lose weight on the Weigh Down™ Diet she got more than she bargained for! In addition to *losing* over 35 pounds and *gaining* a closer relationship with God, Jan discovered a gift— her ability to entertain and comfort fellow dieters! Jan's inspiring website led to the release of her best-selling book, *More of Him, Less of Me.* Jan serves another helping of *her* wit and *His* wisdom in this lovely companion journal. Includes inspiring scripture, insightful comments, stories from readers, room for the reader's personal reflection and *Plenty of **Attitude*** (p-attitude).

(cloth)   ISBN 1892016214 $16.95

Since Life Isn't a Game, These Are God's Rules: Finding Joy & Fulfillment in God's Ten Commandments
Kathy Collard Miller

Life is often referred to as a game, but God didn't create us because he was short on game pieces. To succeed in life, you'll need to know God's rules. In this book, Kathy Collard Miller explains the meaning of each of the Ten Commandments with fresh application for today. Each chapter includes scripture and quotes from some of our most beloved Christian authors including Billy Graham, Patsy Clairmont, Liz Curtis Higgs, and more! Sure to renew your understanding of God's rules.

(cloth)   ISBN 189201615X $16.95

God's Little Rule Book: Simple Rules to Bring Joy & Happiness to Your Life
Starburst Publishers

Let this little book of God's rules be your personal guide to a more joyful life. Brimming with easily applicable rules, this book is sure to inspire and motivate you! Each rule includes corresponding scripture and a practical tip that will help to incorporate God's rules into everyday life. Simple enough to fit into a busy schedule, yet powerful enough to be life changing!

(trade paper)   ISBN 1892016168 $6.95

Life's Little Rule Book: Simple Rules to Bring Joy & Happiness to Your Life
Starburst Publishers

Let this little book inspire you to live a happier life! The pages are filled with timeless rules such as, "Learn to cook, you'll always be in demand!" and "Help something grow." Each rule is combined with a reflective quote and a simple suggestion to help the reader incorporate the rule into everyday life.

(trade paper)   ISBN 1892016176 $6.95

Seasons of a Woman's Heart: A Daybook of Stories and Inspiration
Compiled by Lynn D. Morrissey

A woman's heart is complex. This daybook of stories, quotes, scriptures, and daily reflections will inspire and refresh. Christian women share their heartfelt thoughts on Seasons of Faith, Growth, Guidance, Nurturing, and Victory. Includes Christian writers Kay Arthur, Emilie Barnes, Luci Swindoll, Jill Briscoe, Florence Littauer, and Gigi Graham Tchividjian.

(cloth)   ISBN 1892016036 $18.95

God's Abundance for Women: Devotions for a More Meaningful Life
Compiled by Kathy Collard Miller

Following the success of *God's Abundance*, this book will touch women of all ages as they seek a more meaningful life. Essays from our most beloved Christian authors exemplify how to gain the abundant life that Jesus promised through trusting Him to fulfill our every need. Each story is enhanced with Scripture, quotes, and practical tips providing brief, yet deeply spiritual, reading.

(cloth)   ISBN 1892016141 $19.95

More God's Abundance: Joyful Devotions for Every Season
Compiled by Kathy Collard Miller

Editor Kathy Collard Miller responds to the tremendous success of *God's Abundance* with a fresh collection of stories based on God's Word for a simpler life. Includes stories from our most beloved Christian writers such as Liz Curtis Higgs and Patsy Clairmont that are combined ideas, tips, quotes, and scripture.

(cloth)   ISBN 1892016133 $19.95

God's Abundance
Edited by Kathy Collard Miller

Over 100,000 sold! This day-by-day inspirational is a collection of thoughts by leading Christian writers like Patsy Clairmont, Jill Briscoe, Liz Curtis Higgs, and Naomi Rhode. *God's Abundance* is based on God's Word for a simpler, more abundant life. Learn to make all aspects of your life—personal, business, financial, relationships, even housework—a "spiritual abundance of simplicity."

(cloth)   ISBN 0914984977 $19.95

Promises of God's Abundance
Edited by Kathy Collard Miller

The Bible is filled with God's promises for an abundant life. *Promises of God's Abundance* is written in the same way as the best-selling *God's Abundance*. It will help you discover these promises and show you how simple obedience is the key to an abundant life. Scripture, questions for growth, and a simple thought for the day will guide you to a more meaningful life. (trade paper)   ISBN 0914984-098 $9.95

Stories of God's Abundance for a More Joyful Life
Compiled by Kathy Collard Miller
 Like its successful predecessor, *God's Abundance* (100,000 sold), this book is filled with beautiful, inspirational, real life stories. Those telling their stories of God share scriptures and insights that readers can apply to their daily lives. Renew your faith in life's small miracles and challenge yourself to allow God to lead the way as you find the source of abundant living for all your relationships. (trade paper)   ISBN 1892016060 $12.95

Purchasing Information

www.starburstpublishers.com

Books are available from your favorite bookstore, either from current stock or special order. To assist bookstores in locating your selection, be sure to give title, author, and ISBN. If unable to purchase from a bookstore, you may order direct from STARBURST PUBLISHERS. When ordering please enclose full payment plus shipping and handling as follows:

Post Office (4th class)
$3.00 with a purchase of up to $20.00
$4.00 ($20.01–$50.00)
8% of purchase price for purchases of $50.01 and up

Canada
$5.00 (up to $35.00)
%15 ($35.01 and up)

United Parcel Service (UPS)
$4.50 (up to $20.00)
$6.00 ($20.01–$50.00)
12% ($50.01 and up)

Overseas
$5.00 (up to $25.00)
20% ($25.01 and up)

Payment in U.S. funds only. Please allow two to three weeks minimum (longer overseas) for delivery. Make checks payable to and mail to:

Starburst Publishers®
P.O. Box 4123
Lancaster, PA 17604

Credit card orders may be placed by calling 1-800-441-1456, Mon–Fri, 8:30 A.M. to 5:30 P.M. Eastern Standard Time. Prices are subject to change without notice. Catalogs are available for a 9 x 12 self-addressed envelope with four first-class stamps.

NOTES